MARGARET TUDOR
QUEEN OF SCOTS

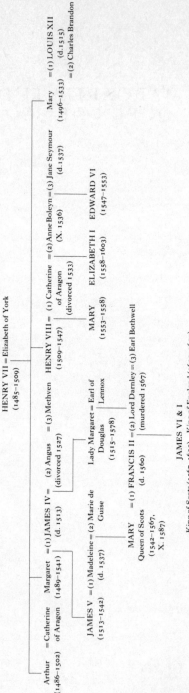

Partial genealogical chart of Britain's royal family, illustrating Margaret's key position in transferring the crown from Tudors to Stuarts (Note: for clarity, and to save space, the last three wives of Henry VIII, none of whom had issue, are omitted from the chart.)

HENRY VII = Elizabeth of York
(1485–1509)

Arthur = Catherine   Margaret = (1)JAMES IV = (2) Angus = (3) Methven   HENRY VIII = (1) Catherine = (2) Anne Boleyn = (3) Jane Seymour   Mary = (1) LOUIS XII
(1486–1502) of Aragon   (1489–1541)   (d. 1513)   (divorced 1527)   (1509–1547)   of Aragon   (X. 1536)   (d.1537)   (1496–1533)   (d.1515)
                                                                                      (divorced 1533)   = (2) Charles Brandon

JAMES V = (1) Madeleine   Lady Margaret = Earl of   MARY   ELIZABETH I   EDWARD VI
(1513–1542) (d. 1537)   Douglas   Lennox   (1553–1558) (1558–1603)   (1547–1553)
        = (2) Marie de   (1515–1578)
              Guise

MARY = (1) FRANCIS II = (2) Lord Darnley = (3) Earl Bothwell
Queen of Scots (d. 1560)   (murdered 1567)
(1542–1567,
X. 1587)

                    JAMES VI & I
                    (1566–1625)   King of England (1603–1625)

King of Scots (1567–1625)

Queen Margaret praying to St. Margaret, from the
Book of Hours given to Margaret by Henry VII.

(*Collection of the Duke of Northumberland*)

MARGARET TUDOR QUEEN OF SCOTS

PATRICIA HILL BUCHANAN

To my husband, L. H. Buchanan

1985

SCOTTISH ACADEMIC PRESS
EDINBURGH AND LONDON

Published by
SCOTTISH ACADEMIC PRESS
33 Montgomery Street, Edinburgh EH7 5JX

ISBN 7073 0424 5

Printed in Great Britain by
Clark Constable, Edinburgh, London, Melbourne

CONTENTS

PRINCIPAL CHARACTERS

in order of their appearance in the book

Henry Tudor (1457–1509) Founder of Tudor dynasty. Ruled 1485–1509 as King Henry VII.

Richard III (1458–85) Yorkist monarch (1483–85), defeated and·slain at Battle of Bosworth Field.

Elizabeth of York (1465–1503) Daughter of Yorkist King Edward IV, Queen of Henry VII.

Prince Arthur (1486–1502) Eldest son of Henry VII and Elizabeth, first husband of Catherine of Aragon.

Catherine of Aragon (1485–1536) Daughter of Ferdinand of Aragon and Isabella of Castille, who married Prince Arthur in 1501, and, as his widow, married Henry VIII in 1509.

Margaret Tudor (1489–1541) Eldest daughter of Henry VII and Elizabeth, who became Queen of James IV of Scotland, mother of James V, grandmother of Mary Queen of Scots.

Henry VIII (1491–1547) Younger son of Henry VII and Elizabeth, who ruled England 1509–47.

Mary Tudor (#1) (1496–1533) Younger daughter of Henry VII and Elizabeth, Queen of Louis XII of France, 1514–15.

William Dunbar (ca. 1460–ca. 1520) Chief poet of court of King James IV and Queen Margaret.

Earl of Surrey (#1) (1443–1520) Official who escorted Princess Margaret to Scotland in 1503; English general at Battle of Flodden Field, 1513.

Lord Dacre (1485–1525) English Warden of the Marches (Borders), who acted as the chief link between Queen Margaret and English court.

King James IV (1473–1513) Ruler of Scotland, 1488–1513, whose brilliant reign ended with his death at Flodden Field. He married Margaret Tudor in 1503.

King James V (1512–1542) Ruler of Scotland, crowned in 1513, after death of his father. Only surviving child of James IV and Margaret, father of Mary Queen of Scots.

Earl of Angus (ca. 1489–1557) Archibald Douglas, Margaret Tudor's second husband, was father of Lady Margaret Douglas.

Duke of Albany (ca. 1484–1536) Heir-presumptive to Scottish throne, reared in France, chosen by Scots Council to replace Queen Margaret as Regent after her second marriage.

Lady Margaret Douglas (1515–1575) Daughter of Margaret and Angus, who married the Earl of Lennox and was mother of Lord Darnley, second husband of Mary Queen of Scots and father of King James VI and I.

Mary Tudor (#2) (1515–1558) Only surviving child of the marriage of Henry VIII and Catherine of Aragon. She ruled England, 1553–58.

Earl of Surrey (#2) (1473–1554) Leader of English troops opposing Scots 1523–24, who corresponded with Queen Margaret.

Henry Stewart, Lord Methven (ca. 1495–ca. 1551) Third husband of Margaret Tudor.

ACKNOWLEDGMENTS

In the preparation of this book I have received the assistance of a number of individuals, to each of whom I am very grateful. I am particularly indebted to the following:

Dr. M. A. Owings, Professor Emeritus and former Head of the English Department of Clemson University, for his helpful critique of my manuscript and his painstaking work in the final proof-reading; Dr. Rosalind Marshall, Assistant Keeper of the Scottish National Portrait Gallery, who helped me immeasurably in locating the portraits of Scottish monarchs; the Duke of Northumberland, for permission to display as frontispiece the previously unpublished miniature of Queen Margaret from the *Book of Hours* in his collection at Alnwick Castle; also his archivist, Mr. Shrimpton, for showing me this rare manuscript; the Earl of Warwick, for permitting me to include the portrait from Warwick Castle of Henry VIII as a small boy.

I am grateful also to those who permitted me to reproduce the following portraits:

(#1) Margaret Tudor Queen of Scots by Daniel Mytens, reproduced by gracious permission of Her Majesty the Queen; (#2) James IV at prayer, from the Österreichische Nationalbibliothek in Vienna; (#3) James IV King of Scots by Daniel Mytens, and (#4) James V as a boy, from the Scottish National Portrait Gallery; (#6) Henry VIII as a young man, from the Royal Portrait Gallery; (#7) Margaret Tudor with the Earl of Angus, from a private collection; (#8) James V as a young man, from the British Museum; (#9) James V King of Scots, from the Scottish National Portrait Gallery.

Part One

THE THISTLE AND THE ROSE

THE TUDOR ROSE (1485)

> We will unite the white rose and the red —
> Smile heaven upon this fair conjunction,
> That long hath frown'd upon their enmity . . .

The time: August 22nd 1485; the place: a battlefield near Market Bosworth, England; the speaker: Henry Tudor, Earl of Richmond. His small army had just won a surprising victory over the forces of King Richard III, who was himself killed in the midst of the melée. The victorious Henry, now wearing the royal crown lost by his defeated foe, had proclaimed his determination to reunite the nation and end thirty years of civil warfare.

The 'Wars of the Roses' were basically a series of contests between two rival families, both descendants of King Edward III. In short, the Yorkists, whose symbol was the white rose, fought the Lancastrians (of the red). The prize, the crown of England, was first snatched by Edward, Duke of York, from the feeble grasp of the last Lancastrian monarch, Henry VI. The latter was a pious but inept ruler, weak-willed and chronically insane. After his death in 1471 (murdered in the Tower of London) and that of his only son (murdered after a battle, aged fourteen), the Yorkists appeared invincible. King Edward IV ruled until 1483, when he died in his forty-second year of natural causes: namely from over-indulgence in food, drink and sex. Since Edward's two sons were still minors, the late King's brother, Richard, was given power to govern as Protector. He soon changed this title to that of King. In the same year the two little Princes perished in the Tower; the causes of their deaths are still unknown and remain one of the fascinating whodunnits of history. At the time, however, rumours that they had been murdered by their uncle spread and soon strengthened the opposition to Richard III. Despite his capable government, plots to overthrow him developed among disgruntled Yorkists, urged on by Edward's widow. These Yorkists finally joined the Lancastrians in focusing their hopes on Henry Tudor, Earl of Richmond.

Henry was the last surviving Lancastrian, although his claim to the throne was shaky, originating from the 'wrong side of the blanket'. His mother's family, the Beauforts, were illegitimate descendants of one of Edward III's sons. They had been legitimized by Parliament with the proviso that this act should not entitle them to inherit the throne. Lady Margaret Beaufort had married Owen Tudor, a Welsh gentleman, and her only son Henry was born and reared in Wales as the Earl of Richmond. He fled the country after the decisive Yorkist victory of 1471, and remained in exile in Brittany, resisting Edward IV's efforts to have him brought back to England. Henry was, after all, the last claimant on the side of the red rose, and Edward had a remarkably flexible conscience. Therefore, the Earl of Richmond wisely avoided repatriation until his chances of survival improved.

By 1485 enough opposition had developed to King Richard to encourage another Lancastrian attempt. Henry Tudor returned from France via Wales. His small force was soon augmented by barons and their retainers who supported the red rose. King Richard hurried to meet this new challenge. His army was larger than that of his foes, but was riddled with traitors, who at the slightest show of success from Henry would cross to the other side. The result was the Battle of Bosworth Field. King Richard died fighting bravely as even his worst defamer, Shakespeare, admits, but the victor took the spoils — and the acclaim of history.

At the time, many expected the Tudor triumph to be as short-lived as the previous coups had been for the past thirty years. In fact, many attempts were made by the Yorkists to recapture the crown. However, none succeeded. This may partially be attributed to the new monarch's ability and forcefulness, but he also had certain advantages over his predecessors. Most of the feudal nobility, leading their own mercenary companies, had fought on one or other side ostensibly out of loyalty to the white rose or the red, but actually for their own personal advantage. Many of these nobles had lost their lives during the fighting; others had lost land and power. They were therefore no longer a formidable group to oppose the royal will. The population as a whole had stood aside during these wars, letting their social betters kill each other off. After thirty years of this, however, the people were tired of the constant turmoil and longed for a strong ruler, no matter whether 'red' or 'white', who would restore law and order.

Their desire was reflected in Parliament, where the Commons were now becoming increasingly important. The latter readily accepted Henry's claim to the throne as based on his victory in 'trial by battle'. His ability to fight and his determination to maintain order mattered far more to them than his ancestry. Moreover, he made every effort to achieve true harmony with his previous opponents, several of whom he even kept on his Council. The corner-stone of his policy of reconciliation was his marriage to Elizabeth of York, daughter of King Edward IV, thus allying

Yorkists with Lancastrians. The marriage took place shortly after Parliament had declared Henry as King and it provided the rationale for the new symbol of national unity that soon decorated almost every public building and every piece of royal property: the red and white Tudor rose.

CHAPTER 1

KING HENRY'S DAUGHTER
(1501–1503)

O n November 19th 1501 the great hall of Westminster Palace glowed in the flickering light of hundreds of torches and candles. Its high-beamed ceiling echoed to the sounds of music, laughter and many voices, for this was a time of joy and merriment — the week after the marriage of the heir to the throne, Prince Arthur, to the Spanish Princess, Catherine of Aragon. Though the wedding itself had been solemnized on Sunday November 15th, the festivities continued unabated through the days that followed. Tournaments, banquets, masques and dances occurred in rapid succession, to prevent any possible ennui among the many high-born guests. Henry Tudor might be careful with his money, but he knew how to spend it lavishly when the occasion called for it, and certainly this one did. The royal houses of Castille and Aragon had many represeı.tatives visiting England for these ceremonials. They must go home thoroughly impressed with the magnificence of their hosts and assure Ferdinand and Isabella that their daughter had married well. The Tudors might have a very recent claim to royalty, but it must be evident that their present estate was splendid, their future assured.

These reflections brought a smile to the thin lips of the King as he sat in the big, carved oak chair on his dais at the upper end of the hall. It was now sixteen years since that eventful day on Bosworth Field when for the first time he had felt the pressure of the royal crown on his brow. Few at that time had been sure it would remain there — so often had it been wrenched by York from Lancaster and back again during the blood-stained thirty years known as the Wars of the Roses. And efforts had been made after Bosworth to seize it once again for York: there had been several plots in the 1480s and the more serious threat in the 1490s, led by an impostor whose real name was Perkin Warbeck. This young man, a haberdasher's model, was told he resembled Prince Richard, the younger of Edward IV's two sons. As nothing had been seen of these little boys since the year 1483, they were naturally presumed dead (although proof of this fact was not to be found until 1674). Nevertheless, in 1491 wheɪ Perkin began to masquerade as Prince Richard, he was soon vigorously supported by leading Yorkists, who proclaimed him as the rightful King. Using troops furnished by King Henry's foreign adversaries, the pretender and his friends made several attempts to invade England. His persistent efforts kept both the country and its King on edge until Perkin was finally eliminated in 1499.

It was unfortunate that mere confiscation of property had been insufficient to prevent new rebellions after Bosworth. At the beginning of his reign Henry had hoped to avoid bloody retribution on the followers of Edward IV and Richard III. The country, he had reasoned, was exhausted by years of violence and cruelty. It needed a period of moderation. Better to play the part of a generous victor, especially since he was married to the Yorkist heiress, Elizabeth. So he had at first spared the lives of his vanquished foes, but had confiscated their property. Bereft of their estates and their retainers, the old nobility would be helpless and, by adding their lands to his, the King would emerge as the wealthiest — hence the most powerful — ruler Britain had seen for centuries.

But widespread confiscations and selective imprisonment had failed to deter all the ruined Yorkists. Sterner measures must be applied; accordingly, after his second breakout from prison, the foolish Perkin Warbeck was at last sent to the scaffold, dragging the hapless young Earl of Warwick, who was implicated in Perkin's last plot, to share his doom. As a direct descendant of King Edward III and a nephew of Edward IV, Warwick had a legitimate claim to the throne and might easily have become the spearhead of future plots by ambitious Yorkists. Until such a threat to Tudor power was permanently removed, the Spanish rulers would not let their daughter marry Henry's son.

King Henry sighed and focused his attention on the entertainment he had ordered for this evening. Masques and 'disguisings' had recently become popular, using elaborate stage devices to portray the theme of every occasion in allegory. He hoped that the Spanish guests would be impressed by the one now in progress. The huge float being drawn into the centre of the great hall was a miniature castle, pulled by four resplendent beasts: a gold and a silver lion, an ibex and a hart. On each of the four towers of the structure stood a child singing lustily, while within the castle walls sat eight ladies presided over by a pretty girl in Spanish dress, representing the Princess of Aragon. Next came a stately ship, fully rigged, bearing eight knights of the 'Mount of Love'. These gentlemen disembarked and sought the ladies' consent to dance. When they coyly refused, the knights attacked and captured the castle. After this victory they succeeded in bearing off the ladies, who gracefully yielded and joined them in a dance, while the 'Spanish lady' smiled approvingly.

The applause accorded this display was as hearty as King Henry could wish for. As the floats and their actors withdrew, the musicians began playing for the dance. The slim young bridegroom left his seat beside his father and crossed the hall to the dais of Queen Elizabeth, where he was joined by one of her ladies. After they had completed two 'bass daunces', the bride and one of her attendants left their seats by the Queen and performed similar dances. Catherine was radiantly lovely, with her slim figure garbed in an elegant Spanish robe and her red hair drawn back under a lace snood. She and Arthur appeared ideally suited for each other. They were almost of an age and both young enough (at fifteen) for many years of ruling and of producing children to ensure the Tudor dynasty. Henry looked across the hall at his own wife. Plump and sweet-faced, Elizabeth of York sat placidly in her royal chair, surrounded by her female court who occupied the cushions provided for them about their mistress. Their union had been a political one (what royal marriage was not?) enabling the 'White Rose and the Red' to join as one, but it had also been a congenial marriage. He and Elizabeth had shared joys and sorrows. Of eight infants born to them, four had survived: Prince Arthur, now fifteen, Princess Margaret, nearly twelve, Henry, Duke of York, aged ten, and little Mary, only four.

At this moment two of the younger members of the family were attracting attention as the Duke of York led his sister Margaret to the dance foor. They made a charming pair, the sturdy, round-faced boy, younger but a shade taller than the girl, who was dimpled and pretty like her mother. Both children were crowned with the red-gold Tudor hair. Their first 'bass dance' was carefully perfect and sedate like those of their elders, but in the second the boy warmed up with enthusiasm. Pulling off his heavy robe of state, he cast it aside and with renewed vigour, 'danced in his jacket with the said Lady Margaret in so goodly and pleasant a Manner, that it was to the King and the Queen great and singular Pleasure'. King Henry joined in the general laughter as his exuberant namesake escorted his sister to her place at her mother's feet, then strode back to his footstool on the masculine side of the dais. The young Duke of York should one day make a good warrior and leader of men. It was too bad that some of his restless energy could not be shared by his elder brother. The young bridegroom now appeared tired. Doubtless six days of constant merry-making after the lengthy ceremony of the wedding, along with its attendant duties as a new husband, had been a strain. He would revive when he reached the bracing airs of mountainous Wales. He was to go there, taking his bride, the following month, to assume his position as Prince of Wales.

In addition to the Spanish match for the heir to the throne, another marriage alliance was to be arranged. A wedding that might prove of equal importance to the one now being celebrated was planned for Princess Margaret. This young lady was now settling herself again on the velvet-cushioned ottoman placed for her at her mother's feet. Flushed and warm from the recent exertions of the dance, she pushed back a strand of golden hair under her snood and carefully smoothed the folds of her elegant, crimson velvet gown. She seemed somewhat annoyed by her brother's recent exhibition. How typical of Harry to throw off his robe and pull her about in that unconventional way! A bass dance, as they had been taught, was supposed to be performed in a gliding motion, with feet never leaving the floor. Instead, he had fairly skipped and pranced. He had trod on her toes once as he flung himself into the dance, but he never cared for his partner's discomfort so long as the spotlight remained on himself. How proud he had been when their father had asked him to escort the Spanish Princess through the streets of London the day after her arrival! He had ridden a splendid horse beside Catherine's more docile mule, and had shared with her the cheers of the crowd. By the way he had gazed at the pretty Princess as they rode through the town, one would have thought he rather than his older brother was to be her bridegroom. Well, very soon Harry would have to take second place not only to Arthur but to his older sister, Margaret, for he was only Duke of York, while she was to become Queen of Scotland. The ambassadors of the Scots King were at that very moment among her father's most honoured guests attending the wedding festivities. They would be discussing the plans for her future as soon as her father had time.

Thus, during the festivities in Westminster Hall, Margaret's thoughts, like her father's, were much occupied with plans for her future. Efforts at arranging a marriage between the English Princess and the King of Scots had begun in 1495, only six years after Margaret's birth. As soon as Henry had established a degree of tranquillity in England's internal affairs, he hastened to safeguard his nation from foreign attack. There was always the danger of hostility from the north. From the time of Edward II, when the Scots had regained independence at Bannockburn under Robert the Bruce, they had been a constant threat to England's security. Raids across the border were frequent. They were especially dangerous when England was at war with a continental foe such as France, which had remained Scotland's 'auld ally' for over two hundred years. Fearing (with some justice) that England wished to eliminate their hard-won independence, the Scots were always looking for chances to weaken their larger southern neighbour.

To establish security in the north by pacific means, English rulers had tried for centuries to arrange a marriage alliance, but for one reason or another such attempts had failed to achieve lasting peace. Now Henry VII was determined to succeed, although not all of his counsellors agreed that this was the wisest course. If, they argued, neither of Henry's sons should leave an heir to the throne, it would mean that Margaret's descendants — the Scottish Stewarts — would eventually rule England as well as Scotland. To this objection the King made a response that has often been quoted to illustrate his remarkable foresight: 'Supposing, which God forbid, that all my male progeny should become extinct, and the kingdom devolve by law to Margaret's heirs, will England be damaged thereby? For since it ever happens that the less becomes subservient to the greater, the accession will be that of Scotland to England, just as formerly happened to Normandy, which devolved upon our ancestors in the same manner, and was happily added to our kingdom by hereditary right — as a rivulet to a fountain'.

With this comfortable self-assurance, King Henry entered into correspondence with James IV. The bachelor King of Scots seemed interested in the project, although the first negotiations of 1495 were interrupted by the attempt of Perkin Warbeck to unseat the Tudor monarch. The impostor gained support from James, who missed no opportunity to sow dissension in the rival kingdom. He welcomed Perkin to Scotland, gave banquets in his honour and even a noble lady for a wife. When Warbeck was finally disposed of, however, negotiations between the two nations were renewed. By 1500 these had gone so far that Margaret was instructed to write to the Pope for a dispensation permitting her marriage to a man related to her 'in the third and fourth degree of consanguinity and affinity'. The pontiff's acquiescence removed any possible obstacle on these grounds. Consequently, James sent his ambassadors in time for them to represent him at the marriage of Arthur and Catherine, and, perhaps more important, to complete his own bethrothal to Arthur's sister.

These Scots had met Margaret, had watched her in the recent dance, and were pleased with the Princess. Although she was perhaps a bit young for their twenty-nine-year-old monarch, she was pretty and accomplished, already moving and speaking with the assurance of royalty. After all, she had been prepared for her role in life almost from the time of her birth. Her grandmother, the scholarly Lady Margaret Beaufort, after whom she was named, had established precise rules for the royal nursery. These included such details as the 'littell cradell', ermine-lined and 'embroidered and painted with fine gold'; and servants who should attend to the child's every need, from the all-important wet-nurse, whose diet was carefully prescribed so that her milk would not injure her infant charge, down to the 'rockers' who must lull her to sleep in the elegant 'cradell'.

Almost as soon as she could walk, Margaret was taught to dance; then she learned to play upon the lute and the clavicord. These accomplishments, which were considered necessary for every high-born lady, apparently were very congenial to her own taste. Like all members of her family, she enjoyed music. How far she advanced in other areas of her education is hard to determine. She shared the tutors who instructed her brothers, who included some of the most intelligent men in England. Among them were Thomas Linacre, John Colet, and William Grocyn, leaders of the northern re-naissance who were attracted to the cultured court of Henry VII. These erudite gentlemen commented on the brilliance of Prince Arthur, evidently the outstanding pupil in the family, but said nothing about Princess Margaret. She certainly learned to read and to write, although her handwriting was atrocious, baffling not only later scholars but even her contemporary correspondents. Her spelling was wildly erratic, but this inconsistency was true of even the learned at that time. She doubtless attained at least a smattering of foreign languages, especially French, which she would need to use living in Scotland, a country which had so much intercourse with France.

So Margaret's charms apparently impressed the Scottish ambassadors, who were already basking in the warm welcome they had received upon their arrival in London in January 1502. The town's hospitality inspired one of these visitors to write an ode of praise to 'London ... the flower of cities all'. This visitor was William Dunbar, the famous rhymer. His poem so pleased the English King that he made the poet several gifts of money, totalling £11 13s 4d. This may appear a trifling amount, but it compares favourably with the £10 gift which the same frugal ruler had bestowed on John Cabot after his famous voyage to North America in 1497. Dunbar seemed well satisfied. At any rate, he became an enthusiastic admirer of Margaret, in whose honour he later wrote many poems.

The ambassadors were successful in their mission, although it took most of the month to complete the marriage treaty. This lengthy document included every detail that the careful Henry could think of in order to make his daughter's future secure. She was to receive dower lands sufficient to yield her an income of £2,000 per year. Her husband was to continue to receive the revenues from these estates throughout his lifetime, but must provide everything necessary for the 'apparatus of her body, the ornamenting of her residences, her vehicles, stud, furniture, utensils, food, dress, private and domestic affairs, and all other things whatsoever, necessary and becoming the honour, state, rank, and dignity of the said Lady Margaret'. She should have plenty of servants, twenty-four of whom must be English if she so desired. In addition, she would receive 500 marks a year as spending money. As her dowry, she would bring her husband 30,000 golden nobles (equal to about £10,000), payable in several instalments: one third at the time of the wedding, one third a year later, and the remainder two years after that. This sum must have helped to reconcile the Scots to the expenses their master would incur for this marriage. Scotland was a poor country, and its King had few of the frugal instincts or abilities of Henry VII.

The signing of the marriage agreement and a separate treaty of permanent peace and friendship between the two kingdoms took place on January 24th 1502. The betrothal itself was performed the very next day at Richmond Palace. The ceremony was a lengthy one. After attending High Mass, the members of the royal family heard a 'notable sermon' by the Bishop of Rochester. Then, with a great company, including the Venetian ambassador, representatives of the Pope and of the French King, the lords spiritual and the lords temporal of the realm, and ladies of highest degree, they proceeded to the Queen's great chamber. Here the matrimonial pledges were made by the bride-elect in person and by Patrick, Earl of Bothwell, as proxy for the bridegroom. Before making these promises, which were considered almost as binding as the marriage vows themselves, twelve-year-old Margaret was given an opportunity to refuse. 'Then the Archbishop of Glasgow [presiding over the solemnities] demanded and speered [asked] the said Princess whether she were content, without compulsion and of her own free will. Then she answered, "If it please my lord my father the King, and my lady mother the Queen"'. When her parents predictably assured her and the company of their approval, the 'fiancells' proceeded. Lord Patrick 'took ... Margaret ... for the wife and spouse of my said sovereign lord, James, King of Scotland, and all for thee (as procurator foresaid) forsake, during his and thine lives natural ...'.

She in turn declared: 'I, Margaret, daughter of the right excellent, right high and mighty Prince and Princess, Henry, by the grace of God, King of England, and Elizabeth, Queen of the same, wittingly and of deliberate mind, having twelve years complete in age, in the month of November last past, contract matrimony with the right excellent, right high and mighty Prince, James, King of Scotland . . .'.

Margaret did not have to endure another ritual which was frequently a feature of such betrothals: the bedding of the bride-to-be. For this ceremony the whole company would repair to a state bed-chamber and watch the newly betrothed lady, clad in an elaborate *déshabillé*, enter and lie down in the big canopied bed. Then the proxy bridegroom, fully clothed, but with his boots removed, would lie down beside her and touch her bare foot with his.

This ritual was carried out fourteen years later in the betrothal of young Princess Mary to Louis XII of France. In her sister Margaret's case, however, this explicit indication of the intimacy of matrimony was omitted. Instead, immediately after the formal espousal, there were dinner parties. Margaret, now formally entitled Queen of Scots, was led by her mother to Queen Elizabeth's table to sit beside her in the place of honour; the King entertained the Scottish and English commissioners and the other masculine guests in another room. A tournament followed, with another great banquet that evening. The joustings and feasts continued for several days, with pageantry, floats and 'disguisings'. The entire town celebrated. A *Te Deum* was sung at St. Paul's; bonfires blazed in the streets; 'and at every fire an hogshead of wine [was] couched, the which in time of the fires burning was drunken of such as would, the which wine was not long in drinking!'

Thus, hailed by populace and poets as the harbinger of peace, the twelve-year-old Queen of Scots presided over all the court festivities, revelling in her new title and her precedence over her younger brother and sister. Margaret would afterwards recall this week as the happiest time of her life. Safe and comfortable in the midst of her family and friends, she could enjoy all the prestige and glamour of the queenly state without bearing any of the duties or responsibilities it was to entail.

This blissful state was short-lived. In April 1502 a messenger arrived from Wales. Soon after his arrival Margaret saw her father's confessor, a Friar Observant, enter King Henry's presence and request to speak to him privately. From the distressed look on the cleric's face it was evident that the message was a sad one, as indeed it was. Prince Arthur was dead. Never robust, he had caught some fever in the damp chill of the Welsh mountains. His bride was recovering from the same contagion, but he had succumbed.

On receiving this tragic news, the King sent for his wife, saying

'that he and his Queen would take the painful Sorrows together'.
Elizabeth, hastening to her husband's side, tried bravely to restrain
her own sobs and comfort her grief-stricken husband. She 'besought his Grace, that he would first after God, remember the Weal
of his own noble Person, the Comfort of his Realm, and of her'. She
reminded him that although his mother had had no other children
but him, God had preserved him and raised him to the throne. He
still had three healthy children, and he and she were young enough
to have more. 'Then the King thanked her of her good Comfort'.
But when she reached the privacy of her own room, the natural grief
of a mother bereft of her first-born overwhelmed her, and she wept
so vehemently that her ladies sent for the King to come and comfort
her. 'Then his Grace of true gentle and faithful Love, in good Haste
came and relieved her, and showed her how wise Counsel she had
given him before; and he for his part would thank God for his son,
and would she should do in like wise'.

This account by the sixteenth-century chronicler portrays the
mutual devotion of Henry and Elizabeth, and makes it difficult to
accept the frequent assertion that he treated his wife with cold
indifference. The unsympathetic view of the King has been
preserved chiefly by historians relying too much on his biography
by Francis Bacon, which has recently been revealed as un-
trustworthy. Most contemporary accounts show that the first
Tudor was a reserved but kindly man, devoted to his wife and
children. Hence it was a truly heartbreaking event for the King, as
well as the rest of the royal family, when Queen Elizabeth herself
died less than a year after her eldest son. Childbirth, so often fatal to
mothers in those days, brought death to gentle Elizabeth of York at
the age of thirty-eight.

The loss of her mother came at a time when Margaret especially
needed her counsel in preparation for her approaching marriage.
This event was scheduled for the autumn of 1503, and as the time
drew near, the Queen of Scots realized that the role for which she
was destined would entail burdens as well as prestige. She must
travel far from her familiar and luxurious home to live in what was
then a completely foreign country, and with a man over twice her
age whom she had never met. True, she had been told that he was
brave, learned and accomplished, popular with men of all classes —
and with women too. The rumours which she had heard about
these ladies were disturbing: he had had many illicit affairs; he
acknowledged a number of illegitimate children; he loved one of his
mistresses so deeply that he had even contemplated marrying her
though she was not of royal birth. Did he still love this paramour?
Would his thirteen-year-old bride have to share his attentions with

a commoner? With all the pride of a Tudor, Margaret rejected this humiliating idea and turned her attention to her new wardrobe.

Fine clothes were her lifelong passion, and as she watched the seamstresses working on the elegant trousseau, she was able to forget her uncertainties. There were gowns of rich velvet, some edged with fur, some with tinsel, some embroidered with gold and silver thread and adorned with gems; robes made of cloth of gold and of silver tissue. She had shoes to match every robe, and hose knitted of wool and of silk, damask kirtles and smocks, and fine linen petticoats. For important public appearances during her journey north she would ride in a litter covered with cloth of gold, fringed with gold silk, and embroidered with the royal coat of arms. The litter bearers would be clad in green and black livery, while her footmen would wear green cloth of gold and white. Her fur-lined coach was painted with the Tudor coat of arms, its horses trapped and harnessed in black and crimson velvet; the riding saddle for her own palfrey was embroidered with red roses. When it came to outfitting his daughter for her marriage, King Henry spared no expense, although he did ask his prospective son-in-law what wages he was going to give Margaret's English servants during their long journey to Scotland. James tactfully evaded this question, although he accepted the responsibility for paying her attendants after they reached his realm. So the servants accompanying the young Queen may have had as much cause to worry about their future as their mistress.

At last the day came for departure. On June 27th 1503 the King accompanied his daughter on the first stage of the journey to Colliweston in Northamptonshire, the home of Henry's mother, Lady Margaret Beaufort. It was said that the shrewd Countess of Richmond had, by clever manoeuvring behind the scenes, been the real mainspring for her son's success in gaining the throne. The King was devoted to her and often sought her counsel. It was natural that he should take his daughter for a last visit to the Countess before the long journey north, especially since the Princess was Lady Beaufort's namesake.

Doubtless the young girl received much good advice, both worldly and spiritual, from her grandmother, who was noted for piety and scholarship as well as for political cleverness. Henry also gave her a fatherly admonition, reminding her of her obligations to her family and her nation. To help her remember all these injunctions, he gave her a beautiful Book of Hours, inscribed on the flyleaf with his own signature. His mother had probably helped plan the content of this illuminated manuscript, since it contained many lofty precepts for the sort of behaviour for which Lady Margaret was noted, including benevolence to religious institutions and especially to centres of learning.

The model held up throughout the book was Saint Margaret, a peculiarly appropriate model for the Princess to imitate, since this eleventh-century saint had also been reared as an English Princess and had married Malcolm III (Canmore), King of Scots, after the death of Macbeth. She was remembered for her softening influence upon her crude warrior husband and for her many good works in caring for the poor, establishing religious houses and spreading culture. Did Lady Margaret fondly imagine that her granddaughter would achieve a similar reputation? At any rate, the Book of Hours shows the young Margaret receiving inspiration from the saint. The Princess is pictured wearing a gold crown and royal robes. Kneeling at a gold-draped table with her hand on a large open book, she gazes up at Saint Margaret, who floats above the table in the centre of a dazzling halo.

The same picture appears at intervals throughout the volume, which also contains scenes from Saint Margaret's life and the lives of other saints. Margaret was delighted with the book, and especially with the flattering portraits of herself. But if she was inspired to emulate the model held up for her, she was foredoomed to failure; as a typical Tudor, she had some admirable traits of character, but none likely to lead to canonization. Moreover, the future which the fates had in store for her would have tried the patience of even a saint.

Fortunately that future was well hidden as she said farewell to her grandmother and her father. Parting from him must have been especially painful, for she had always been very close to him, particularly since her mother's death. She must have realized that this was a final goodbye, for with the great distance she was to travel and the many uncertainties of the day, it seemed unlikely that she would return within his lifetime, if ever. But if she wept, she managed to hide her tears from her companions. At least, none are mentioned in the lengthy and detailed account which was written of the entire journey by one of her retinue, Somerset Herald, John Young. His journal gives a day-by-day description of the trip, making it evident that he thoroughly enjoyed being a part of the magnificent train acompanying the young Queen.

He first lists all the important members of the company, starting with the Earl of Surrey, Treasurer of England. To this foremost member of his court, his most capable general, King Henry had given the task of supervising his daughter's journey. His wife, the Countess of Surrey, acted as duenna to the young girl. Like many in such a position, she and her husband became somewhat irritating to their charge, as is clearly indicated in the letter Margaret sent to her father after her wedding.

Nevertheless, Margaret managed to hide her annoyance, at least from the notice of the observant young Somerset Herald. According to his journal the 'Quene of the Scotts' behaved with perfect propriety on every occasion, enacting the role assigned her with poise and graciousness which were remarkable in a thirteen-year-old. As a matter of fact, Margaret thoroughly enjoyed participating in most of the ceremonies. All her life she was to exhibit the love of finery and display that was so typical of the Tudors, along with her family's ability to dramatize any situation to her own enhancement. Therefore she naturally responded to this opportunity to make herself the centre of attention, and, suppressing the pangs of grief at parting from her father, she rode to the head of the procession, 'richly dressed, mounted upon a fair Palfrey'.

She was 'very nobly accompanied, in fair order and array, of the said Lords, Knights, Ladies and others'. John Young continues to name each of these important individuals, describing in detail their gorgeous apparel and outstanding attributes. The Earl of Surrey led the nobles, followed in order by knights, squires and yeomen. Even on such a trip over hundreds of miles, social rank and precedence were carefully maintained.

After this military vanguard came the young Queen of Scots, surrounded by liveried footmen wearing the Tudor emblem on their jackets. An extra palfrey was led behind for use whenever she might require it, as well as her 'very rich litter borne by two coursers, very nobly dressed'. Next came the ladies on horseback, accompanied by a number of squires; than a carriage drawn by six horses and bearing four more ladies, whose servants followed on horseback.

There were minstrels and other musicians to enliven the parade through each town, while officers of arms and sergeants of arms marched along close to Margaret to protect her from being jostled by the crowds. When necessary other officials brandished their maces in order to create sufficient space around her to enable the crowds to see the Queen and her company plainly. Behind this troop of females and their servants came the retainers of the lords and knights, each retainer dressed in the livery of his master. The nobles' carriages were likewise adorned with the coats of arms of their owners. Margaret's green and white carriage bore the 'Arms of Scotland and of England . . . with red roses and portcullis crowned' (these being symbols of the Tudors).

As she traversed each county, its sheriff, with a company of thirty horsemen dressed in his livery, would ride before her holding up a white rod of office. Each time she approached a town, its officials would come forth to meet her, along with all the chief persons of the town, sometimes a company of friars singing *Laudes*, sometimes the bishop of the town's cathedral bringing a cross for her to kiss.

'Through all the good Towns and Villages where she passed, all the Bells rang daily. And by the way came the Habitants of the Country for to see the noble Company, bringing great vessels full of drink, and giving the same to them that need had of it. . . .' Lodgings for the night varied according to where they stopped: sometimes the home of the most important official was used, sometimes an abbey, sometimes a bishop's palace, or, if none of these were available, an inn.

The elaborate procession greatly impressed the people who flocked to see it, thus fulfilling one of its chief purposes. The image of Tudor greatness must be made clear to all, especially in the northern parts of the country where there had been most disaffection for the new monarchy. In particular, it was important to strengthen the dynasty's hold in York, the very centre of the White Rose's strength. But here, if there were still lingering die-hard followers of Edward IV or Richard III, they were certainly not evident. The whole shire turned out to welcome the daughter of Henry VII in a celebration that outshone all the preceding ones.

First the two sheriffs came out to welcome her to their franchises, along with other town officers and a crowd of burgers and common habitants. Soon afterwards Percy, the Earl of Northumberland, appeared. Margaret remembered him from the time of her bethrothal. As usual he was magnificently arrayed and wore crimson velvet with 'sleeves and collar bordered with gems, his Boots of Velvet black, his Spurs gilt'. He cantered up, causing his spirited horse to make frequent 'gambades pleasant for to see'. He was followed by a company of footmen, knights and gentlemen who were elegantly accoutred and splendidly mounted.

However, Earl Percy and his party could not outdo the Queen and her companions in magnificence. Before arriving in the vicinity of York, her entire company had stopped in order to change their travel-stained clothes for fresh and more costly garb. Bathing facilities were never plentiful in the sixteenth century and were almost non-existent here on the moors, but their absence did not bother anyone. In spite of their unwashed bodies, lords and ladies put on beautiful garments of silk, satin or velvet in the vivid colours which were so popular at the time. For the occasion Margaret chose a gown of cloth of gold, with a close-fitting bodice which was low-cut at the neck to display a choker and pendant of sparkling emeralds.

As the procession moved along, the music of trumpets, sackbuts and hautboys signalled its approach to the waiting town. In an expansive gesture of welcome, the mayor had ordered one of the city gates to be widened so that the Queen's equipage could pass through it. (The spot is still marked on the ancient city wall by a bronze plate which reads, Queen Margaret's Gate.) Church bells throughout the town rang out a welcome as King Henry's daughter made her entrance, ensconced in the horse litter that was lined and fringed in gold.

Immediately inside the high crenellated town walls she was greeted by the Lord Mayor, robed in crimson satin, riding a sturdy horse and accompanied by his aldermen. Then, bearing his great mace of office, he preceded her to the 'mother church' of all northern England. The narrow streets leading to the great cathedral were thronged with citizens and 'All the windows were so full of Nobles, Ladies, Gentlemen, Burgesses, and others in so great Multitude, that it was a fair sight for to see'. The Archbishop of York received her at the Minster, together with the Bishop of Durham, the Abbot of St. Mary's and other clergymen, all in their pontifical robes. After kissing the cross near the font, she proceeded to the altar to make her offering, giving thanks for the safe journey.

She spent the night in the Archbishop's palace. The next day, Sunday, the company remained in York, where they attended Mass and took part in a magnificent procession at the Minister. The Princess was dressed for this occasion in another gown of cloth of gold, with a collar of precious stones and a golden girdle. Her heavy train was borne by the Countess of Surrey, with the assistance of a gentleman-usher. They were followed by all the ladies and gentlemen of her retinue, wearing their richest garments, with 'great collars, great chains and girdles of gold'. Other nobles, knights and squires brought up the rear. The huge church was so filled with townsfolk that 'it would be impossible for them to be numbered'. Nevertheless, 'so good Order there was, that no cry nor noise was made'. After a lengthy service, dinner was served for the royal party in the Archbishop's palace. Here the Countess of Northumberland came to be presented to the Princess and to receive her kiss of welcome. The dinner was a splendid one, with hundreds of different dishes. Each time a new course was served 'Trumpets and other Instruments rang to the Ancient Manner'.

On the following day the great procession departed from York and continued the long trek northwards. The vastness of Northumberland amazed the Princess as they spent day after day crossing its great moorlands. Percy, lord of all these domains, also impressed everyone with the magnificence of his dress and retinue, the excellence of his steeds, and his expert horsemanship. He rode beside Margaret much of the way and entertained her by showing her interesting features of his homeland. Just beyond the little market town of Hexham, where they spent one night in the abbey, he pointed out the ruins of Hadrian's Wall which had been constructed in the second century A.D. by the Roman conquerors of Britain. Margaret gazed at the remnants of this ancient barricade which stretched far into the distance over the rolling Northumbrian hills. It had been built to defend the fertile lands of the south against the marauding Picts and Scots of those long-ago days. Now here was she, a representative of that southern kingdom, *en route* to wed the present ruler of those wild tribesmen of the north. Would she, through her marriage, be able to bring to an end the international conflict which had recurred so often from the second century to the sixteenth?

At the 'New Castell' on the Tyne, Earl Percy provided a lavish banquet for the entire company 'which lasted to midnight, for cause of Games, Daunces, Sports, and Songs'. Small wonder that the open-handed host was gaining the title of 'Percy the Magnificent'! One new addition to the party here was Lord Dacre, King Henry's chief representative in the Borders, charged with holding this strategic area for the English. Despite the obsequious manner with which he addressed the daughter of his monarch, the Princess felt a vague sense of distrust. Little did she then guess how many times their paths would cross in the future, nor could she realize how correct the sense of foreboding which she felt on first meeting the Warden of the North would prove.

The next night they were again guests of Percy, this time at his great castle of Alnwick. Here the Earl provided the young Queen of Scots with a form of entertainment which she enjoyed more than all the elaborate festivities and formal ceremonies that had been her daily fare ever since leaving Colliweston. He took her to his park to let her engage in her favourite outdoor exercise, hunting. She had learned this sport from her father, with whom she had spent many happy hours of her childhood in woods and fields. Now she was delighted to be able to exhibit her skill with bow and arrow by shooting a large buck. This recreation was a welcome relief from the tedium of constant travel. However, the end of the long journey was at last in sight.

On July 30th they reached Berwick. This Border stronghold had changed hands many times in the past, but was now under firm English control. As they entered the fortified town, they were greeted by the boom of cannon. This was still rather an unusual sound, for although gunpowder had been introduced into Europe over a century earlier, it was not yet widely used. The reverberations delighted youthful members of the party like John Young, who declared it 'was fair for to hear'. The Countess of Surrey, on the contrary, clasped her hands over her ears and shuddered. Looking at her husband's martial frame as he rode at the head of the procession, she wondered how long it would be before he might be called on again to lead an English party into Scotland; next time he came would the cannon still be signalling a joyful welcome, or something more serious and deadly?

CHAPTER 2

COURTSHIP IN THE ROYAL MANNER (1503)

Thirty-four days after they had left London, the cortège left Berwick, the last English town, and crossed over into Scotland. As they drew near to Lamberton Kirk, they were met by emissaries of the King of Scots. The Archbishop of Glasgow led a company of mounted noblemen, knights and squires, all handsomely dressed in velvet or damask, and followed by the usual 'great multitude of people'. As the two groups came together, the trumpets of the Scots blew a welcome, 'the which melody was good to hear'.

The Queen was led to a pavilion. Here she and her train were brought refreshment, served from three more pavilions. 'There was plenty of bread and wine' for all — a notable achievement, since nearly 1,000 Scots had met them and the English party alone now numbered about 1,800. Most of the latter, however, soon left, having seen their Princess safely across the Border. Percy of Northumberland made his exit as magnificently as he had made his first entrance, causing his steed to perform more 'gambades and leaps'. Over 500 of her original company continued with the Princess. They spent that night at the Priory of Coldingham.

Next day, passing Dunbar, where ordnance was fired to welcome them, they came to Haddington and were lodged at a nunnery. Their progress through the country was slowed by the rough and very narrow roads, but local countrymen rushed forward to clear the path. For many others the sight of their future Queen and her vast company was an exciting event in their monotonous lives. It was the first time they had seen so many Englishmen traversing their often-disputed area on a peaceful mission. Usually, they came galloping across the Borders brandishing swords and leaving a trail of devastation in their wake. Some of the country folk now offered flagons of beer to the travellers, but, adds Somerset Herald, this was not a free treat. Each drinker was expected to pay for his draught. These peasants were, after all, very poor, and the passage of the wealthy Englishmen was an opportunity for the thrifty Scots to get a little of their own back again from the southerners who had so often devastated their land.

On August 3rd, Margaret and her great train arrived at the castle of the Earl of Morton in Dalkeith. Its lord presented his new Queen with the keys of the well-kept stronghold. As Margaret was being freshly robed for supper, there was a clatter of hooves in the courtyard outside. Several of her ladies, sitting close to the window, looked out and jumped up exclaiming, 'The King! 'Tis the King of Scots!'

Edinburgh was the place officially scheduled for their meeting, but the prospective groom could not restrain his eagerness to meet his bride. His surprise visit was not, however, entirely spontaneous, but followed a well-established rule of courtship in the sixteenth century, based on the popular literature of the day. All chivalric romances told how the eager monarch and his retinue would go disguised as a hunting party and intercept the path of his intended. So, although none in the English party knew where or when he would make his appearance, the coming of King James that evening was not entirely unexpected.

Nevertheless, even the carefully trained Margaret could not repress a quick gasp at the news that the long-expected moment was actually at hand. How glad she was that she had donned for this evening the green velvet gown with low-cut neck that displayed her beautiful pearl necklace, wound about her throat! With a fast-beating heart she heard the tread of many footsteps coming up the stairway towards her chamber. Forcing herself to walk unhurriedly, she now moved to the doorway, surrounded by the throng of her curious ladies. The door opened and there, in the forefront of a group of gentlemen dressed in hunting garb, stood the man who was to share her life from this time forward 'forever after'. She saw a well-knit man of medium height, with shoulder-length auburn hair already slightly touched with gray, and, to her dismay, with a beard 'something long'. His jacket of crimson velvet, bordered with cloth of gold, was over elaborate for a hunting expedition. Nevertheless, he wore boots and spurs and, as tradition also required, his lute was slung across his shoulders. She at once dropped into a deep curtsy, while he bowed low. Lifting her from her obeisance, he kissed her gently, then turned to kiss each of her ladies and particularly to welcome the Earl of Surrey and his wife.

'Then the Queen and he went aside and communed together a while. She held good manner, and he bare-headed during the time and many courtesies passed'. As they talked Margaret found herself able to look at him more closely. Despite her aversion to his beard, the smile behind it was warm, and the hazel eyes were kind as they looked down at her. He, for his part, saw a girl who, though rather tall and well-proportioned for her age, was not much older than his own eldest daughter. Beneath the snood her hair shone red-gold in the torchlight. Her face, still childishly round, was clear-skinned, pink and white. A dimple appeared in her cheek as she smiled uncertainly up at him.

He asked her about her father, her younger brother, now Prince of Wales, and her little sister. Once again, as he had already done by letter and messengers, he expressed his sympathy for the deaths of Prince Arthur and 'Queen Elizabeth. He also had lost his mother at an early age, he told her. Then, turning to more cheerful subjects, he asked about the journey from London. He hoped it had not been too tiring for her. It surely had taken an extraordinarily long time. He had been sending messengers for days to inquire when they would reach Scotland.

She answered his questions, giving all the proper responses as she had been schooled to do. She then asked him about his hunting, a natural topic since he and his men had come in the guise of a hunting party. Noting her apparent interest in the subject, James pursued it further and was delighted to hear her lively description of killing the large stag in Percy of Northumberland's park. He promised soon to provide her with much more sport of this kind — a prospect that had her smiling in anticipation by the time that a blast of trumpets announced supper.

They moved from her chamber to the great hall, where the meal was to be served. Having 'washed their hands in humble reverence, and after set them down together', James insisted that his bride-to-be take the seat of honour and be served first with every dish. After a bounteous repast, 'Minstrels began to blow, where danced the Queen, accompanied of my Lady of Surrey'. Margaret performed with the grace instilled by years of practice, well pleased with this opportunity to display her accomplishments. She accepted as her rightful due the monarch's lavish compliments. Yet, she could not help blushing a little with pleasure as James praised her. Then he turned to compliment her partner, Lady Surrey, and Margaret bit her lip and gave a sigh of weariness. Taking this as a hint that she was growing tired, her suitor rose and declared that the hour was late; he and his party must be off. Thus 'he went to his bed at Edinburgh very well content of so fair meeting . . .'. As soon as he had left, her ladies crowded about her exclaiming over her good fortune in having acquired so attractive a bridegroom. 'Was he not handsome?' they asked Margaret. But she refused to agree so readily. His 'beard is too long', was her only comment.

That night a fire broke out in the castle stables. To the Princess's horror, she learned that a number of her horses had died in the smoke and flames, including her own favourite palfrey. She was still grieving over this loss the next day as the party moved on to the

Opposite: Henry VIII as a small boy

(Collection of the Earl of Warwick)

Below: Henry VIII as a young man
Artist unknown, *c.* 1520

(National Portrait Gallery, London)

Abbey of Newbattle, where they were to sojourn for several days. In the evening, hearing that the King was again coming to see his fiancée and to express his sympathy for the loss of her horses, a number of English lords set out to meet him. However, he, 'flying as the bird that seeks her prey . . .', took a different route and came alone to the abbey. Hence once again he was able to take Margaret by surprise. Accompanied by several noblemen, he entered her chamber and found her playing cards with some of her ladies. In spite of herself, Margaret felt her spirits lift with excitement as he strode into the room, wearing a black velvet jacket bordered with crimson velvet and white fur. She walked across the room to meet him and, records the ubiquitous John Young, 'of good will kissing him'.

Later the minstrels played for a bass dance, and again Margaret performed, first with the Countess of Surrey, then with Lord Grey, while several other couples joined in. Bread and wine were served, with which the King 'first served the said Queen' before he would partake of any. Then it was James's turn to perform. At his fiancée's request, he drew out his lute and played first it, then the clavichord, 'which pleased her very much'. Various noblemen, both English and Scottish, were next called on to play and sing popular ballads to entertain the company.

The evening passed so pleasantly that Margaret was regretful when the King at last asked her leave to depart. Kissing her good night, he ran down the stone steps to the courtyard, where a waiting squire stood holding his horse. Looking down after him, the Princess saw him vault lightly into the saddle, without even touching the stirrups, though his steed was very mettlesome and responded instantly to the rider's spurs. 'Follow who might', the King galloped away from the abbey. The Earl of Surrey and other nobles came after him more slowly, so James courteously reined in his horse and waited for them to join him. He and the Earl rode together for a short distance, talking. Then the English returned to the castle while the Scots rode on to Edinburgh.

James's visits continued every evening for the remainder of the four-day stay in Newbattle. Each time he and his betrothed sat together, with the Queen in the place of honour, in the only chair the house afforded. This seat was intended for the King, but 'because the stool of the Queen was not for her ease, he gave her the said chair', while he took the lower stool beside her. James continued always to insist that she be served first from every dish. Margaret was pleased with this deference, but annoyed because he also invited the Earl of Surrey and his wife to sit with them. James and the Earl had much in common, both being military men with plenty of experience in knightly tournament and in actual combat. In fact, in 1497, during one of the chronic Anglo-Scottish disputes, they had actually led opposing forces. James's men had raided across the Border, and Surrey, then Henry VII's commander in the north, had retaliated, driving the Scots back into their own territory. James next had challenged the English general to a jousting match — the prize, if Surrey won, a King's ransom, but if James was the victor, Scotland would regain the city of Berwick, along with nearby fishing rights. The Earl had refused to hazard his monarch's possessions on such individual trial by combat, though he agreed to accept the personal challenge at some other time. Subsequently, peace had been restored between the two realms and the marriage alliance established. Since that occasion, however, James had always wanted to meet Surrey personally and he enjoyed all the more the opportunities which he now had to converse with so renowned a fellow warrior. Each time they were together during banquets or other festivities, they would talk enthusiastically about outstanding champions they had watched in the lists, or would exchange views about new weapons being introduced into warfare. While they enjoyed this masculine conversation, the Princess found herself having to pass the time in tedious gossip with her daily companion, Lady Surrey. The young girl welcomed the moment, therefore, when the last course was cleared from the board so that the remainder of the evening could be spent in music, dancing and games.

She was, however, genuinely touched by James's generosity when, one morning, his emissaries arrived leading a string of handsome horses, each one equipped with expensive saddle and trappings. These were to compensate for the loss of her horses in the disastrous fire. He pleased her even more by sending a tame hart for her to enjoy hunting. The Earl of Surrey intervened and decreed that the deer should be saved for a later occasion when the King also could enjoy the sport of chasing it. Margaret was annoyed by Surrey's presumption in giving this order, but there would hardly have been time to enjoy a hunt, since the English company were due to enter Edinburgh itself that day.

For this occasion everyone dressed in his or her best. Most of the nobles, knights and gentlemen wore robes of crimson velvet, with their steeds trapped in matching velvet or gold-embroidered linen. The Queen was dazzling in a gown of her favourite fabric, cloth of gold, trimmed with black velvet; round her neck was a choker of rubies and pearls. She was borne in her litter, while the fine horse that James had given her was led after it. Halfway to the city the King came to meet her, accompanied by a retinue of gentlemen. He galloped up to her party on his spirited bay. He too was dressed in cloth of gold, bordered with purple velvet and fine black fur; his 'doublet of violet satin, his hose of scarlet', and his fine linen shirt edged with pearls. His steed was also trapped in cloth of gold, and his bridle was fringed with gold.

As he approached the Queen he doffed his flat velvet cap and bowed low to her. Then leaping from his horse, he kissed her as she sat in her litter. Next he remounted and rode beside her, conversing with her as the procession moved on. A gentleman now preceded the King, carrying his sword upraised. 'The said Sword covered with a Scabbard of Purple Velvet, which was written upon with pearls, "God my Defender"'. Behind them came the Archbishop of Glasgow, the Bishop of Moray and Earl Bothwell.

En route to Edinburgh James had provided several diversions to entertain his fiancée. First, they paused to watch an elaborate play in which two armed knights came out of a pavilion and battled over a 'fair Lady Paramour' until the King and Queen called upon the knights to cease fighting and present their cases for royal judgement. The antagonists agreed to suspend their quarrel until a certain day, when the King promised them a fair trial. Next the tame hart, which James had sent to Margaret, was brought out and loosed. A greyhound was allowed to chase it, but the deer was the swifter of the two. Having won the race to the town, the deer was given protection.

The time came for the grand entrance into the capital city. When they reached the town a gentleman brought the King a handsome courser, trapped in cloth of gold and crimson velvet. 'Upon the which Horse the King mounted, without putting the Foot within the Stirrup, in the Presence of them all'. He then made a gentleman mount behind him to see whether or not the horse would carry two. However, since the horse was not trained for the purpose, James returned it to the care of his equerry. Instead, he mounted the palfrey he had sent the Queen, and Margaret was placed on the pillion behind him. Thus together they 'rode through the said Town of Edinburgh' with Earl Bothwell now carrying the upraised sword ahead of them.

Two hundred Scottish knights, led by James's cousin Lord Hamilton, accompanied them through the city, 'some in jackets of Cloth of Gold, of Velvet, and of Damask, figured of Gold, and of many Colours'. These knights 'were commanded by the King that they should not go before, but only in the Company of the said Queen, that it might be seen that she was well accompanied and richly'.

Music for the parade was provided by companies of pipers and by minstrels and trumpeters of both nations. They performed equally well, although Somerset Herald adds scornfully that the Scottish ones 'had no new banners'. There were no Scottish officers at arms in attendance, as there were for the English. Except for these small details, however, the English herald could find nothing to criticize in Edinburgh. He appeared to be quite impressed by the show put on by the Scots King for his English guests.

At the town entrance had been erected a big wooden gate with two towers. Angels appeared at the windows of these towers 'singing joyously for the Coming of so noble a Lady', while another angel in the centre window presented Margaret with the keys of the town. Later on, there was a freshly painted cross and beside it 'a Fountain casting forth wine, and each one drank that would'. Near this wine fountain was a platform on which Paris could be seen handing the goddess Venus a golden apple 'for the fairest'. Other mimes on the same platform represented the Annunciation of the Virgin Mary and the marriage of Joseph and Mary. At another corner of the town a series of tableaux portrayed the four Virtues: Justice, holding sword and scales, stamping down King Nero; Force armed with a spear, trampling Holofernes; Temperance grasping the reins of a horse which was suppressing Epicurus; Prudence holding a wax taper, crushing Sardanapalus. On every street corner musicians hailed the advance of the long parade.

Somerset Herald notes with approval that the whole town had been decorated in honour of the new Queen. Tapestry hung from many walls; windows and doors were festooned with flowers. Every window was filled with 'Lords, Ladies, Gentlewomen and Gentlemen' watching the English procession, 'and in the streets was so great a multitude of people without number, that it was a fair thing to see. The which People were very glad of the coming of the said Queen. And in the Churches of the said Town Bells rang for Mirth'.

The college of St. Giles' Church came out to meet them, bringing sacred relics and presenting them to the King. He gave them to Margaret to kiss first, before doing so himself. The procession moved on down the steep hill of the Canongate, pressed upon by crowds of Scots in holiday attire. Their shouts of welcome to the English Princess were echoed by those of watchers gazing from the windows of all the gaily decorated homes and shops on each side of the narrow street. Crossing a meadow at the bottom of the Canongate, they entered the precincts of Holyrood. From the Church of the Holy Cross 'came the Archbishop of St. Andrews, Brother to the said King, his Cross borne before him, accompanied of the Reverend Fathers in God the Bishop of Aberdeen, Lord

Privy Seal of Scotland, the Bishops of Orkney, Caithness, Ross, Dunblane, and Dunkeld, and many Abbots, all in their pontificals, with the priests and canons richly revested, preceded by their Cross'. The Archbishop gave this cross to the King to kiss, but, as before, he passed it first to his betrothed.

Everyone now dismounted and entered the church. James, putting his arm about his young Queen, led her to the great altar, where cushions covered with cloth of gold had been placed for them. 'But the King would never kneel down first, but both together'. As they rose from their devotions a joyous *Te Deum* rang out. 'After all Reverences done at the Church' the King passed through the cloisters and into his palace, 'holding always the Queen by the Body, and his Head bare'. A group of important officials now approached to bow low before their new Queen: the Earls of Huntly, of Lennox, and of Morton, the Earl of Erroll, Constable of Scotland, the Earl Marischal of Scotland, the Earl of Argyll, Steward of the House, 'accompanied of many Lords, Knights, and gentlemen, well arrayed'. Then, as they entered the King's great chamber, they were greeted by 'many Ladies of great Name, wives to divers of the said Lords, and others, accompanied of many Gentlemen and Gentlewomen, arrayed very nobly after their Guise'. While the King went about the room greeting and kissing each lady, the Bishop of Moray escorted Margaret around, introducing her to each of them. 'After she had kissed them all, the King kissed her for her Labour'. Finally, with his arm about her again, he conducted her to her own apartments 'and kissed her again'. He then went to his rooms to entertain the nobles with a dinner, while a similar meal was served in the Queen's quarters for her and her ladies.

After supper that evening, James again went to visit the Queen. They danced several bass dances, this time as partners, before he 'took his Leave, and bade her good Night joyously'. The brief period of courtship was now ended.

CHAPTER 3

QUEEN OF SCOTS (1503)

'The eighth Day of the said Month every Man appointed himself richly for the Honour of the noble Marriage'. Some wore robes made of velvet of vivid shades; others, cloth of gold. The Earl of Surrey displayed about his neck the rich collar of the Garter, as did every other nobleman belonging to that prestigious order, while those not so privileged wore heavy gold chains as adornment. The King was resplendent in a gown of white damask embroidered with gold and lined with sarcenet. The sleeves of his jacket were of black velvet slashed with crimson satin, his doublet was cloth of gold, his hose, scarlet. A black velvet cap upon his auburn hair and a jewelled sword belted about his waist completed his costume.

The bride was dressed in a rich robe of the same colour and materials as her groom's; it was a gift from him for this important occasion and had cost £219, according to the royal accounts. He had also given her the beautiful gold and pearl collar and the golden crown, studded with gems. Beneath the crown, her long golden hair fell loosely to her shoulders as was the usual style for a bride, symbolic of virgin purity. Over it a coif of netted tissue hung to her heels.

Before the ceremony itself, the English bishops and nobles were conducted by their Scottish counterparts into the palace, where the King awaited them in his presence chamber. Here an English clergyman read aloud the conditions of the marriage and James's secretary accepted them in his master's name. Next the whole company, led by the Archbishop of St. Andrews and the Bishop of Aberdeen, entered the Queen's apartments to conduct her to the church. She was escorted by the Archbishop of York on her right and the Earl of Surrey on her left. Lady Surrey, with the help of a gentleman usher, carried the Queen's heavy train. On entering the chapel of Holyrood Abbey, this group occupied the left side of the church. The King and his entourage soon afterwards arrived to take up their stand on the opposite side.

After the Archbishops of York and Glasgow had taken their places in front of the altar, James walked across the aisle to Margaret. He bowed low, she curtsyed, and he then led her to the altar, his arm again about her waist. Here the marriage rites were finally performed by the two archbishops. Next the Pope's letter confirming the marriage was read out. 'This done, the Trumpets blew for Joy'. The King, still bareheaded, as he had been from the beginning of the ceremony, led the Queen up to the high altar in silent devotion. Here, as usual, James gave her precedence in kneeling on the cushions, covered in cloth of gold, 'paying her the most great Humility and Reverence, as possible might be'. Next came the Litany, followed by the Mass. Then after the new Queen had been anointed, James handed her the heavy sceptre. As the loud *Te Deum* rang out, Margaret, sceptre in hand, realized that at last she was in very truth, Queen of Scots.

Immediately after the church ceremony, the groom led his new bride to her chamber while he went to his own apartment to hold 'Estate Royal for that Day'. Dinner was first served to the Queen before being taken to the King. She was treated 'with all the Honour that might be done', and her chamber had been newly decorated. The tapestries covering the walls depicted the history of Troy; the glass windows were adorned with the Arms of Scotland and of England, with the addition of a rose and a thistle interlaced through a crown as a fitting symbol for the present marriage. Draped from the ceiling above her head and covering the wall directly behind her was her cloth of estate in richly embroidered cloth of gold. The only guest at her own table was the Archbishop of Glasgow. At the next table sat the highest ranking ladies who had accompanied Margaret from England, along with the high-born ladies of Scotland. Next there was a board for the Queen's Chamberlain, together with her nobles and knights; at a third and fourth board were the ladies and gentlemen of lesser rank.

The meal itself was prodigious. The first course alone consisted of twelve dishes, beginning with a wild boar's head, 'gilt within a fair platter', then a 'fair piece of brawn and in the third place with a Gambon'. The second course presented 'forty or fifty messes'. Meanwhile the King was served similar fare in his apartment, where he had as special guests at his table the Earl of Surrey, the Archbishops of St. Andrews and of York, and the Bishop of Durham. His chamber was hung with red and blue draperies, with a ceiling, or cloth of estate, fashioned like the Queen's of cloth of gold; and the walls were covered by tapestries depicting the story of Hercules. His Chamberlain and others of high rank sat at another board in the same room. As John Young describes the scene: 'In the King's Hall were three Rows of Tables, and one above in the Front, where was sat the Prelates', then, in descending order of importance, 'the great Lords, Nobles, Knights, Squires, Gentlemen, and other honourable Persons, at double Dinner'.

During the second service 'Officers of Arms presented them-selves' at the King's table to cry, 'Largesse'. But James commanded them instead to perform this ceremony for his bride. Consequently, in a few minutes, Margaret was honoured by the cry of 'Largesse, to the high and mighty Princess Margaret, by the Grace of God, Queen of Scotland, and first Daughter engendered of the very high and very mighty Prince Henry the VIIth, by that same self Grace, King of England'. This cry was repeated three times, 'in the King's Chamber, in the Great Chamber that is nigh, and in the Hall of the King and of the Queen'. And although it was James who gave the expected reward to his heralds, he would not let them cry out his own high honours, 'saying that it sufficed to cry hers'. Certainly the Scottish King was making every effort to please his new bride and her English friends. He succeeded completely with her company, at least if Somerset Herald's account correctly mirrors their senti-ments. How well did he please Margaret herself?

At that moment, she was too exhausted by the lengthy ceremonies, deafened by the continual fanfare, and surfeited with the enormous banquets, to give much thought to her own feelings. Like a well-trained actress, she went through the motions of her role, uttered the proper phrases for each required speech, and accepted with aplomb every tribute laid at her feet by her gallant husband. But how she must have longed for a moment of calm, at least a few hours in which to relax and to stop carefully acting out her part in this brilliant drama!

But the role of Queen was an exacting one, with little time for personal relaxation and scarcely even a moment of silence. Trumpets rang out during the meal as every course was carried in, minstrels played and sang, and a company of players enacted mimes. Like King Henry at Prince Arthur's wedding, King James was determined to impress his foreign visitors. Accordingly, as soon as the lengthy dinner was finished, the boards were removed and in the great hall 'the minstrels played, and the King and the Queen, the Ladies, Knights, Gentlemen, and Gentlewomen danced; also some good bodies made Games of Pass Pass, and did very well'.

Finally, however, the exhausted young Queen was given a respite. When Evensong was held, John Young describes how the King went 'to the Church, where the Abbot of the Place did the service'. James went with his 'Noblesse, and those of the Queen, but without her'. Margaret had had enough services for one day. During Evensong she snatched a few moments of rest. Even this stolen reprieve was short enough as supper came immediately after the service. There is no account of what dishes were served this time — surely little was needed after the lavish dinner — but once again the Queen was served first 'and the Personnages above said, again held their Places'. That night, bonfires blazed throughout all Edinburgh, as the entire populace celebrated the joyous wedding which they hoped would mean lasting peace.

The Somerset Herald was much pleased, as were his fellow English officers of arms when the Scottish King presented them with his magnificent marriage gown, while he himself now donned more sober garb. The next day, John Young and his friends went to thank their gracious host for this generous gift. Margaret in turn gave her gorgeous marriage gown to the Scottish heralds, but her husband retrieved it for her, redeeming it with a large sum of money so that she could keep the dress for her own wardrobe.

The next day the King again went to Mass, with his entourage of nobility, but again without his wife. Instead, the Earl of Surrey and his English followers accompanied him, and James had another opportunity for conversing with King Henry's general on the way back to their apartments. After dinner that day an Italian youth 'played before the King on a corde very well', and there was dancing. But 'touching the Queen, I say nothing, for that same Day I saw her not, but I understand that she was in good health and Mere [merry]'. Margaret therefore remained apart from these activities. According to some authorities, etiquette forbade the bride to show herself in public the day after the wedding. If so, this custom must have been a welcome one, since it allowed her to relax after the constant public appearance.

The following morning, however, St. Lawrence's day, the Queen again appeared on her way to the High Kirk, 'accompanied of her noble Train' of English and Scottish ladies. She was beautifully dressed in another 'Robe of Cloth of Gold with a rich Collar'. She was followed by the King with his company of noblemen, the Lord Huntly bearing the sword ahead of him. James wore a gown of crimson figured velvet edged with fur, a black satin doublet, scarlet hose, a black velvet cap, 'and his Beard kyted of Sheers'. This cutting of James's beard had been performed the previous day. Having learnt, when he went to visit his new wife the day after the wedding, that she much disliked his long beard, the good-natured monarch had permitted two of her ladies to trim it to his wife's taste. Lady Surrey and her daughter, Lady Grey, had volunteered to do the cutting, and the job was carried out immediately under Margaret's supervision. Not only did he thus acquiesce in her whim, but he also paid the two lady barbers magnificently. His treasurer's accounts record that cloth of gold worth £330 was delivered to Lady Surrey and gold damask worth £180 to Lady Grey.

That same day James knighted forty-one men in honour of his new Queen. As soon as he had given them the accolade, he told Margaret, '"These are your knights", and taking her by the Hand, led her to the Door of her Chamber'. Here the whole company were 'well and honestly served, as was also all the Fellowship, with plenty of Hippocras'. Later on, jousts were held to celebrate these events. Thus, with tournaments and feastings, church services and knightly ceremonies, dancing, music, and dramatic performances, every day was filled during the week following August 8th. Finally, the time came for the English guests to depart. Laden with gifts presented to them by their gracious host, they took their leave of the Scottish monarch and his youthful bride, 'and, that done, every Man went his Way'.

As she watched her companions of the long journey north turning back to retrace their steps to London, the English Princess must have had difficulty restraining her tears. Of course, she was left with English servants, as stipulated in her marriage contract. Some of her ladies also stayed, a number of whom remained permanently in Scotland and eventually married noblemen there. But their presence could not counteract the realization that she was now permanently settled in another world from the one in which she had always lived. The letter she sent to her father at this time is eloquent testimony to her feelings:

Sir, as for news I have none to send, but that my lord of Surrey is in great favour with the King here, that he cannot forbear the company of him no time of the day. He and the Bishop of Moray ordereth everything as nigh as they can to the King's pleasure: I pray God it may be for my hearts's ease in time to come. They call not my chamberlain to them which I am sure will speak better for my part than any of them that be of that counsel. And if he speak anything for my cause, my Lord of Surrey hath such words unto him that he dare speak no further. God send me comfort to his pleasure, and that I and mine that be left here with me be well entreated, such ways as they have taken. For God's sake, sir, hold me excused that I write not myself to your grace, for I have no leisure this time, but with a wish I would I were with your grace, now, and many times more, when I would answer. As for this that I have written to your grace, it is very true, but I pray God I may find it well for my welfare hereafter. No more to your grace at this time, but our Lord have you in his keeping. Written with the hand of your humble daughter, —

MARGARET

This passage is often quoted as evidence of Margaret's selfishness, showing as it does a total lack of appreciation for all the kindness with which James had treated her. Her petulant complaint about his attentions to the Surreys shows, it is said, that she had been badly spoiled, demanding that all attention be riveted on herself alone. The letter certainly does give this impression, but there are also other very plausible reasons for the newly crowned Queen's unhappiness.

An obvious one is the quite natural homesickness of a thirteen-year-old who, finding herself for the first time in her life living in a new and alien environment, realized that there was no escaping this fate. Another is the sheer physical exhaustion which must have overcome her by this time. As pointed out earlier, the thirty-four-day trip from London was one long series of public appearances interspersed with the discomforts of riding constantly, whether by carriage or on horseback, over rough roads in all kinds of weather. Then followed the entry into Scotland, the meetings with her husband-to-be, the wedding itself and all its attendant festivities.

But there was a further problem for the new Queen, completely ignored by most of Margaret Tudor's biographers. Somerset Herald's account of the wedding day concludes with this paragraph:

> After the supper, the night approached, therefore each one withdrew him to his Lodging for to take his Rest, and the King had the Queen apart, and they went together. God by his Grace will hold them in long Prosperity.

Thus John Young gracefully draws the curtain on the private life of the King and his new wife. However, in order to understand Margaret's unhappiness during her first days as Queen of Scots, it may be necessary to consider this occasion more closely. The first night of marriage is seldom one of perfect ease for a young bride. How especially difficult it must have been for a girl still thirteen, married to a thirty-year-old man she had met only a week before, and with whom she had had almost no private conversation, and had only been together on very public appearances! Knowing almost nothing of his private character, she was now to experience an even greater shock. Beneath his clothing, next to his skin, James wore a heavy chain of iron.

As she recoiled from the sight of these rusty links about his waist, her new husband tried to explain. It was penance, he told her, carried out as a permanent reminder of the mortal sin he had committed when he was fifteen years old. At that time a group of nobles had rebelled against his father, James III. These men had seized the young Prince and persuaded him that his sire was ruining the country by his ineptitude and had convinced him that, under their leadership, James III could be led to improve and reform affairs. Beguiled by their arguments and at all events unable to escape their control, the boy had permitted himself to act as their puppet leader, and had ridden in their ranks as they marched against the monarch. Defeated by rebels at Sauchieburn, near Bannockburn, the King had fled on a borrowed horse which then threw him. He was carried to the house of a miller and there called for a priest to shrive him lest he might die from his injury. The 'priest', however, on learning who had called for him, immediately stabbed him to death and carried his body for a reward to the victorious rebels. Thus James III had been treacherously slain in spite of the solemn promise the rebels had given his son that his father would not be harmed.

Margaret could not understand how James could feel he was to blame for this dreadful murder, since it was the nobles who had forced him into the war against his father, and he had had their promise that his father would be unharmed. But her husband could not absolve himself so easily for the part he had played in the tragedy of Sauchieburn. He had, in effect, been accessory to the murder, and to a person of his deep religious convictions this meant a lifetime spent in penance. He would never remove the iron chain; instead, he added a new link to it every year. He would go to his grave with it still about his waist.

Grim as this revelation was, it was not the only one that the new Queen was to hear. She learned that the rebellion that overthrew James III was only one of many such episodes in Scotland's past. One reason for this chronic turbulence was that the nation had had a series of child-rulers who had started their reigns with the disadvantage of lengthy minorities. During such periods, ambitious nobles would frequently try to seize or manipulate the youthful monarchs to their own advantage, with little regard for the welfare of Scotland as a whole.

Another problem was the division of the population into two separate elements. The Lowlanders, descended from the early invaders from the continent, were the more cultured, settled population who inhabited the fertile southern and eastern area. They dressed and behaved much like the nearby English and engaged in farming or commerce. But to the north and west, in the vast expanse of the Highlands lived the 'wild Scots', as they were called by foreign observers. Their ancestors were the savage Picts and Scots who had held the Romans at bay.

In many ways the Highlanders had retained the manners and customs of that early period. Their language was still the ancient Gaelic, a language similar to that of Wales, the home of Margaret's grandparents. The Highlands, like Ireland and Wales, were part of the 'Celtic Fringe' to which the early inhabitants of all Britain had fled when the invaders came. The area they inhabited was so barren and rocky that it was difficult even for sheep to find sustenance in many parts. Hence the people still lived by hunting and fishing, rather than by settled cultivation of the land. Unfortunately, the land which belonged to their more fortunate neighbours in the Lowlands was a favourite hunting area for the Highlanders. Flocks and herds from Lowland farms were frequently driven back up to the hills by these wild marauders, and luckless owners who tried to guard their property often lost their lives, while their homes and barns were looted and burned.

This sort of disorder, however, was no longer prevalent, as James reassured his bride. Justice was now maintained both in Highlands and Lowlands, though it took constant vigilance on the part of the ruler to maintain good order. He had been constantly engaged in this work ever since he had first wrested control of affairs from the nobles who had governed during his own minority. He had no fear of the 'Wild Scots', but travelled freely among them, talking with them in their own Gaelic, which he spoke fluently, discussing their grievances and giving them the same justice he gave all his people.

Despite his reassurances, however, the English Princess could not forget the fact that she was now in a land which was truly foreign to her own. Her role as Queen was not going to be as easy as it had seemed at that happy time of her 'fiancells' back in Westminster. Moreover, there were other matters to cause her anxiety, matters brought to her knowledge, not by her husband, but by her ladies-in-waiting. They had of course quickly learned from their Scottish counterparts tales of the many extra-marital affairs the bachelor King had enjoyed. One of his earliest mistresses, Lady Margaret Drummond, was the one he had even contemplated marrying. Beautiful and charming, she kept a pre-eminence in his affections so that even after a dalliance with some new charmer, he would return to her. But the Queen need not fear her, for she had died just a little over a year before. She had been poisoned, they said, along with her two sisters, Lady Fleming and Isabella Drummond. This dreadful crime, it was rumoured, was committed by the Kennedys, the family of James's next mistress, Lady Jane Bothwell, who feared that the King might leave Lady Jane and return to Lady Drummond. Lady Jane now lived at Dernaway, an estate near Elgin

which the King had given her. However, James had not been to see
her lately. Would the Kennedy family now decide to get rid of the
King's new wife as they had his former mistress? Perhaps there was
in fact ample reason for the new bride to be wishing herself back in
England with her father.

CHAPTER 4

KING JAMIE'S BRIDE (1503–1504)

> Nor hold no other flower in such dainty,
> As the fresh Rose of colour red and white
> For if thou dost, hurt is thine honesty,
> Considering that no flower is so perfite,
> So full of virtue, pleasance and delight,
> So full of blissful angelic beauty,
> Imperial birth, honour, and dignity.

Thus William Dunbar urged King James to be true to his English bride, whose marriage he now hailed in *The Thistle and the Rose*. This poem is famous because it makes the first formal use of the thistle as Scotland's emblem. Here this thorny plant represents James as the warlike Scot, bristling with weapons, marrying Margaret, the red and white Tudor rose.

With a poet's licence, Dunbar was certainly extravagant in his praise of the royal bride. Never in her life could Margaret have been described as full of 'angelic beauty'. Yet she does appear quite pretty in the portrait painted at about this age, her figure still trim, with only a suggestion of girlish plumpness. With her fresh complexion and long golden hair, she apparently won the admiration of the crowds who witnessed her entry into Edinburgh and later public appearances. Everywhere she was hailed as the symbol of lasting peace with England, and as the wife of Scotland's best-loved monarch in many years.

Responding to the cheers with smiling grace, she soon exhibited the Tudor knack of appealing to the common folk. The evidence of her popularity acted as a tonic to the young Queen, and helped her to overcome the pangs of homesickness which had engulfed her immediately after the marriage.

More important to her new-found happiness than the plaudits of the crowd, however, was her husband's attentiveness. He who had charmed every woman he met now set out to win the love of this thirteen-year-old. He would spend every evening in her apartments, entering with zest into the card games she enjoyed, and making small wagers with her and her attendants who were invited to participate, playing at her invitation on the lute and the clavichord and urging her to play. Sometimes a minstrel entertained them with ballads; at others, the musicians played for dancing, or wandering players were invited to perform. By day, whenever he had leisure, James took her out hunting or hawking in the fields and woods beyong the palace. These were, of course, favourite sports for him also; thus the sharing of mutual enthusiasm helped to strengthen her attachment to her husband. Almost against her will she found herself joyfully expecting his next visit, turning to receive his praise after she had killed a stag, choosing his favourite selection to play upon the clavichord.

It was easy for James to acquiesce in these matters, since his own interests were many and varied. Not only did he excel in all the usual sports and accomplishments expected of gentlemen of that day, but he also tried his hand at more lowly occupations, such as carpentry, barbering, and even dentistry. In the latter he developed some skill, practising upon such of his subjects as would permit it. It must have taken a courageous man to complain of an aching tooth to this King, for he would at once insist on drawing it for him! Afterwards, however, contrary to the common practice of dentists, the royal surgeon would then pay his patient. So his account books frequently show such extracts as this: 'Item: to ane fellow because the King pullit furth his tooth — 14 s.'.

His private account book also illustrates the simple, unostentatious kindness of his nature: 'To a monk of Arbroath, that lay sick in Edinburgh, by the King's command — 4s, 4d.'; 'To an Englishman that was ship broken [shipwrecked] — 28s.'; 'Given to an Irishman that said his silver was stolen — 2s.'; 'When the King departed, to the boy that brake his leg and lay still, there, to his expenses, and to pay for his leeching — 22s.', and one especially touching item: 'To a poor bairn that took the King by the hand — 3s.'.

His open, extrovert nature made it easy for him to win friends. The Lowland nobility who had been constantly critical of James III, opposing him and eventually rebelling against him, were loyal to his son even to the extent of following him finally into a war which many of them felt was folly. They had despised James III because he spent his time with special favourites on whom he showered gifts and titles, and because he appeared to prefer dabbling in the arts to the more masculine pursuits of joust and battle. Young James, on the contrary, showed such zeal for the exercises of knighthood that there were few who would dare challenge him in the lists, and in combat he was criticized not for cowardice like his father, but for the impetuous ardour that always made him rush to the forefront of battle. He never allowed his enjoyment of a wide variety of hobbies to interfere with his duties as monarch, but was instead constantly vigilant in maintaining order throughout his kingdom.

Margaret Tudor, Queen of Scots
by Daniel Mytens

*(With gracious permission of
Her Majesty the Queen)*

When on expeditions to supervise his government, he endeavoured to hear the viewpoint of all his subjects. He loved to mingle freely with the crowds, asking questions of humble citizens and encouraging frank answers. Apparently many individuals used such opportunities to ask for redress of personal grievances, as is shown from his own account book: 'Item — Paid to an Englishman and a woman that were spoiled [robbed] passing to Whitehern, by an Englishman and a Scotchman, which were *justified* [hanged] in Lochmabon — 14s.'; 'Item — to the man that hanged the thieves at the Hullibuss — 14s.'; 'Item — for ane rape [rope] to hang them in — 8p.'.

To help humble folk to overcome their reticence in the presence of their ruler, he would occasionally go incognito among his subjects. Disguised as an ordinary huntsman he might ride through the Highlands, seeking shelter in the home of some petty chief, conversing with him in his native Gaelic. Thus, he gathered from the 'grass roots' opinions of various policies.

Another role he would assume was that of a pilgrim, adopting this guise for personal and religious motives rather than political ones. For frequently in the very midst of court functions and pleasures, James would suffer an attack of acute melancholia. In the depths of depression he would relive the horror of Sauchieburn and its sequel, feeling anew the pangs of remorse. The only palliative for such guilt was immediate penance. In the medieval fashion, which was so characteristic of his nature, he would don sackcloth and ashes, take up the pilgrim's staff, and trudge barefoot and alone to one of the many shrines with which Scotland abounded, such as that of Saint Ninian. This saint, who first established Christianity in Scotland, was James IV's favourite. He made these pilgrimages in as private and unostentatious a manner as was possible for one of his position. Yet he hoped one day to fulfil the ambition of his heroes of the Middle Ages, by making the supreme gesture of medieval piety: a crusade to the Holy Land. Meanwhile, he carried out the other rituals classed by the medieval Church as 'good works', gifts to clerical foundations and faithful observance of all religious occasions, fasting and prayer, even retreating for days during Lent into a monastery for complete separation from the world.

Margaret gradually discovered all these facets of her husband's character and personality as she lived with him. She was far too practical and self-centred to share his idealistic views on life, or his religious enthusiasm, yet she appreciated his kindliness and responded to it with all the affection of which she was capable. She accompanied him wherever he went, and that meant almost constant travel, for like most successful monarchs of that time, he was always on the move.

There were several reasons for royal progresses in time of peace. First, the King's personal presence was needed to ensure obedience to his law, especially by the powerful nobles. This was particularly true in a nation like Scotland where native chieftains still held the prime loyalty of all those living on their own vast estates. A second reason for royal travel was the revenue system. Feudal dues owed to an overlord were paid mostly in kind, since coined money remained rather scarce. With completely inadequate transport facilities, it was difficult to send wagonloads of produce long distances to the capital city. The easiest way for the King to collect them, therefore, was to go to the source and consume them there. When a ruler travelled, he was accompanied not only by his family and personal servants, but by all the officials of his personal government with their servants, and by an armed retinue of knights, squires and yeomen. With such a horde to be housed and fed, a great quantity of taxes in the form of produce could be collected in a very short visit.

A third reason why all who could afford several estates moved frequently from one household to another was the very primitive sanitary system then prevailing. The *garderobe* was a sort of stone privy usually built far up in the corner of a turret. The reason for its height above the ground was to permit the excretions to ooze down over the walls for some distance before falling into the moat. Every castle had several of these *garderobes*, but not nearly enough to accommodate the crowds of people who would accompany a royal progress. So, with unfortunate frequency, emergency use was instead made of any inconspicuous spot, such as a chimney corner, an embrasure or an entrance to a winding stone staircase.

Obviously no house could remain hygienic for more than a month or so at a time when occupied by a fairly large number of people. It had to be almost literally 'hosed down' with many buckets of water from turret to foundation in order to cleanse it of the accumulated filth, then allowed to remain vacant (or nearly so) long enough to dry out and regain a more wholesome atmosphere. Fortunately permanent furniture was then quite scarce. Stone walls were left bare. So were the wooden floors, which would usually be strewn with fresh rushes or fragrant grasses, easily swept out and later replenished during preparation for new occupancy. The few benches, boards and trestles used for dining seats and tables were easy to move about and to scrub, as were also the rare bedstead and chair. Other furnishings, hangings to cover the walls, mattresses and covers for the beds, would be carried along with personal clothing in the many wagons that made up a King's caravan. A Queen like Margaret, who loved clothes, added considerably to the extent of the royal entourage. As many as thirty-five wagons were needed to contain her apparel on one progress. James, no slacker himself when it came to magnificent dress, rarely needed more than seven.

The first long journey they undertook together was early in September 1503. The monarch took his bride to visit many parts of her new country, starting with his favourite manor-house, Linlithgow, seventeen miles from Edinburgh. At first sight of this palace, Margaret loved it. She was impressed by its situation, on a low hill above a beautiful loch, and by the high entrance gate, crowned by a carving of the Scottish royal arms. As they crossed the drawbridge over the moat and rode in through the stone gateway, James briefly told her the history of the building.

In the twelfth century a wooden manor-house and a stone church had been built on the site. In 1301-1302, her own distant ancestor, Edward I, had put a peel, or palisade, around these buildings, but as soon as the Scottish Kings regained independence for their nation, they destroyed this evidence of English work. Several manor-houses in succession had subsequently been constructed and later demolished, until, early in the fifteenth century, James I had begun the present one. James IV himself had added considerably to the structure, putting in new passages and stairways and most recently building the south façade in preparation for his marriage. In her honour, he told her, he had had it constructed in the English style, and he proudly pointed out some of its features. Above the arched entrance was a beautifully carved scene of the Annunciation of the Virgin Mary. Margaret admired this and the other carvings, but she was especially pleased to find floor tiles decorated with love-knots encircling an 'I' (for 'J') and an 'M' in the King's presence chamber. She liked the great hall or 'Lyon Chalmer', so called from the great wall-hanging of satin emblazoned with the Lion of Scotland. This drapery, which had been sent from Edinburgh for their coming, covered the wall above the huge fireplace at the south end of the hall, the end in which the royal table was set. Here there were two high-backed chairs, made of oak, but cushioned with cloth of gold and fringed with gold silk, for although for formal occasions the King and the Queen each had a separate table, under more ordinary circumstances they would dine together. Seated at their table on the dais, with their feet resting on thick fur or woollen rugs and the great fire blazing behind them, they would look across the long room where the boards were laid for the diners of lesser rank. At the opposite end of the chamber a carved screen covered the passage to the kitchens. Above this partition was the gallery for the musicians who played throughout the meal.

Before the meal, however, a silver basin of scented water would be brought to the King and Queen. A high-born page or squire would kneel to hold this so that they could wash their hands before eating, one of the few hygienic customs of the time. A similar hand-washing ceremony followed the meal, and was necessitated by the fact that forks then were non-existent, so that everything had to be eaten with the fingers. Meat was cut for them by the royal carvers (usually members of the nobility). Meanwhile, the less exalted diners at the ordinary tables had to 'spear' their own meat from the common platters with their daggers. Gravy was sopped up with bread, but vegetables must have presented a problem for dainty eaters. However, there were not many vegetables available then, mostly beans, peas, carrots and beets. Other food was plentiful. There were always several kinds of meat and fowl, including game, venison, wild boar, pheasant, grouse and partridge. Some of these might have been killed by James and Margaret themselves, for Linlighgow had a park to which deer and boars were brought from Falkland and other royal preserves to provide hunting pleasure for the royal pair. Also there were fish from the adjacent lake, and apples, pears or cherries from the surrounding orchards. All these viands were washed down with wine which had been diluted with water and sweetened with honey.

The monarch and his wife partook moderately of the offerings of this great table. James has been praised by contemporary writers for notable temperance in both eating and drinking, and for not caring to linger long over his dining. Moreover, much of the time at the table was spent in conversation with the frequent guests, in watching the antics of the pair of court fools, Currie and his wife, 'Daft Ann', or in listening to the music of the minstrels. A quartet of Italian musicians customarily accompanied the King on his travels, and any wandering minstrel was sure of a welcome at the royal dining hall. After the meal was cleared away and the boards and trestles used for tables removed, a pantomime or a 'disguising' might be put on in front of the screen at the far end of the hall. Sometimes there was a miracle play depicting biblical events. At other times there could be dancing, or the entire company might lounge about the roaring fire to listen to tale-tellers who recounted the favourite stories about ancient heroes or the well-loved legends of King Arthur and his knights. As she relaxed in this pleasant atmosphere and looked about the torchlit hall, Margaret felt a sense of happy ownership, for Linlithgow was part of her own property, designated by James as one of her dower houses.

After several days spent pleasantly here, hunting and hawking by day and enjoying music in the evenings, the royal couple continued their progress northwards, visiting Falkland, Perth, Aberdeen and Elgin. Outside Perth, the new Queen saw the famous 'Moot Hill', where Scottish rulers were always crowned. She didn't know whether or not to believe the story James told her of the origin of this mound. He said that in ancient times a new Scottish monarch was supposed to travel to each district of the land to receive the homage of its chief. Later, to save the expense of a retinue sufficient to protect the ruler on such an extensive journey, it was decreed that the chiefs should instead gather at Scone, the approximate centre of the country, to swear their allegiance. In order to stand on his own property while pledging this loyalty, each nobleman would fill his boots with earth from his home. After giving the oath of fealty while standing on this soil each would then empty his boots on to the ground. Hence the name — 'Boot Hill' or 'Moot Hill'.

Whether or not this old legend was true, Scone, where James IV had been crowned, remained the chief meeting place for the Scottish Parliament. The chapel bell of the nearby Abbey of Scone was always rung before any new law was promulgated; thus, the 'bell of Scone' had come to be synonymous with the law of the land. Many important decisions had been made here: for example, the Great Council of 1318 had voted to establish the house of Stewart as the royal dynasty to succeed that of Robert Bruce. For many years every new King had sat for his inauguration on the Stone of Destiny, brought hither in 843 by Kenneth MacAlpin, who joined the Picts and the Scots into a unified kingdom. Then in 1296 Edward I seized the stone and transported it to England, in an effort to prevent the rule of further independent Scottish Kings. This attempt was unsuccessful of course, and, James added, one day Scotland would regain the stone, its rightful property. As he made this statement his tone was such that even Margaret was prudent enough to refrain from any reply.

At Scone Abbey they were entertained by the Abbot. Their next important stopping place was Aberdeen. The wind from the North Sea was wintry-cold when they went to the harbour to view the fishing boats and other ships, though it was still early in October. Nevertheless, after a short stay in Aberdeen, they continued northwards, but towards the interior, to Elgin. There they finally turned south, and by the middle of the month had reached Stirling, another of Margaret's dower houses.

She admired its size and its commanding location: a tremendous castle, perched high on a plateau with views of all the surrounding countryside, including the nearby battlefield of Bannockburn, where Edward II had been defeated by Robert Bruce in 1314. However, she did not enjoy her stay there. It was unmistakably built for defence rather than comfort, with stone walls fifteen feet thick at the base. Even the huge tapestries hanging from the walls could not keep out the damp chill. Also she was shocked to find that this, her dower house, was being used as the chief residence for a number of her husband's illegitimate offspring. James greeted them with warm affection, and they evidently were devoted to their father, who often came from Edinburgh to visit them. His new wife could not bring herself to share in this family scene. Her thoughts kept returning to the mother of each of these youngsters. The eldest, Lord Alexander Stewart, was the son of James's first mistress, Mary Boyd; Lady Margaret Stewart was the daughter of the unfortunate Margaret Drummond. Looking at this girl, only a year or so younger than herself, the new Queen wondered if she knew of her mother's fate. The unhappiness that had overwhelmed her at the time of her marriage once more engulfed her, and she fled to her own apartment, not waiting to make the acquaintance of still more children of her various rivals.

Despite the King's own enjoyment of his 'bairns', he could not be comfortable when his wife was so distraught. He soon gave orders that all their baggage was to be loaded once again for a return to Linlithgow. Three weeks here in the pleasant apartments looking out over the gracious lawns and the rippling waters of the loch, restored Margaret's spirits. On November 7th, the royal entourage at last returned to the capital city.

Margaret's fourteenth birthday was on November 29th, and the day was celebrated with feasting, tourneys and music. Her most impressive gift was a magnificent folio Book of Hours. James had ordered it and had it made over a year before, intending it as a wedding gift, but it had been delayed in coming from Flanders, and therefore he had kept it for her birthday instead. It was larger than the one which her father had given her as she was leaving for Scotland, but similar to it in its painstaking and beautiful manuscript and exquisite coloured miniatures. Every page was bordered with flowers, fruits and butterflies. The frontispiece was of the royal arms of Scotland, bearing the motto, 'In my defens God us defend', set within a frame of love-knots entwined with thistles and daisies (the French for daisy being *marguerite*). Two of the nineteen full-page illustrations portrayed the Queen and her husband, each kneeling in private devotions. The one of James showed him, in state dress of cloth of gold under an ermine-lined cloak, being presented to Christ by Saint James. That of the young Queen showed her dressed in rich purple and gold, kneeling before the Virgin and Child, while behind her stood Saint Cyriac, the martyr whose feast day was August 8th, the date of their wedding.

Her birthday was barely over before Yuletide began. James thoroughly enjoyed celebrating the Christmas season, planning not only many extra devotionals, but also additional merry-making, to keep the entire court occupied with as much festivity, feasting, music and dancing as had taken place in the week following their wedding. The master of the revels this year was Master John, a French physician who dabbled in alchemy. This pseudo-science fascinated the King who, being always short of money, felt that a new, cheap way to produce gold would solve all his financial woes. Like other impecunious rulers, he preferred to find ways of making new money rather than stretch his available income by careful economizing.

Unfortunately, Master John never succeeded in alchemy, but he proved very capable in devising revels to entertain the court. A morris dance was performed by six men and one woman dressed in red and white taffeta; miracle plays depicted the birth of the Saviour; 'disguisings' with elaborate stage settings were produced; and the music of harps, lutes, pipes and trumpets resounded throughout the palace during the traditional Twelve Days of Christmas. New Year was the day on which gifts were exchanged (in commemoration of the Feast of the Epiphany — the visit of the three Wise Men to the infant Jesus). James, generous as always, gave his wife a 'heavy ducat' (an ounce of gold), two magnificent sapphire rings and two crosses set with pearls. He also remembered each of her attendants and gave them presents of jewellery. Thus, with all the activity and celebration, Margaret had no time to feel homesick on this first Christmas away from her own family and England.

Shortly after New Year 1504, sorrow struck the Scottish royal family with the death of James's younger brother, Alexander, Duke of Ross, heir-presumptive to the throne. Despite his youth, he had been Archbishop of St. Andrews, since it was customary for important clerical appointments to be granted in accordance with royal influence rather than ecclesiastical vocation. This cynical disregard for merit when filling church offices was commonplace in Renaissance Europe and is illustrated by the fact that even the pious King James had no compunction whatever in establishing his relatives in lucrative church positions. As a result of the scandalously corrupt practices current in the sixteenth-century church, critics in Scotland, as elsewhere, demanded drastic reform of such abuses. Like the English Lollards, these Scottish reformers were termed heretics by the Catholic hierarchy and were persecuted. To

James's credit, he refused to countenance the demands made by many that such critics should be put to death. When he attended a trial where Scottish Lollards were being judged, he managed to turn the whole procedure into a farce and so avoided sending the accused to the stake.

His leniency to heretics notwithstanding, the King did not go so far as to agree with their demands for church reform, but continued to play a part in some of the corrupt practices. Thus, on the death of his younger brother, he obtained Papal approval to grant the archbishopric of St. Andrews to his own eldest bastard, Alexander. This boy, still in his early teens, showed, it is true, much intellectual promise. To prepare him for the dignity in store for him, his father soon sent him, along with Lady Bothwell's son, his younger half-brother, the Earl of Moray, to be educated in Padua under the celebrated Erasmus. At about the same time, young Lady Margaret Stewart was taken to Edinburgh Castle to be reared as befitted a King's daughter. Since Queen Margaret lived in Holyrood Palace while she was in Edinburgh, she apparently did not object to the girl's appearance in the capital city. The other royal children were also removed from Stirling so that their presence in her dower-house would not upset the Queen when she was in residence there.

Margaret stayed at Stirling for some time during the summer of 1504, while her husband went to attend the ayre of Dumfries. Personal supervision of his courts of justice was one feature of his government that helped make it effective, and he never neglected this important duty. Sometimes he also personally led his armed forces when they were needed to track down dangerous criminals. Thus, in 1504 he conducted the 'raid of Eskdale', to chase some notorious thieves and outlaws out of the area.

Before making this raid, the Scottish monarch had taken the precaution of notifying his father-in-law of his plans, to preclude an English attack on his party if they should inadvertently cross into English territory. Trouble was therefore averted and several English Border notables even came forward with gifts of food and drink for the husband of their King's daughter. The raid was successful in capturing the rebels, some of whom were immediately tried and executed, while others were held for a later court of justice at Dumfries.

During his absence, the Queen supervised changes being made to Stirling Castle, but had plenty of time to enjoy herself in such pastimes as riding, archery, and even such childish sport as running foot-races with some of her attendants. Records of these activities are available from her husband's account book, since he paid for the expenses she incurred, even including the wagers she lost to her attendants. She doubtless spent additional sums from her own purse, but since she failed to keep such meticulous accounts as did her spouse, there is no record of these.

The year 1504 marked an additional milestone in the Queen's career. When the Scottish Parliament met in March, the King presented his English bride to the assembled estates; she was then formally crowned. Other provisions of the marriage agreement were likewise concluded in this period. Her dower rights were confirmed by the Scottish Parliament, and a copy of this document of confirmation was sent to her father. King Henry, in turn, having received a parliamentary grant for the purpose, now made prompt payment of the part of her wedding portion that was by then due, and even went so far as to repay his son-in-law the expenses of Margaret's wedding journey incurred after she and her followers had crossed over into Scotland. Obviously the English monarch felt well satisfied with the treatment his daughter had received in Scotland. Margaret's letters home during the year since her wedding had evidently convinced her father that she was well contented. Although royal expense accounts record payments to messengers that carried her correspondence to and from England, the letters themselves are unfortunately missing for this period. However, one written by her to her brother, shortly after he had become King of England, indicates that she was happy in her marriage: '. . . Our husband is ever the longer the better to us, and we lack nothing'.

CHAPTER 5

SUNSHINE AND SHADOWS
(1504–1512)

Several years after his marriage, King James set out on one of his solitary excursions — this time to the north. Stopping only to change horses at intervals, he made the entire journey from Edinburgh to Elgin in one day, going by way of Perth and Aberdeen — a total distance of 187 miles. This remarkable feat proved the extraordinary endurance of the monarch (and of his steeds), although it hardly gave the ruler an opportunity of talking informally with his subjects, his usual objective on these incognito trips. He was able to spend the night after his arrival in Elgin in the home of a humble priest. Here he slept on a hard board instead of a comfortable bed. The next day he rode on to Tain in Ross where he worshipped at Saint Duthac's shrine. After he had thus combined a religious pilgrimage with a governmental inspection tour, he threw off his disguise and announced his presence to the people of the area. This gave the noblemen of that vicinity an opportunity to do him honour, and to escort him on his more leisurely journey home.

The ostensible aim of this expedition had been to check personally the safety of his highways from brigands. It also gave the restless monarch a chance to enjoy adventure away from the usual pressure of courtiers and the formality of palace functions. Margaret was concerned while her husband was away on quixotic excursions of this sort, needlessly exposing himself to danger from highway robbers or from accidental injury. She was even more worried, however, by another sort of excursion on which he went from time to time, again without her company. Like the knights-errant of the medieval romances whom he admired, James loved to go in person to right injustice, punish evildoers or assist the oppressed. He was especially responsive to a call for help from ladies in distress.

In the spring of 1504 he received word that Lady Bothwell was very ill. He responded by immediately dispatching his personal physician to attend his former paramour. Next, to make quite certain that she was recovering, he went to visit her himself, and finding that her health had amended he lingered on to enjoy the good hunting in the woods around Dernaway. The following year it was Lady Bothwell's 'bairn', the Earl of Moray, who, she said,

needed his father's presence at Dernaway, the manor-house which
James had given her years before when their relationship first
began. He had made this gift with the proviso that it would be hers
so long as she remained true to him: she had been mistress to the
Earl of Angus, Archibald Bell-the-Cat, before she had met and
charmed the monarch.

Of course, there was no reciprocity in this agreement. As in most
affairs of this sort, only the woman was expected to remain faithful.
Between his two visits to Jane, her royal lover spent considerable
time with another woman, known only by her initials, 'L. of A.'.
That this was a woman is clear because the King's Treasurer always
indicated such recipients of royal bounty in this manner. It is, of
course, through these account books that the ruler's various amours
can now be traced. So, in 1505 many expensive gifts of jewellery and
clothes were recorded for 'L. of A.'.

Although Margaret probably had no access to these tell-tale
records, she could not be kept in complete ignorance of her
husband's philandering. His unexplained (or poorly explained)
absence on trips from which she was definitely excluded, roused her
suspicions. Also the court which always surrounded the couple,
whether they were at Holyrood, Linlithgow or Stirling, was too
numerous and close-knit for even the ruler to keep many secrets.
Her faithful ladies-in-waiting were only too ready to whisper to
their mistress every rumour that was circulating.

Nevertheless, James tried to keep his young wife happy. He
continued to shower her with gifts on every occasion, magnificent
gems and the rich velvet gowns that she loved. He was unfailingly
generous too in providing her with money. The marriage contract
had stated that he was to continue receiving the revenue from her
dower lands throughout his lifetime, but should maintain his wife
meanwhile by providing for all her needs. This arrangement proved
to be far from a bargain for the husband. The sums he supplied to
keep Margaret in the style to which she was accustomed far
exceeded the income derived from her dower lands at Linlithgow,
Stirling and Kilmarnock. In addition to paying her pension and the
salaries of her attendants, he maintained her stables, furnished the
manor-houses where she resided and paid an average of £1,000
annually for her clothing and other paraphernalia.

Besides giving her as luxurious a life-style as sixteenth-century
Scotland could provide, he also continued to pay her a great deal of
personal attention. In addition to arranging hunting expeditions by
day and card-playing and music in the evenings, he thought of other
forms of entertainment for diversity. Special dances were performed in her apartments, with minstrels from England and a

dancing master from France, who showed them all the latest steps from the continent. The 'bass dance', still in favour throughout western Europe, was now enlivened by more rapid steps and more swaying. Together, the King and the Queen experimented with these innovations, while the musicians played '*L'amour de moi*', '*Helas, Madame*', and '*Joussance vous donneray*'. The courtiers applauded and, at the royal invitation, joined in the dance.

An amusing description of one of these sessions is given by Margaret's favourite poet, William Dunbar. In verses too bawdy to be quoted by Margaret's Victorian biographers, he ridicules the performance of several participants: Sir John Sinclair, the dancing master, whose 'one foot always went unright and with t'other would not agree'; or Master Robert Shaw, the Queen's physician, who 'staggered like a lame horse'. One lady, whom Dunbar called 'Dame Dounteboir' (a word meaning courtesan) 'made such motions with her hips, from laughter none could hold their lips: while she was dancing busily, a blast of wind sound from her slips'. On the contrary, however, he is generous in his praise of 'Dame Musgrave' for her 'trimly dance, her good convoy and countenance', and wishes he might marry this graceful lady-in-waiting. Altogether he declares, 'a merrier dance might no man see'.

Another form of amusement which was extremely popular with both royalty and commoner was the tournament. This violent sport was one the King loved not only to watch, but to participate in. Many a joust was held during his reign. It was still considered useful as a military exercise, giving the knights an opportunity to practise their feats of arms. It was more important, however, as a festivity, the crowning entertainment for any special occasion, to celebrate holidays, birthdays, weddings, or the presence of important visitors.

The most delightful example of tourneys during this period is the one held in June 1507. This joust was planned by the Queen in honour of her favourite attendant, Black Ellen. Ellen was one of two Moorish girls who had been brought to Scotland from Portugal in 1504 by the famous sea captain, Robert Barton. He had presented them to the Queen, and had brought a red-tailed Portuguese horse and a musk cat for her husband. Margaret immediately adopted the two dark-skinned girls into her household. They were converted to Christianity and baptized as Margaret and Ellen. The latter became the Queen's favourite. She now made her the heroine of a special entertainment which combined the features of a masque and a tournament. With the enthusiastic assistance of the King, a great spectacle was prepared. Invitations were sent out to knights all over Scotland, and as far-off as France, urging them to pit their skill against an unknown warrior; known as 'the wild knight', the champion of a beauty from far-off Africa, he would fight all comers.

On the appointed day a number of skilled competitors appeared at the lists drawn up before Edinburgh Castle. A large assembly of notables watched from seats erected for their comfort, while Queen Margaret presided from a special box provided for her and her court. Meanwhile a throng of the less privileged peered through the barriers erected on all sides of the mock battlefield. Brilliant pennants floated over the arena; a number of bronze cannon, the King's most prized new weapons, were displayed on the walls; an artificial 'tree of esperance' shimmered in the sunlight, its metal leaves and golden pears and flowers glittering, while on its branches crouched improbable winged 'beasts'.

Trumpets blew to herald the arrival of the dark beauty, who was drawn in a gilded chariot to the place of honour on the edge of the lists. She wore a robe of gold-flowered damask, trimmed with yellow and green taffeta and black velvet. Two maids of honour in similar dress attended her, while two knights clad in white damask acted as her squires. Again the trumpets blew, and in galloped the 'wild knight', on a magnificent war-horse, both steed and rider clad in shining steel. The knight, whose helmet was closed to hide his identity, brandished a gilded battle-axe. He was accompanied by two burly 'Germans' clad in black and yellow velvet and cloth of gold, and followed by several 'wild men' in shaggy goat-skin coats and helmets decorated with stag horns.

The challengers then came forward to contest the field with the unknown champion, but he bested each of them in turn. Proclaimed the victor, the 'wild knight' at last dramatically pulled off his helmet, and revealed the King of Scots himself. Though this revelation was probably a complete surprise only to the more lowly of the spectators, the entire crowd politely feigned amazement and applauded enthusiastically. These feats of arms were succeeded by a great banquet, over which the Moorish maiden presided as 'Queen of love and beauty'. The irrepressible William Dunbar as usual recorded the occasion in verse:

> When she is clad in rich apparel
> She blinks as bright as ane tar-barrel;
> And how she shines like any soap,
> The lady with the mickle lips.

The whole pageant won so much acclaim that a second tournament was performed several years later. Black Ellen was once again the honoured lady and the 'wild knight' predictably won against all comers, though it must have taken a good bit of acting on

the part of the spectators to show surprise when the unknown
champion again turned out to be the King.

Performances of this sort were often put on as part of the
entertainment for distinguished foreign guests. Among the visitors
from overseas who came to Scotland during this period were
representatives from the papal court. In April 1507 James was
presented with particular marks of favour from his Holiness: a
purple diadem surrounded with a gold-flowered wreath and a
magnificent sword with a golden hilt and sheath, studded with gems
(both are still to be seen in Edinburgh Castle among the Honours of
Scotland). Even more important than these costly gifts was the title,
'Protector of the Christian Religion', which was conferred on James
by the Pope. Inspired by this honour, the pious King of Scots
resolved even more firmly to follow the *via crucis* to Jerusalem.

Meanwhile his wife had in a less dramatic but more substantial
way shown her devotion to her duties as Queen. On February 21st
1507 she had presented her husband with an heir to the throne. The
infant was baptized two days later in a magnificent ceremony.
Robed in white silk and borne on a pillow covered with cloth of gold
and ermine, he was given his father's name and proclaimed Prince
of Scotland and of the Isles. The celebration of these happy events
included dancing to the music of drums and trumpets, songs by
minstrels and the distribution of money to the poor of Edinburgh.
Messengers were sent to carry the news to all parts of the kingdom,
as well as to London to let King Henry know he was now a
grandfather. The nursery established for the little Prince was
elegant enough to have won the stamp of approval of even Lady
Margaret Beaufort. Its furnishings included two cradles with
rockers to keep them in motion when occupied by his royal
highness. Silver utensils were to be used in preparing his food,
although for a while a wet-nurse, carefully selected for good health
and clean habits, was to provide his nourishment.

The baby's father, rejoicing with all his court and nation over the
arrival of his first legitimate child, was soon afterwards driven to the
opposite extreme of intense anxiety. His wife fell victim to 'a most
violent disease incident to child-birth'. Every remedy known to the
doctors of that time was tried without noticeable effect. James was
completely distraught. '. . . Yielding himself up to anguish', wrote
the historian, Lesley, 'he would not be soothed by any human
consolation. Wherefore, since he placed all hope of his wife's
recovery in God alone', he went on foot to the shrine of Saint
Ninian. This was a considerable distance from Edinburgh, located
at Whithorn in Galloway. However, the royal pilgrim felt that his
efforts had been worthwhile, for when he returned to Holyrood he

was greeted by the joyous news that the Queen had improved and was now expected to survive.

Meanwhile Margaret had been suffering not only from the difficult birth and subsequent fever (as well as the ministrations of the learned men of medicine), but also from mental anxiety. She recalled the fate of her mother. Was she also to succumb to the death that overtook so many women? She called out for James, who, despite all his faults, was ever kind and loving. When she was told that he had gone on a pilgrimage for her benefit, she burst into tears. Surely, she cried, he would be of more solace to her here by her bedside than traipsing across the land to the shrine of a long-dead saint. However, by the time he returned she was feeling much better. When she was triumphantly told by him and her nurses that her fever had broken at the very moment when he had fallen on his knees at Saint Ninian's tomb, even she was convinced it had been a miracle. In gratitude she now returned his kisses and smiled with relief and pride as he joined her in admiration of their infant son.

In July 1507, the Queen, having fully recuperated, agreed to her husband's suggestion that she ought to personally thank good Saint Ninian for her miraculous recovery. James would accompany her so that they might express their gratitude together. This pilgrimage was far removed from the lonely trek which the King had made in the depths of the preceding winter. Instead of trudging on foot, they rode on horseback, fully attended by ladies-in-waiting, servants, minstrels and other entertainers. There being this time no real urgency in their expedition, they broke the long trip by frequent overnight stops at such commodious resting places as Blackness, Stirling Castle, the Bishop's Palace in Glasgow, and even found time for several hunting excursions at some of their stops. It took seventeen horses to carry the Queen's baggage, though four were sufficient for her husband. Along the way they were entertained by musicians sent by noblemen through whose districts they passed, while countryfolk met them from time to time, bringing gifts of food and drink to refresh them. This leisurely itinerary brought them to Whithorn in a little over two weeks. Here they performed their devotions and left their offerings at the shrine. Their mission accomplished, they then spent another fortnight on the return journey.

The happiness of the royal family was short-lived. On February 27th 1508, the little Prince, who was just over one year old, died. By this time the young mother was already expecting another child, who arrived in July of that same year. But this baby girl expired almost as soon as she was born. Then came the birth of a boy in

October 1509. Tragically, little Arthur (named after the King's favourite hero of antiquity) lived only nine months.

Perhaps a miracle would still provide the grieving couple with the longed-for heir. In the spring of 1511 Margaret again made a pilgrimage, this time to the shrine of another of her husband's favourite saints, Saint Duthac, far to the north of Edinburgh. As on her previous trips, the Queen travelled in style. Apparently she agreed with Chaucer's Canterbury pilgrims, that a visit to a 'holy blissful Martyr' need not be devoid of earthly comforts. Her usual train of pack-horses carried a full wardrobe with outfits for almost every occasion, but almost certainly it did not include one of sack-cloth and ashes. Nor was this a solitary journey. Along with a military escort of knights and squires, an entourage of ladies-in-waiting and servants surrounded her. Even her favourite poet, William Dunbar, went along, to record in rhyme the reception accorded her at stops along the way. The town of Aberdeen made especially great efforts to greet their Queen in proper style. The High Street was cleared of pig-sties and other unsightly features, and instead was draped with tapestries and festooned with flowers. She was met by the chief officials of the city, attired in velvet and bearing a red-velvet canopy to shade her while her retinue paraded through the city. Several mystery plays were put on for her entertainment depicting biblical scenes such as Adam and Eve being ousted from Eden and the visit of the Three Wise Men to the Christ-child. Historical pantomimes were also included: Robert the Bruce rode up in martial array, followed by later Scottish monarchs. The whole occasion was vividly described by Dunbar:

> Then came there 4 and 20 maidens young,
> All clad in green of marvellous beauty,
>
> .   .   .   .   .
>
> Playing on timbrels and singing right sweetly
>
> .   .   .   .   .
>
> The lieges all did to their lady *lout* (bow)
> Who was conveyed with a royal rout
> Of great barons and lusty ladies *schene* (beautiful)
> 'Welcome our queen'; the commons gave a shout;
> Be blythe and blissful, burgh of Aberdeen.

After spending a night in this 'blythe burgh', she and her company went on their leisurely way, finally reaching the goal of their journey at Tain in Ross. Here the Queen worshipped and made offerings to Saint Duthac, along with her fervent petition for a child, living and healthy and preferably male.

James IV at prayer, from the *Book of Hours of James IV and Margaret Tudor*

(*Österreichische Nationalbibliothek, Vienna*)

Perhaps the good saint heard her prayers. Maybe the unusual number of devotions and offerings she and her husband made that year at the shrines around Linlithgow and Edinburgh helped. Or it may have been the supernatural effect of her acquiring the *sark* (shirt) of Saint Margaret. The timely discovery of such an important relic of the eleventh-century Queen of Scots was considered an excellent omen for the sixteenth-century Queen. Whatever the explanation, on April 10th 1512, another Prince was born, who was destined to survive the hazardous years of childhood and to become known in history as King James V.

Throughout these years of travail Margaret's health suffered. Every birth cost her intense pain and illness more severe than was usual in childbirth even in those days. Her life was despaired of more than once, causing her devout husband again and again to seek divine intervention through vigil, fasting and pilgrimage.

While the Queen was thus painfully fulfilling her chief duty by assuring the continuity of the royal house of Stewart, the King was working to improve his nation for his successors. More than any previous Scottish monarch, he endeavoured to develop commerce. The middle class, emerging at this time as an important factor in politics as well as in economics, benefited as a result of his efforts, just as the English bourgeoisie benefited from the Tudor regime.

To protect his merchants from attacks by pirates as well as by rival trading nations, James began building a strong navy. Three of his 'great and costly' ships were the *James*, the *Margaret* and the *Great Michael*. The third of these was his especial pride, intended to outdo all previous vessels in size and equipment. Its construction, according to contemporary accounts, 'wasted all the wood in Fife', despite the importation of much timber from Norway. The completed ship measured 120 feet by 36 feet — dimensions which were considered almost incredible at that time. While it was being completed, James spent much time at the shipyards of Leith. Margaret paid him a surprise visit there in October 1511; they ate several meals on board and spent the night there.

The building of a navy increased James's prestige in Europe. His assistance was sought more and more frequently by other rulers. His uncle, the King of Denmark, asked for and received Scottish help against Sweden in 1509. Then in 1506, James's cousin, the Duke of Gueldres, threatened by a coalition of powerful states, besought his help. James leapt to the defence of this relative and at once wrote to the rulers involved, who included his English father-in-law. To him James wrote, '. . . If you, unmindful of any ties of blood, affinity, and alliance with him, should endeavour to prostrate my cousin, the Duke of Gueldres . . . and, contrary to law and justice, expel him from his paternal seat, I, who believe that in war justice will prevail over wrong, shall be sorrowfully compelled to esteem you, my most illustrious father, as my enemy; and ... to oppose your troops and for the sake of justice and necessity to repel force'. He added a reminder of the sorrow such a collision between her father and her husband would cause 'our dearest wife, your sweetest daughter'. Henry gave up his plans to attack the Duke, and the coalition against Gueldres was broken up.

Friction with England also arose for other reasons during this time. In 1507 two of James's cousins, the Earl of Arran and his brother, Sir Patrick Hamilton, journeying from France home to Scotland, crossed over English territory without first obtaining a safe conduct, and were seized by border authorities. Sir Patrick was paroled and permitted to return home, but the Earl of Arran was held hostage. To assuage his son-in-law's enraged reaction to this hostile act, King Henry sent Dr. Nicholas West to Edinburgh in 1508. The emissary complained to his monarch by letter that, although Queen Margaret tried to get her husband to see him, James took his own good time in granting him an interview. For five days, the ambassador said, he was kept waiting because the Scottish King 'was so greatly busied in shooting guns and making gunpowder'.

When finally he gained an audience, he could not get James to agree to anything less than the immediate and unconditional release of the Earl of Arran. West suggested this could be arranged if Arran would first take an oath to return to England later in case this were required. James retorted that if his kinsman should be so pusillanimous as to take such an oath, he would have him hanged the minute he entered Scotland. It would be sensible, the emissary advised Henry, to yield to his son-in-law's demands and thus prevent him not only from armed retaliation but, he hoped, from renewing the 'Auld Alliance' with France. Representatives of King Louis XII had been busy in Scotland lately and were still pressing for a renewal of the Franco-Scottish league, which England wanted to avoid at all costs. Two individuals who shared this view and were very kind to Dr. West were Queen Margaret and the Bishop of Moray. The prelate was one of Margaret's favourite Scottish associates. He had recently been to London on a diplomatic mission and could tell the Queen about recent events and personalities in her father's court. West was most grateful for the kindness of these two pro-English leaders, for the general feeling in Edinburgh then was so vehemently anti-English that he declared 'there was never man worse welcome into Scotland' than himself. But their intercession smoothed things over with James, who finally assured the ambassador he would be a faithful son to King Henry so long as the latter proved 'loving, kind, and like a good father'.

Nevertheless, King Louis persisted in his efforts to get the Franco-Scottish pact renewed. In the spring of 1508, Lord d'Aubigny and Sir Anthony d'Arcy, Sieur de la Bastie, arrived in Edinburgh and were welcomed with a series of tournaments and banquets. The strain of attending all these magnificent functions may have been too overwhelming for the very elderly Lord d'Aubigny, whose sudden death brought all the celebrations to an end.

An account of all these events in the intercourse between Scotland and France was taken to England in May. James had promised West to keep his father-in-law informed of his relations with Louis's court. Therefore, after a little prodding by his anxious English wife, he sent the Bishop of Moray to London to tell Henry about the visit of the two distinguished French noblemen. In response, King Henry at once sent as a gift to his son-in-law a string of handsome horses, complete with trappings. James reciprocated by sending some steeds from Galloway and several falcons to the English ruler. This interchange of presents and assurances of affection marked the conclusion of Scottish-English affairs for the year 1508. In April 1509, King Henry VII died.

CHAPTER 6

THE ROYAL ROAD TO DISASTER
(1509–1513)

The accession of Henry VIII to the English throne was an event fraught with significance not only for Britain but for Europe as a whole. His reign was to bring about a complete breach with the past — a break which none living in 1509 could possibly have foreseen. Even before the beginning of the famous divorce case, which ended in the religious separation from Rome, his actions in another sphere had already disturbed the European balance of power. His prudent father had avoided warfare wherever possible; young Henry welcomed it as an opportunity to win renown. The first Tudor had become unpopular by his methods of acquiring wealth and establishing a well-filled treasury; his son won quick popularity by executing the agents who had helped his father amass millions; then he turned to the pleasant occupation of spending those riches.

At first his aim appeared to be simply to turn his court into the most brilliant example of Renaissance magnificence. Acclaimed by scholars like More and Erasmus, the eighteen-year-old ruler patronized the arts. To the delight of young courtiers, each evening at his palace was enlivened with music, dancing and extravagant masques. Sports-lovers applauded as he sponsored great athletic contests, from wrestling bouts to tournaments, in all of which he personally participated and excelled.

But mock battles failed to satisfy his restless energy. Only by combat in actual war could he win the worldly fame desired by the true Renaissance Prince. Hence, when the so-called Holy League was formed against France in 1511 the English King was happy to join it, for France was England's ancient foe. Unfortunately, France was also Scotland's ancient ally. Thus the fate of Scotland was also to be affected by the accession of Henry VIII.

None of these developments, however, was apparent in 1509. Margaret, though saddened by the death of her father, felt no qualms about the future. She joined in her husband's message of congratulation to the new English monarch, and was pleased when news came of her brother's marriage, a month later, to Catherine of Aragon. This union seemed appropriate, indicating that the new ruler would follow the plans laid out by his father. Also, Margaret felt it should be a happy marriage, for she recalled that her brother had developed quite a boyish crush on the pretty Spanish Princess at the time of her marriage to Prince Arthur. She remembered the pride with which the ten-year-old boy had escorted fifteen-year-old Catherine as she rode through the streets of London, his round face turned admiringly towards the lovely lady who was to be his older brother's bride. Margaret smiled, recollecting the energetic way he had danced that evening with his sister. Probably he had been boyishly showing off for the benefit of the Spanish Princess. Little could she imagine, while engaged in this reminiscing, the effects their marriage was to have.

At first, indeed, the new reign in England appeared serene, and relations with the northern kingdom progressed even better than during the last years of Henry VII. Existing treaties of peace and friendship were renewed. The young Tudor promised to send to Margaret certain jewels that had been left to her by Prince Arthur. According to his will, these gems were to be held by their father until his death, then handed over to his older sister. At her urging, James asked Henry now to send her this bequest. The newly crowned monarch promised to do so as soon as an inventory could be taken of them. Other matters which arose causing friction were quickly smoothed over. But by 1511 several eposodes had occurred that caused a ruffling of tempers on both sides of the border. The Scottish Warden of the Marches, Sir Robert Kerr, had been assassinated by Englishmen, and the government appeared to be slothful in punishing the assassins. In a separate incident Captain Andrew Barton, one of James's best naval leaders, had received, along with his brother, royal permission to seek out and punish the Portuguese who had killed their father. Unfortunately, the Barton brothers had interpreted this permission as a licence to attack ships of all nations. Consequently, an English family, the Howards, set out to end these depredations. They captured the marauding ships in an action during which Captain Andrew Barton was killed.

James sent his herald to the English court to complain of these injuries. Henry's immediate reply was a lofty statement that such affairs as the punishment of pirates were beneath royal notice. A few months later, nevertheless, he did send agents to try to conciliate the angry Scottish monarch.

Meanwhile, a far more significant controversy between the two Kings had arisen: the 'matter of France'. It was ironic that the originator of this conflict should have been the Pope. The same Julius II, who had honoured James in 1507 for being the European monarch most successful in promoting peace, seemed himself to be most notable in fomenting war. First, in 1508 he had organized the League of Cambrai, which included France, in order to gain territory from Venice. Then in 1511 he proposed the Holy League to drive the French out of the territory which they had just won in Italy. He quickly gained Venice, Switzerland and Spain as allies. Ferdinand of Aragon is considered responsible for persuading his son-in-law to join this coalition, but, as indicated earlier, Henry needed no urging. Here was his opportunity to restore to England the Angevin Empire which had been lost in the preceding century. As he joyously entered the League, he pictured himself as the reincarnation of that earlier King Hal, the victor of Agincourt.

Before galloping off to war and glory, however, he realized he should secure his northern frontiers against attack. It was chiefly this consideration that prompted him to send Lord Dacre and Dean West as ambassadors to Edinburgh in June 1512. On their arrival they went first to see the Queen. It was natural that they should do so, expecting this English Princess to support her native land in the quarrel. Also they may have heard that she took some small part in diplomacy herself. In 1510 she had been approached by the Danish emissary asking her to remind her husband of King John's request for aid. In her reply, she stated that James needed no such prodding and was fully ready to help his Scandinavian relative.

Again in March 1512, she had written to Ferdinand of Aragon to second her husband's appeal for peace, on which James was entirely bent, and urging Ferdinand to dissuade his English ally from plans to attack France. This appeal, of course, fell on deaf ears, since the Spanish monarch himself was egging Henry on to war.

Perhaps Lord Dacre and Dr. West had learned of the letter she had written to Ferdinand and wanted to give her their master's side of the matter. In any event, they were warmly welcomed by the Queen, who invited them to dinner. She was eager for news from home and was much delighted by their descriptions of her brother's court, the brilliant dress, the elaborate 'disguisings', and the tournaments. She was told that, just as she had surmised, the new King seemed deeply in love with his wife. Turning then to their errand in Scotland, she advised the two gentlemen how best to approach her husband in order to conciliate him and assured them that he sincerely desired an amicable settlement of all differences. They might have succeeded in settling the causes of friction between the two nations on land and on the high seas, but on the main issue there could be no agreement. Henry was planning to attack France, a nation which James felt bound to defend.

His determination to support his 'auld ally' (with whom he had recently signed a new pact of friendship) has been much criticized by historians. With hindsight, his course certainly appears disastrous. Yet from his immediate point of view, the alternative would have presented dangers just as grave. In practical terms he stood to lose his one faithful ally if he deserted France. Suppose the young Tudor King, with the help of his European allies, succeeded in crushing the forces of Louis XII. Who would then come to the aid of Scotland in case it should be the next victim of Henry's aggression? He might easily decide to reaffirm Edward I's claim to suzerainty over his northern neighbour. (In actual fact, Henry did later assert this very claim.)

On the other hand, there were many practical reasons for maintaining good relations with England. There was, for example, the possibility that Henry might die without heirs. In this eventuality the next in line for the English throne would be Margaret or her children. However, in 1512 this possibility appeared exceedingly remote. True, Catherine of Aragon had been unable so far to produce a living, healthy child, but, as Margaret and James knew only too well, it sometimes took years to achieve this happy result, and both Henry and his wife were still young. So it was not primarily this prospect that caused James to continue seeking peace. Instead of an earthly inheritance, it was a heavenly kingdom for which he most deeply longed. Like the medieval knights he emulated, he was fascinated by the vision of restoring the Holy Land to Christendom. His intense desire to go on an actual crusade underlay most of his actions during these years. It was chiefly for this purpose that he built his great ships and tried to win promises of support from wealthier rulers, such as Louis XII. But before any such crusade could materialize, it was necessary for the monarchs of Europe to cease their petty quarrels with each other and join forces against the infidel. This desire was then the basic reason underlying the efforts James made to restore peace in Europe in the years just before Flodden.

James's sincerity in these efforts is proved by a careful survey of his correspondence from 1511 to August 1513, much of which is calendered in the *Letters and Papers of Henry VIII* for these years. The Scottish monarch appealed to one potentate after another. In 1511 he asked both the Holy Roman Emperor, Maximilian, and the College of Cardinals to try to reconcile Pope Julius with the French; next he sent the Bishop of Moray as his personal representative to endeavour to effect this reconciliation. The only result was that Julius sent his own envoy to Edinburgh, where he requested that James's pacifying influence be used on France. Actually, however, the aim of this manoeuvre was not to achieve European peace, but simply to prevent the Scots from helping Julius's enemy, Louis XII, in the war that seemed imminent. James replied that it was the Pope's ally, Henry VIII, who was endangering the general tranquillity, for he was simultaneously threatening to invade France and permitting English forces to ravage Scotland both on land and at sea.

In 1512 the Scottish ruler wrote to beg the 'most Catholic King', Ferdinand of Aragon, not to make war on his fellow Catholic, Louis of France. In the same month he wrote to Julius again, reproving him for his recently announced plans to attack France. What could be worse, asked James, 'than for a Holy Father and a Christian son to war with each other'? Instead, let all Christian Princes now join forces for a crusade against the unbelievers. For his part, he would personally urge Louis to restore all his Italian acquisitions to the Pope, if only there were no recourse to arms.

Meanwhile, he kept trying to negotiate on his own with King Henry, suggesting a meeting of the commissioners of their two nations to settle all Anglo-Scottish points of contention. To prove his own sincere good will towards his brother-in-law, he himself had just instructed his ambassador to France to beg Louis to expel Richard de la Pole, the latest Yorkist pretender to the English throne, from France. (This indeed appears a reversal of the usual Scottish policies toward England; in the 1490s James had been a strong supporter of that earlier Yorkist pretender, Perkin Warbeck.) He added that, despite Henry's refusal to co-operate with him, he was going to continue working for a settlement of the controversy among the European powers.

The King of Scots did in truth continue these efforts, but it was discouraging work, as he confessed to his uncle, King John of Denmark, towards the end of 1512. The French had now authorized him to mediate with the English, but his attempts to do so had been rebuffed, even though he had offered to forgo his own just claims against England if Henry would try to work for universal peace. Instead, the English Parliament voted to wage war against France and even to make a pre-emptive strike against Scotland beforehand, to prevent its endangering the northern parts of England during the proposed invasion of France.

Then for a time it appeared hopeful that the Pope might at last exert his spiritual influence in favour of peace, for during 1512 the French had been forced out of Italy. Consequently, early in 1513, papal briefs requested James to persuade Louis to agree on a plan of pacification. The delighted Scottish monarch promptly sent these briefs to Henry. But the latter replied that Julius had now changed his mind to the extent of joining England and all the other nations bent on renewed war against France. In dismay, James at once wrote to the Pope asking whether this was true and begging him once more to help prevent a conflict. However, even if peace had been the Holy Father's sincere aim, he would have had difficulty in dissuading the young English King from his determined course. For Henry had been humiliated in 1512. He had sent troops to southern France to aid his ally, Ferdinand of Aragon. This wily monarch had used the English forces simply to protect his northern borders, while he himself invaded Navarre. Henry's army, poorly provisioned and miserable, had mutinied and returned home. Predictably, their young King was furious. Determined to redeem his reputation, he now prepared for a great invasion of France which he would lead in person.

Before his departure, however, he had to ensure the safety of his northern borders. Accordingly, he once again tried diplomacy and in March 1513 Dr. West was dispatched to Edinburgh. As on his previous visits, he went first to see the Queen, who was then in residence at Stirling. Margaret had suffered from ill health since the envoy's last visit, and in November 1512 she had borne a premature child. This infant, conceived the same month as the birth of little James V, had died almost immediately. Having recovered more rapidly than usual, the Queen had then fallen victim to a serious malady which threatened her life. Her ever-solicitous husband had, as on previous occasions, resorted to acts of piety, offering many prayers at saints' shrines and masses for her restoration to health. She was at prayer herself when Dr. West arrived, giving thanks for her recuperation and joining in the Good Friday service being held in the chapel.

Dr. West attended the service, at the conclusion of which the Queen saw him and invited him to sit with her in her private pew. He gave her the letters from her brother and his wife, in which they expressed concern for her during her recent illness and sent wishes for her speedy return to health. She was most grateful for these messages. Dr. West wrote to his sovereign afterwards to tell him that she had read the letter 'with such a manner as I cannot declare unto your grace, it was so joyfully and lovingly received, saying these words: "If I were now in my great sickness again, this were enough to make me whole", seeing that your grace did so remember her'.

The church service then recommenced, so the envoy took his leave after Margaret had told him that she hoped to hold a longer conversation with him soon. The King was not available at this time. During Lent he always retired to the monastery of the Friars Observant, where he spent his time in vigil, prayer and fasting. He would rejoin his Queen and court at the close of this penitential season.

A few days later, on Easter Sunday, the Queen invited Dr. West to dine with her. She was eager for more news from her homeland. The emissary wrote a lengthy account of the occasion to his King: 'All the dinner, she passed the time very joyously, with honourable communication of your grace; and specially she enquired of your stature and goodly personage'. He told her all about her brother, his good looks and fine stature now that he was grown. He also told her how the young ruler no longer spent his time just in masques and joustings, but also attended to the more serious business of government.

She seemed pleased when West described Henry's pride in the great ships he was having built. It reminded her of her husband's enthusiasm for his navy, and she recounted the various feasts she and James had shared aboard the *Great Michael*. But when she learned that the purpose of Henry's navy was to carry his army across the Channel to France, her happiness vanished. At this news, wrote West, 'she was right heavy'. He then reminded her that the purpose of her marriage was to keep peace between England and Scotland, and urged her to persuade her husband to 'keep the peace in your [Henry's] absence . . . and she said she would do so, to the best of her power, and she doubted not but he would so do, so that he might have justice'. Evidently the Queen was loyal to her husband in this controversy.

Next she brought up another point, an issue in which she was particularly involved: the jewels bequeathed to her by Prince Arthur. Although Henry had, at the time of his accession, promised to forward to her either the jewels themselves or the money they were worth, he had as yet failed to fulfil this pledge. 'And therewith she asked if your grace had sent her legacy'. Dr. West replied that he was ready to deliver the legacy to her immediately, on condition that James 'would promise to keep the treaty of peace'. 'And not else?' asked the Queen. 'No', was the firm reply; if James made war, Henry would not only withhold his sister's jewels from her, but also would take from her and her husband 'the best towns that they had'.

Before Margaret could recover from the shock of this brusque statement sufficiently to reply to it, her husband entered the room, interrupting her tête-à-tête with the envoy. James had returned from his monastic Lenten vigil to join his Queen and court in the celebration of Easter. There was no more talk of business that day, and by the time the Queen next had an opportunity to converse privately with Dr. West, she had been able to compose a re-markably temperate speech, saying that 'albeit her brother was unkind to her, she would keep her kindness to him, and do her best to entertain the same'. Nevertheless, she personally wrote a letter to

Henry for West to deliver on his return, in which she expressed herself more freely, though in the formal language required of all diplomatic correspondence. Addressing him as, 'Right excellent, right high and mighty Prince, our dearest and best beloved brother', she first thanked him for his concern for her in her recent illness. Then she continued: 'We cannot believe that of your mind, or by your command, we are so *fremdly* [strangely] dealt with in our father's legacy. . . . Our husband knows it is withholden for his sake, and will recompense us so far as the Doctor shews him. We are *aschamit* [ashamed] therewith, and would God never word had been thereof. It is not worth such estimation as it is in your divers letters of the same; and we lack nothing; our husband is ever the longer the better to us, as knows God, who, right high and mighty Prince, our dearest and best beloved brother, have you in governance'.

Her husband was far more outspoken in his own reaction to Henry's mean behaviour. In the letter he sent the English monarch he said he had spoken to Dr. West 'of our dearest fellow the Queen', who 'for our sake gets not her father's legacy promised in our divers letters. Ye may do to your own as ye think best. She shall have no loss thereof'. Thus he scornfully announced his intention to repay Margaret himself for the legacy withheld by her brother. Then he went on to the more important issues between them: the redress he had been demanding for injuries done to Scots on land and sea by the English. In spite of Henry's failure to do justice, James continued to work for peace by sending the Bishop of Moray to France. He would have to make the entire journey by sea, since Henry refused to grant him a safe conduct across England. Once again, the Scottish King begged his brother-in-law to delay his intended attack on France.

When Dr. West took these messages back to Westminster, he had to confess that he had had no success during his long stay in Scotland, and that he felt sure the Scots King meant to support his 'auld ally'. The clever Louis had meanwhile appealed to James in ways sure to find a ready response. Not only did he offer to ward off future attacks from across the border, in return for Scottish support for France, but also promised to underwrite the expenses James would incur for the great crusade against the infidel which Louis realized was so close to James's heart. Above all, he appealed to the honour and chivalry of this most chivalrous King, to come to the aid of an imperilled and faithful friend. The only way he could avoid going to war and keep his honour, James felt, was to prevent the war entirely.

In this endeavour he was encouraged by a truce which was made in April between France and Spain. The English and French might be included in this truce if they wished, through the mediation of their respective allies. Louis had written to James urging him to enter this truce if England agreed. In James's subsequent letter exhorting Henry to join this general peace, the Scots King reminded him of the valiant knights who would perish on both sides if the war continued — soldiers who instead should be going to fight together against the infidel. He sent condolences to Henry on the recent death in a sea battle of his admiral, whom he knew 'through acquaintance we had of his father [the Earl of Surrey] that noble knight, who convoyed our dearest fellow the Queen unto us'.

James's last effort to dissuade Henry from war fell, like his previous attempts, on deaf ears. On June 30th 1513 the young English King, with a vast martial array, sailed for France. He left Queen Catherine in charge of England, with the ageing, but still very competent, Earl of Surrey to take active command of forces that were to be levied from the northern shires to repel any attack from across the Border. He hoped, however, that the Scots King might be withheld from such action by the threat he had instructed Dr. West to make plain on his last visit to Edinburgh. West had on that occasion reminded James that if he invaded England during the King's absence, he would be breaking the treaty which he had made first with Henry VII and then renewed on the accession of Henry VIII. This promise had been made under oath; therefore, if he broke it he would be excommunicated. The papal mandate to this very effect was then produced by West. James drily remarked that Henry was fortunate in having such an acquiescent Pope. (Indeed it must have been pleasant to be in Henry's position with written assurance from God's representative on earth that he was in the right, his opponent in the wrong.)

Faced with this threat of papal anathema, James had responded scornfully that he would not attack English territory without warning, for this would be contrary to the code of chivalry. If he found war inevitable, he would send a message and warning to this effect to the English monarch, wherever he might be at the time, so that he could return home and defend his lands. This virtual declaration of war was delivered on July 26th. Lyon Herald, the royal messenger, was sent across the Channel to give Henry his master's ultimatum. The English must at once cease their invasion of France, or else King James, as the ally of Louis XII, would feel obliged to retaliate by carrying war and destruction into England. Henry was with his army besieging Thérouanne. He received the message with defiant scorn, replying that not only was James breaking his sworn pledge of peace, but that Scotland was only a fief of the English crown. Therefore, on his eventual return from

France, he would deal out to the Scottish ruler the punishment deserved by any rebellious vassal.

Before sending his herald to Henry, James had of course, sought the counsel of his nobles. A large majority of them agreed with their sovereign that he must remain true to the 'Auld Alliance'. (One reason for their support was probably the generous pensions many of them received from their 'auld ally'.) On the other hand, a vocal minority opposed war with the ancient foe south of the Border. The venerable Elphinstone, Bishop of Aberdeen, sincerely doubted the wisdom of this war. Other opposition to it came from the Earl of Angus. This nobleman is portrayed in Scott's *Marmion* as an heroic and ageing male Cassandra, warning his impetuous young monarch against the folly of his course, with tears streaming down his cheeks. A less glamorous picture of the 'doughty Douglas' emerges from a more realistic scrutiny. He was nicknamed Archibald 'Bell-the-Cat' because, many years earlier, at the time of the overthrow of King James III, he had volunteered to take the challenge of the rebellious nobles to the threatened King in person. Later, during the reign of James IV, the same 'Bell-the-Cat' was again accused of treason. The English *State Papers* for this period prove that he was actually guilty of promising to turn his border fortress over to the foe in the event of a conflict. So, just as some nobles were bribed by France, others were in the pay of England.

Throughout this whole period the most energetic advocate of peace was, understandably, the English-born Queen. She had proved totally loyal to her husband in her conversations with Dr. West, and she deeply appreciated the way James championed her in her own quarrel with her brother over her legacy. Nevertheless, she was appalled by the likelihood of war between her husband and her brother. Personal anxiety for the possible outcome of this conflict doubtless was a stronger motivation than the fate of either nation in such a war, and it was this personal aspect of the affair that she presented to James in her pleas.

First she reminded him of the dire predicament in which he would leave her if he himself died in battle. She was once again pregnant. Could she survive childbirth — always so perilous for her — without his prayers and personal intercession with the saints? Then, even if she recovered, how would she, a lone woman, look after his nation during their son's minority?

Contrary to her husband's rejoinder that Louis had hinted that, after defeating Henry VIII, he might help James to attain the English throne, she pointed out the complete unlikelihood of any such development; the strength of the English nation defending itself against Franco-Scottish aggression made such an idea merest fantasy. Also Louis had promised to underwrite James's expedition to the Holy Land, but how could James profit by that promise if he and the knights who were to participate in it were killed in this futile expedition against England?

The most subtle approach used by the French, and one which had even more success with the romantic admirer of King Arthur, was an appeal made to his chivalry by Louis's Queen, Anne of Brittany, She had written to him begging him as her knight to rescue her from Henry's invasion. Scott puts it thus:

> For the fair Queen of France
> Sent him a turquoise ring and glove
> And charged him as her knight and love,
> For her to break a lance,
> And strike three strokes with Scottish brand,
> And march three miles on Southron land,
> And bid the banners of his band
> In English breezes dance.

Faced with this romantic foolery, Margaret tartly reminded her husband that Queen Anne was middle-aged, 'a woman twice married [the first time half in adultery, the last almost in incest], whom ye did never, nor shall ever see' — scarcely the fairy-tale damsel in distress. Should her letters 'prove more powerful with you than the cries of your little son and mine — than the tears, complaints, and curses of the orphans and widows which you are to make'? Moreover it was scarcely chivalrous to invade England leaving a woman to rule it alone during the absence of its monarch. 'If ye will go, suffer me to accompany you; . . . I hear the Queen my sister will be with the army in her husband's absence; if we shall meet, who knows what God, by our means may bring about?'

Seeing that none of these appeals to his reason had any effect, Margaret tried another tack: she played on his superstition. She recounted to him daily the fearful dreams with which she was afflicted each night: 'that she had seen him fall from a great precipice; she had lost one of her eyes', that she had seen his naked corpse bleeding and pierced with many arrows.

Next she induced him to see visions. A few days before he joined his army, as he arose one evening from prayer in the Church of Linlithgow, a ghostly stranger appeared before him. He was dressed in flowing robes of blue and white and carried a great staff. With his high forehead and golden hair he looked precisely like the nearby painting of Saint John. In hollow tones the vision warned the monarch to give up his plans of war and to avoid commerce with women. While the King stared in amazement, a young companion tried to seize the apparition, but it vanished. The 'ghost' may have disappeared through a private door in the north side of the church, adjacent to the palace. In any case, Margaret was almost certainly the *dea ex machina* behind the episode. It is amusing to note that she managed to include in the apparition's advice to her husband a warning not only against warfare, but also against dalliance with ladies.

Another strange phenomenon occurred a few days later, at the time of his army's assemblage on the Burgh Muir outside Edinburgh. A sepulchral voice shouted at midnight from the market-cross, calling each of the leading personages in the army by name, and summoning them to the gates of Hades within forty days. Unfortunately none of these stratagems succeeded, although the King seemed struck by each when it occurred. He still felt obliged by his pledges of loyalty to his ally to turn his promises into facts, though probably all he intended to do was to create a diversion which would force Henry to give up his attack on France.

While awaiting the arrival of his troops, the King stayed for several days at Linlithgow with his wife, where, as they had done so often in the past, they boated together on the loch and enjoyed watching the progress of their child. Little James had been quite sickly at first and one wet-nurse after another had been tried. Finally, a healthy Irish girl had proved capable of giving him milk of the proper 'formula', so that he grew quite strong. Now in his second year, he was large for his age and 'right life-like' in appearance, as Dr. West had reported to the child's uncle, Henry VIII, after seeing the boy with Margaret at Linlithgow. Before leaving, James had made provisions for his son's care in case he did not return from battle. As tutor he had selected the Bishop of Aberdeen, William Elphinstone. Although this cleric had opposed the King's decision regarding the war with England, James respected him. He was reputed to be the wisest man in the kingdom and was Keeper of the Privy Seal.

The King also showed great respect for his wife's judgement by making her in his will not only guardian of their son, but also Regent of Scotland should he be killed. This was a somewhat unusual position to be granted to a woman, since by custom the Regent was the one nearest in line to actual succession to the throne. James also gave an order for her to receive 18,000 crowns sent by King Louis to finance the war.

Having made his will, James went to Edinburgh to meet his army. Immediately after having sent his warning to Henry, he had summoned his leaders and their followers to the capital. There in the third week of August he reviewed his troops, a magnificent array, including all the foremost nobles of the kingdom and representing Scots of all regions from the northern Highlands and the Western Isles to the Lowlands around the Firth of Forth.

While this army prepared to march southwards to the Border, the King himself took a brief ride to the north, to the oft-visited shrine of Saint Duthac, for he could not undertake anything of such importance without first appealing for divine support, especially since he knew that he had incurred papal anathema by his actions. Pope Julius II had recently died, but his successor was continuing his policies, including the excommunication of the Scottish King if he should attack the Pope's ally, Henry VIII. Although James, like all good Catholics of the time, took such decrees very seriously, he had more confidence in Saint Duthac and in the dictates of his own conscience than he had in such politically motivated churchmen. From Tain he returned south and rode to rejoin his forces. Margaret accompanied her husband to Dunfermline, then, at his insistence, went back to Linlithgow. Here, in her favourite palace, she now assumed the traditional role of women in time of war, waiting, praying and weeping.

The first actual fighting had already begun in early August. Lord Home, Scottish Warden of the Marches, had led a successful foray into Northumberland, seizing quantities of booty. On his return home, however, he was surprised by an English force and, hampered by his loot, had lost most of his men and all of the stolen goods. Small wonder that his expedition acquired the name of 'Home's ill Raid'. Action had also taken place on the sea, though it had been no more successful. James had sent his little fleet, including the *Margaret*, the *James* and the *Great Michael*, to the assistance of his ally, Louis. Unfortunately its commander, the Earl of Arran, took a detour by way of Ireland, where he stormed Carrickfergus. This inept admiral was replaced, but the Scottish navy was of little use in this war. These unsatisfactory beginnings should have been yet a further warning to James to give up his intended advance, but now there could be no turning back as he went to meet his destiny.

The Battle of Flodden Field is difficult to describe with any accuracy. There are many accounts, but all are based on first-hand accounts from the English, since no Scottish survivor ever narrated this national disaster. Many rumours spread throughout Scotland, stories which never were authenticated, but which gave rise to widely differing versions of the entire fray. Some of these were chronicled as 'accurate history' by such early writers as Pitscottie and Buchanan, neither of whom is now accepted as completely reliable. In Buchanan's version, especially, the King's blame is

James IV, King of Scots
Artist unknown

(Scottish National Portrait Gallery)

emphasized. He is accused of causing over-lengthy delays before the battle, then of foolishly accepting his enemy's challenge to come down and fight in the open, losing his advantageous position on the impregnable heights. It is even alleged that he refused to permit his artillery to fire upon the English until they had crossed a narrow defile and were in a position to defend themselves in fair fight. All these allegations bear out the usual charge against James that his devotion to medieval standards of honour prevented his taking advantage of opportunities to defeat his enemy by any means other than those approved by the laws of *noblesse oblige*.

However, more recent and careful analyses of the events before and during the final battle disprove this somewhat romantic version. True enough, James was delighted when he learned that the Engish leader was his old acquaintance, the Earl of Surrey. His admiration for this nobleman was that of one good knight for another's fighting ability and reputation. He had in fact often expressed a desire to meet him in tournament or combat. Nevertheless, he did not allow his respect for this opponent to endanger his own success nor put the lives of his followers into jeopardy.

Also, the delays in coming to meet Surrey were not, as some have felt, foolishly prolonged. Before hastening to meet the English army, it was wise of him to safeguard his rear by capturing several strongholds in the vicinity. Consequently James captured the castles of Wark and Etal, and, after a five-day siege, the almost impregnable fortress of Norham. Then, taking several more strongholds, including Chillingham and Ford, he made his headquarters on Flodden Ridge.

Another of the rumours about this expedition is that at Ford Castle the King frittered away precious time enjoying the charms of its chatelaine, Lady Heron. Whether or not this English lady indeed tried to entice the romantic monarch into sparing her home and also into delaying his advance against Surrey, is impossible to prove. On leaving he had her castle burned, scarcely a very lover-like gesture! And in any case, the dalliance (if there was any) lasted not for weeks, as has been charged, but for only three or four days. The delay was necessitated by the fact that numbers of his soldiers had deserted, some of them sick with a pestilence which had just swept down from the north, others discouraged by the drenching rains with which the country was deluged for weeks. Hence the King waited for some new contingents to arrive. The delay probably hurt the Earl of Surrey even more than the Scots. The English were running out of provisions. Food was getting scarce, and far more serious, so was their ale. How long could they hold out drinking nothing but water?

Perhaps James should have postponed his advance even longer!

The comparative size of the two armies is difficult to ascertain, since the English accounts (the only ones available) would naturally exaggerate the size of the enemy they defeated. Surrey's force may have numbered about 20,000, and the size of the Scots army was probably about the same. The English were armed chiefly with halberds, whose heavy, sharp bills were of deadly effectiveness in the hand-to-hand combat that decided the day. Their archery was less damaging to the heavily armoured Scots, whose armour proved detrimental in weighting down the wearers. The chief weapon of the Scots was a spear, five yards or more in length. With these spears out-thrust they would form a ring to provide a constant barrier against attack. But their opponents hacked down these long and unwieldy weapons and then went on to clash with the swords raised by the Scots against their foes.

Both sides had some artillery. James had had all his prized cannon hauled from Edinburgh and emplaced on Flodden Ridge. Unfortunately, his best gunners had been sent with his fleet to France, and those he had with him proved poor marksmen. Most of their shots went over the heads of their foes. Surrey, on the other hand, had German gunners who fired with deadly accuracy and soon silenced the Scottish cannon.

After leaving his temporary headquarters at Ford Castle, James maintained his position on Flodden Ridge. This was so impregnable that his opponents tried to get him to come down and meet them on the plain, where they were encamped about six miles away. Surrey, knowing the King's chivalrous nature, challenged him to come down and fight in the open, and his son, now Admiral of England, taunted James to come and seek his desired vengeance for the death of Captain Andrew Barton. James scornfully refused, declaring that he would choose his own ground for fighting.

He did, however, accept the challenge to fight not later than September 9th if his opponents arrived to do battle by that date. Surrey had sent him this challenge for fear that otherwise James and his army would simply return across the Border and wait until the English host had dwindled away as a result of their lack of provisions and of desertions, before renewing their invasion of England.

Since he could not lure his opponent from his strong position by guile, Surrey decided to outflank him. By moving secretly, he planned to cut him off from return to Scotland and surprise him from the rear. He and his men therefore crossed the Till early on the morning of September 9th. This change of position was at first hidden from the Scots. When James discovered it he realized he must move at once, before his foes themselves reached a superior vantage point on Branxton Hill. He at once set fire to his camp, and under cover of smoke moved to meet the enemy on the northern slope of Branxton Hill. His position here was excellent; if he could have held it, Surrey's men would have been forced to climb the hill to attack, and the Scots could have maintained their close-packed squares bristling with spears. Unfortunately, the English artillery, after silencing the opposing cannon, next turned their fire directly on these spearmen, and they soon opened great holes in the Scottish ranks, especially in the centre which was commanded by the King. James was thus forced to move and called for a charge down the hillside out of cannon range.

The slopes were wet, for it had been raining steadily ever since the armies had first begun moving weeks ago. To keep their footing on this muddy terrain, the men removed their shoes and came down the hillside in utter silence. James had arranged his force in five main bodies, himself leading the centre. Surrey meantime was seated in a chariot a little apart from the mêlée. The reason for this position was neither cowardice nor infirmity, though he was now seventy years old. Instead, as general, he must maintain command of the entire field, so that he could order changes to be made wherever necessary and send each contingent to the place where it was most needed. In this position he was far wiser than his opponent. In fact, the most just criticism that has been made of the Scottish King in battle is that, instead of directing his army, he led it both in person and on foot, wading into the very forefront of battle, thereby leaving each leader to make his own decisions as to the next move. Hence, units that might have been useful in another area simply rushed down, fought and killed a few enemies, took their booty and left. It was for this reason that Home and his Borderers gave no help to the centre when it was so desperately needed, but simply plundered for themselves. In the aftermath of the battle, when Home and his band returned alive and booty-laden from the field where most of their compatriots had died, charges of treachery were made against them, but were never proved.

James was not a good general. Yet it was his impetuous bravery, sharing every bit of the danger with his soldiers, that endeared this King to his people. Paying no heed to his nobles' entreaties that he remain mounted and stay apart from the fray, he sent his battlehorse to the rear. Like his men, he removed his shoes, gripped sword and spear, and plunged down the hillside. He led the charge in person, heading straight for the standard of the English leader, and so he fell, still rushing onward, within a spear-length of the Earl of Surrey.

No prisoners were taken from the central band which surrounded the King. Nobles, bishops, knights, squires and yeomen, all fought to the finish. Among them fell James's son, the young Archbishop of St. Andrews, fighting alongside his father. James's body was found the next day by the English. (No Scottish survivors remained in the vicinity.) It was naked, stripped like the other corpses by the booty-seekers, but Lord Dacre, who knew James well, identified the body which had been pierced by several arrows and the left hand almost hacked off. His coat was found and sent by Queen Catherine to her husband (now victorious in France) as a trophy of her success in guarding his realm during his absence.

Lord Dacre had the monarch's body conveyed to Berwick and encased in lead. No immediate burial could take place, since he had died excommunicate and was therefore forbidden to lie in consecrated soil. However, the Pope generously permitted the ban to be lifted at the request of his ally, Henry VIII, so that the brother-in-law of the English King could receive Christian burial. His coffin was therefore taken to England and buried at the monastery in Richmond.

Yet there were Scots who refused to believe that this was the end of their well-loved ruler. The iron belt, they said, had not been found on the body that was encased in the leaden coffin. Therefore it could not have been his corpse, but that of some other with whom he had exchanged coats to fool the enemy. Some said that, seeing Lord Home staying apart from the thick of the battle, James had ridden over to command Home's immediate assistance in the centre, or else be hanged as a traitor. According to this tale, Home then seized his King and had him carried to his castle, where later he was murdered. Other, even less probable rumours spread among the common folk. Their King, they said, was not killed, but only stunned in the fray. Recovering afterwards to view the ruin all about him, he had gone off on a pilgrimage to the Holy Land to pray for his people. He would return one day and restore his country to the glory which it had known during his reign.

This glory was now ended; of that there was no doubt. Looking back over the series of developments that ended Scotland's brief Renaissance, one is reminded of an ancient Greek tragedy, in which one event follows another in a predetermined course leading on to final disaster. The key role played by King James was one for which he seemed doomed, if not from birth, at least from the age of fifteen when he unwittingly took part in the murder of his father. His outstanding attributes, of leadership and courage, of piety and kindliness, his patronage of the arts and his skill in government, were all outweighed in the end by a fatal flaw. This weakness — in itself a virtue — was his chivalry. His devotion to the code of *noblesse oblige* made him susceptible to manipulation by the true Renaissance Princes of the period. Pope Julius II, Louis XII, Henry VIII and others paid lip service to the ideals of the past and displayed them in vivid pageantry, but in fact they were flint-hard realists of the new era. Recognizing the sincerity of James's chivalry, they appealed to it for their own purposes and thus led him on to his destiny.

Louis XII was the most successful in manipulating the Scottish King. During the long negotiations before Flodden, he emphasized France's need for help in its desperate struggle; his appeal to *noblesse oblige* was dramatized by his Queen's plea for James to be her knight. Likewise, Louis realized the genuineness of James's zeal for a crusade, as a means of wiping out, once and for all, the greatest blot on his life: the guilt that remained after his sinful rebellion against his father. Seen in this light, it is clear that the road to Flodden Field began at Sauchieburn.

Part Two

DOUBLE, DOUBLE, TOIL AND TROUBLE (1513–1528)

CHAPTER 7

THE REGENCY (1513–1514)

> To tell red Flodden's dismal tale,
> And raise the universal wail,
> Tradition, legend, tune, and song
> Shall many an age that wail prolong.

The 'universal wail' described by Sir Walter Scott began the very day after the fatal battle. Rumours reached Edinburgh on September 10th, causing crowds to gather in the streets demanding news. The chief magistrates, along with the leading nobility, were absent, having accompanied their King to war, but those bailies who had remained in the city ordered the men to return to their work and urged the women to go to the churches to pray. They also had a guard mounted against a possible attack from the south.

The first vague rumours were only too soon followed by direct reports which confirmed the earlier suspicions of disaster. As it became known that their King had indeed perished along with most of his splendid army, many citizens began urging that immediate steps be taken to protect the city. It certainly seemed likely that the English would follow up their victory in Northumberland by invading the virtually defenceless northern nation. Fortunately, however, the Earl of Surrey had not enough horses for such an attempt. Also, his army had sustained severe losses in the fray of September 9th. Therefore, he disbanded the levies which had been raised for the defence of northern England, although Lord Dacre, English Warden of the North, conducted raids across the Border, burning villages and destroying crops.

As soon as the report of Flodden arrived at the capital, a messenger was dispatched to Linlithgow to notify the Queen. She had spent the anxious days in her favourite palace, trying to pass the time by playing with her little boy, a diversion for which she ordinarily had little opportunity with all the pressure of court functions. He was, at a little over a year and a half of of age, a lively, handsome child, and Margaret loved him with the devotion natural to a mother who had lost so many children in their infancy. But even the pleasure of his company could not divert her thoughts from her main concern: the fate of her husband and his expedition against her native land and the armies of her brother.

The rain that had been drenching the two armies for the past weeks also fell unceasingly at Linlithgow, deepening the sense of gloom that had afflicted all those left behind after the army's departure. When finally, after many days of foreboding, the messengers arrrived bringing the woeful tidings, Margaret felt no shock. It was news she had most dreaded, but had expected almost constantly from the time James first sent his ultimatum to Henry. Those nightmares which she had recounted to James were not fictitious, but dreams which she had actually experienced. Confirmation of her worst fears could scarcely increase the bitter sense of hopelessness which she had felt during these past weeks. Therefore she wasted little time now in additional mourning. From the time she left James at Dunfermline she had felt certain he was lost — 'fey' [doomed to die young], as the Scots expressed it.

Consequently, she had wept bitterly during the previous months while she was still futilely trying to dissuade him from this war. Her tears had fallen often while she waited for the news from his army, but now that the dreaded blow had struck, her eyes soon dried and a new resolve stiffened the twenty-three-year-old widow. James IV was dead, but his son lived. She would live henceforth for James V. It was well for Margaret that she had the resolute will of a Tudor; she would need it in the days to come. For her the golden days were past. No longer would she be protected and coddled, as she had been all her life, first by royal parents, then by a royal husband. She was now on her own. Henceforth it was she who must be the protector, the guardian, of herself, of her infant son and of the unborn child of James IV now in her womb.

Her first move was to leave Linlithgow at once. It had been her favourite residence, but now it held too many reminders of the good old days, her happy times with James. Also, on more practical grounds, this palace was too vulnerable to attack. Stirling, that great stone fortress on the steep hilltop, was almost impregnable, and it was another of her dower houses, now hers since her husband's death. So she gave the orders, and carts and pack-horses laden with furniture and clothing began the familiar process of moving from one dwelling to another. She did not wait for all the paraphernalia to be transported. She and her child, with their most essential attendants, left at once for the stronghold and within hours were secure behind its fifteen-foot-thick walls.

Now she and her son were safe from an English attack, but what of the Scots? Would they prove loyal to the English widow of their well-loved ruler? She did not hesitate, but sent an immediate call for a Council meeting. Summons were issued to all the nobility and high clergy in the area who had survived Flodden. Alas, there were many gaps in their ranks! An archbishop, 'two bishops, two abbots, eleven earls, and fifteen lords', as well as about ten thousand men of lesser rank (according to English calculations) had perished with the King. The sad remnants of the Council met, however, on September 19th, and agreed that the heir to the throne must be crowned at once. There was no time to journey to Perth or to arrange for a magnificent ceremony at Scone. On September 21st, the coronation of eighteen-month-old James V was held in the chapel of Stirling Castle. At the same time his mother was recognized as Regent during his minority, in accordance with the will of the late King. So she and her son were proclaimed 'James, by God's grace, King of the Scots, and Margaret, Queen of Scotland and testamentary *tutrix* of the same'. The nobles appointed the Earl of Angus (Archibald, old 'Bell-the-Cat') to assist her in her regency. The Earls of Arran, Huntly, Morton, Argyll, Lennox, Eglinton and Glencairn, Lord Drummond, the Archbishop of Glasgow and the Bishop of Aberdeen (William Elphinstone, whom James V had designated as his son's tutor) were similarly appointed. Until the lords decided to change it, Stirling was to be the royal residence with Lord Borthwick as its captain.

The next necessity was to re-establish peace, but this proved more difficult. Queen Catherine, still acting as Regent for England during her husband's absence in France, sent a court chaplain, Friar Langley, to comfort her sister-in-law and to arrange for a truce. Margaret submitted this proposal to a Council which she called to meet at Perth. The nobles, however, wanted revenge for the recent defeat, and were encouraged in this belligerence by a ship-load of munitions which had just arrived from France. Accordingly, the Council sent a request for additional help from Denmark and notified all the Scottish shires to prepare for war.

Louis XII sent an offer of further help by messengers who soon arrived from his court, together with Lord John Fleming and the Earl of Arran, under whom the Scottish fleet had finally reached France in September 1513. A letter was brought by them from John Stuart,* Duke of Albany, who proposed to convoy the war munitions to Scotland. This nobleman was the son of James III's younger brother who had rebelled against his royal uncle and had been banished to France. Hence the present Duke was by birth heir-presumptive to the Scottish throne, although he had spent his entire life in France, where he now held high office.

His offer to bring aid from Louis and to assist in the war with England was eagerly accepted by the Council. It was made clear that this acceptance entailed no threat to the authority of young King

* Although his family name was *Stewart*, he spelled it in the French style, *Stuart*.

James or of his mother, and therefore Margaret also agreed, albeit reluctantly, since her aim was to conclude peace with England, rather than to continue the war. Despite the promises of Louis and Albany, the proffered assistance was delayed time after time, while Lord Dacre's raids continued to cause suffering along the Border. Margaret therefore wrote to her brother to ask for peace. Henry answered that 'the Scots should have peace or war from him, according to their own choice and behaviour'. However, since he was still at war with France, he would certainly benefit by the cessation of hostilities with Scotland. A truce was therefore arranged to last for a year and a day, starting in February 1514. The Council agreed to this, although Margaret's plan to send deputies to sue for a permanent peace agreement aroused antagonism. Being English and sister to Henry VIII, she was naturally suspected of favouring her own native land.

As time passed she found the Council, which had split into factions, increasingly difficult to deal with. The older members wanted peace, but the younger and more aggressive ones were determined to strengthen the French connection and to avenge their fathers' deaths at Flodden. As the Queen kept talking of peace, they linked her with the older group and accused her of disloyalty to Scotland. In March 1514, Parliament took over the control of the chief fortresses of Scotland, which until then had been at the disposal of the monarch. Margaret was understandably angered by this diminution of her authority. However, at the time she was unable to take any action. On April 8th, Lord Dacre (who kept up with Scottish affairs through paid agents in Edinburgh) informed Henry that his sister had 'taken her chamber' at Stirling Castle. Three weeks later she bore the posthumous son of James IV, whom she named Alexander. The infant was immediately proclaimed as the Duke of Ross, the traditional title of the second in line to the throne, and was first baptized by James, Abbot of Dunfermline, and by Gavin Dunbar, Archdeacon of St. Andrews, then confirmed by the Bishop of Caithness.

His birth did not incapacitate his mother as completely as on previous occasions. This was fortunate, for she needed all her strength to deal with the problems that by now were growing on all sides. That a woman who was not even Scottish, but the sister of the hated King of England, should govern in the name of her infant son, was itself distasteful to many of the noblemen. They were ready to dispute any measure by which she appeared to be overreaching her authority. For example, a quarrel soon arose over her attempt to nominate new bishops to those sees left vacant after Flodden. Although the nomination of bishops had for some time been a royal prerogative, many lords objected to its being used by the female Regent. While this question was still being argued over, Margaret learned that members of the pro-French faction were urging the Duke of Albany to come to Scotland, not just as a leader of auxiliary troops, but as Regent in her place. Moreover, as heir-presumptive to the Scottish throne, he might well try to supplant his infant nephew and become King himself. This dire possibility was suggested to Margaret by Henry who, jealous of France's strengthening influence in the northern kingdom, urged his sister to prevent the coming of this Franco-Scot.

Margaret needed no encouragement on this score, but found it a task which was most difficult to carry out, although for a short while she appeared to be winning general acceptance among the nobility, while with the common folk she still maintained her original popularity. She demonstrated her ability to charm and to conciliate the opposition during the July meetings of Convocation and Parliament. The nobles were willing to sign a statement of unamimous support for their current administration: 'Madam, We are content to ... concur with all the lords of the realm, to the pleasure of our master the King's grace, your grace, and for the common weal ...'. They also agreed finally to send messengers to England to arrange for a peace treaty. This arrangement was facilitated by the current negotiations between England and France leading towards a general accord in which Scotland could be included.

Despite this evidence of concord, there were still rumblings of discontent. Moreover, an agreement in Parliament and the Council that all would work 'for the common weal' did not guarantee the maintenance of order at the local level. Even a strong ruler like James IV had needed to be constantly vigilant to preserve the King's peace, and had been called on frequently to travel from one end of the kingdom to the other to see to the 'justification' of evil-doers. With a child monarch and an inexperienced woman in authority, things rapidly went downhill. Lord Dacre observed to King Henry at this time: 'Of a surety there is neither law, reason, nor justice at this day used nor kept in Scotland, but get that get may'.

What could Margaret do? Her presence in the Council chamber might temporarily conciliate the opposition there, but she had neither experience nor temperament to fit her for the task of constantly rushing from one trouble-spot to another. And, even if she had tried to do this, it was unlikely that her arrival on the scene of the crime would restore law and order. In fact, even on her own estates she could not enforce obedience. The tenants on her dower lands refused to pay their rents, so that she was actually in dire financial straits. Never accustomed to economize, she found she had soon spent the £8,000 James had left to her from King Louis's advance payment, and was forced to pawn her jewels in order to pay expenses. Royal expenses of course were always high, with all the estates to be kept up and the servants, retainers and officers to be paid. And even in the seat of authority itself, in Parliament or the Council, she could not be sure of control. She might win support briefly, but unanimity seldom lasted over a week. Each nobleman appeared to be interested solely in the personal benefit which he would derive from measures taken. Only in the face of a real emergency would they work together. The longer Margaret wrestled with these problems, the more she became convinced that what she needed was a strong arm to carry out her decrees, a firm voice to urge agreement with her policies, a reliable companion to sustain her in adverse circumstances — in short, a husband.

Everyone had expected that she would marry again. During the winter after Flodden, William Dunbar urged her to think of the future:

> O, fair sweet blossom, now in beauty's flower,
> Unfaded both of colour and virtue
> Thy noble lord that died, has done *devoir*,
> Fade not with weeping thy visage fair of hue;
> O lovesome, lusty lady, wise and true,
> Cast out all care, and comfort do increase,
> Exile all sighing, on thy servant *rue*, [lay aside]
> Devoid languor and live in lustiness.

Even before her poet's attempt to turn her thoughts to matrimony, speculation had been rife on the subject of her next choice. The Venetian news-letter of September 18th 1512, reporting the English victory at Flodden, added, 'the Queen widow of Scotland would make a good match for the Emperor'. Emperor Maximilian even sent his secretary to Edinburgh to investigate this possibility in the summer of 1514, although his ostensible errand was to carry his master's condolences to the widow and congratulations to the new King, James V. Another possible suitor was the French King. His wife, Anne of Brittany, had barely been pronounced dead before three ladies were mentioned as suitable to succeed her: '... the Emperor's daughter or one of the King of England's two sisters'. As it turned out, it was the younger of these sisters, pretty little Princess Mary, whom Henry decided to sacrifice for the benefit of an alliance with his erstwhile foe. It is certain that the choice of her younger sister did not cause Margaret any pangs of jealousy. She still harboured a grudge against the wily French monarch who had pushed her husband to his ruin (and hers and their country's). Also the decrepit fifty-two-year-old was certainly not the type of man she had in mind; neither was middle-aged, lantern-jawed Maximilian. Even if either monarch had been youthful and attractive, marriage to a foreign ruler would have necessitated her leaving Scotland and giving up her children.

Some of the pro-French nobles contemplated arranging her marriage to the Duke of Albany. This would nicely resolve the question of the regency, but completely ignored the fact that the Duke was already happily married and had no desire to abandon his charming French wife. It also overlooked the fact that Margaret had no desire to marry Albany.

It may be that rumours of this proposed match reached the Queen and finally persuaded her to take matters into her own hands. Probably she would have done so without any of these pressures, because the man she chose had all the attributions sure to please a woman of her taste. He was young, handsome and accomplished as a sportsman and a courtier. He was Archibald Douglas, whose father and uncle had been killed at Flodden. Hence, when his grandfather, old 'Bell-the-Cat', died in 1514, the nineteen-year-old boy succeeded to the title of Earl of Angus and became one of the principal members of the Council chosen by Parliament to advise the Queen Regent. In appearance, he must have somewhat resembled James IV, being of medium height and build, with reddish hair and dark eyes. However, in contrast to James's shoulder-length hair and beard 'something long', Angus's hair was short and his beard close-trimmed. In facial expression too, there is nothing in Angus which is reminiscent of the gently smiling lips and eyes that can be seen in pictures of the dead King. Instead, an intent and somewhat piercing gaze and a stubborn set of mouth indicate a more ruthless character. But this portrait was painted some years later. At the time when Archibald first arrived at the Council table, the young Earl appeared gracious and completely submissive to the Queen Regent. At any rate, she apparently fell in love with him, if not at first sight, certainly after a very short acquaintance. Margaret was, after all, still quite young, and, according to Dunbar and other contemporaries, still pretty at twenty-four, with a bright, fresh colour and glowing vitality. It took little urging for her to follow the poet's advice to 'live in lustiness'.

As has been noted by other historians, Margaret's second

marriage has marked similarity to that, fifty-three years later, of her granddaughter, Mary Stuart,* to Lord Darnley. In each case, the Queen seems to have been infatuated with a young man simply on the basis of physical attraction. And in each case precipitancy in fulfilling her desire ended in disaster. In each case too, it must be admitted, there appeared at first to be some fairly sensible reasons for the Queen to choose her consort. In the case of Margaret there was her great need for a man to assist her with the management of the country. Since young Angus headed one of the most powerful families in Scotland, it seemed to her that he was the very one she needed. Aided by his kinsmen, he would fight her battles, carry justice throughout her dominions and force her unruly tenants to pay their rents. The fact that he fulfilled not one of these hopes and on the contrary exacerbated all her problems, even adding new ones, has caused historians to condemn her second marriage as the foolish leap of a sex-starved nymphomaniac into the arms of the first good-looking courtier she saw.

Seen in the light of history, Margaret certainly made a bad mistake. Yet, in August 1514, this was not evident. Her brother, for example, approved her choice, even though he had not been consulted in advance. In fact, no one was consulted. The marriage took place secretly on August 6th 1514, in a small parish church in Kinnoul near Perth. The fact that the priest who officiated was John Drummond, a relative of the groom, adds to the likelihood that young Angus's maternal grandfather, Lord Drummond, helped to sponsor this match which seemed to offer so many advantages to his family. Lord Drummond was already Justice General. He had risen politically many years earlier because his daughter, Lady Margaret, was the best-loved mistress of James IV. Oddly enough, the young Earl's other grandsire, old 'Bell-the-Cat', was the first lover of Jane Kennedy (Lady Bothwell) who also became a mistress of James IV. In fact, it was rumoured that her family murdered Lady Margaret Drummond. If the Queen Regent was aware of these strange coincidences in her new husband's background, she was unconcerned by them. These ghosts of the past had no relevance whatsoever to her present situation. Of immediate concern, however, was the fact that by roughly asserting the power his family had attained by his grandson's marriage, Lord Drummond soon increased friction among the nobles.

The secrecy of the ceremony was due to the fact that Margaret had been widowed less than a year and that her bridegroom had just broken off his previously contracted engagement to Lady Jane

---

* Since Mary was reared in France, her name is customarily spelled in the French style *Stuart* rather than *Stewart*.

Stewart of Traquair. Although not yet twenty at this time, the young Earl had already been married, but his first wife had died in childbirth some years earlier.

Margaret's new-found happiness was soon marred by the vehement opposition which her marriage aroused among the nobles. Far from strengthening her position, it lost her most of the support she had had on the Council. The Douglases and Drummonds were delighted by having their youthful representative raised to the position of co-Regent, a title soon given by the Queen to her husband, but most others were furiously jealous of his new pre-eminence. Efforts to invite the Duke of Albany to Scotland as Regent in Margaret's place were now redoubled. Her opponents maintained that the Queen mother had forfeited her right to the guardianship of her sons through her re-marriage. Hence, she no longer had any claim to the regency, and her rights as *tutrix* to the King were suspended until eight days after the Council meeting on September 12th. She must also give up the great seal of office and had no authority to dispose of any of the royal plate or jewellery. At the Council meeting, where Margaret was represented by several members of her new husband's family, it was agreed to send a request to Albany to come and assume the regency at once. Meanwhile, he was simply referred to as the Lord Governor. The Queen signed this request because she saw that opposition was futile at that moment. Later, she hoped to gain enough support to restore her former authority. She had enough of the Tudor pragmatism to bend with the wind of opposition when necessary — a quality that her future niece, Queen Elizabeth, was to demonstrate to perfection, though her granddaughter, Mary Stuart, never mastered it.

When Parliament met in Edinburgh, Margaret found the opposition led by James Hamilton, Earl of Arran, as strong as it had been in the Council. Being a grandson of James II's sister and consequently of royal blood, Hamilton felt he deserved a position of more authority than the mere Earl of Angus. So vehement did he and some other disgruntled noblemen (such as Lord Home and the Bothwells) become against the upstart who had married the King's mother that the royal couple and their servants fled from the capital to Stirling Castle.

Safe behind the walls of this fortress, Margaret sent a memorial to the remnants of the Parliament, now meeting at Dunfermline. Signed by the few who still rallied around her, this document stated that the Queen and her party were ready to compromise, if only their opponents would be reasonable. The latter replied with an offer allowing her to keep the guardianship of her sons if she relinquished the regency. The representative whom she chose to discuss this proposition was Gavin Douglas, her husband's uncle, whom she now designated as Chancellor in place of the titular chancellor who had deserted her for the 'Governor's party'. Gavin's efforts to reach a compromise were, however, unsuccessful. The faction supporting Albany as the new Regent formally declared that the Queen's second marriage had destroyed any claims to regality which she had held through James's will, including that of being 'tutrix of the King's grace our sovereign Lord, her son'. This right was, of course, one that Margaret was particularly determined to maintain. She might relinquish royal control of the nation (at least temporarily), but not maternal supervision of her children. Hence the negotiations broke down.

When the lords of the opposition refused her offer to compromise, Margaret felt that they had forfeited the right to dictate to her in any way. She would therefore maintain not only possession of her children, but also her rights of sovereignty. Consequently she continued to issue commands and to sign orders as *Regina Scotiae et testamentaria regis tutrix*. One such order was for a Parliament to be convened at Perth on October 20th. The opposition forbade anyone to attend this 'unlawful assembly' and ordered the immediate publication of the Council's declaration which in effect had deposed her.

Subsequent attempts by the representatives of the two rival governments to meet and resolve their differences were complete failures. Finally, word came from the Duke of Albany. He accepted the regency, with the proviso that the lords were to 'offer all good ways to the Queen' and her party. This evidence of his chivalrous concern encouraged Margaret, although the opposition nobles still refused to restore the guardianship of her son. She therefore refused to negotiate with them, hoping that the Duke's arrival might turn events in her favour.

Meanwhile, she had aroused a new storm of controversy by seeking to have her husband's uncle, Gavin Douglas, appointed to the primacy of Scotland. This important Church post had been vacant since the former Archbishop of St. Andrews, Alexander Stewart, had perished at Flodden. For a time the contention among applicants for this post was forestalled by the choice of William Elphinstone, Bishop of Aberdeen. This clergyman was so universally revered that no one would contest his elevation to St. Andrews. Also his age encouraged younger applicants in the expectation that he would not long obstruct their own ambitions to obtain this see. Sure enough, late in 1514, before papal confirmation had arrived, the elderly prelate died.

To prevent an immediate resurgence of competition for the vacated post, the Council forbade anyone to apply for it without their permission. Nevertheless, three candidates at once renewed their efforts undercover: Forman, Bishop of Moray; John Hepburn, already at St. Andrews as Prior; and Gavin Douglas. The latter was the choice of the Queen and her husband, but was supported by neither the Pope (who favoured Forman) nor the chapter of St. Andrews (who elected Hepburn). Given this state of affairs, Douglas's men took the forthright step of seizing the castle of St. Andrews (the Archbishop's residence). Naturally this use of force brought events to a climax. The Council denounced the Queen and her hated Douglas connections. They repeated that she had no right to nominate even bishops, let alone archbishops. Margaret wrote to the Pope to ask him to accept Gavin, and to her brother for direct aid. In response to his sister's appeal for help, Henry promised her troops and ships. Margaret accepted the offers with pleasure and urged that they should be sent at once. In reply to his message (received through the medium of Lord Dacre who conveyed secret letters back and forth between the Queen and her brother), she wrote: 'I and my party were in great trouble of mind till we knew what help you would do to us'. She had shown his letter to 'all my lords which were with me in my castle of Stirling . . . whereof they were greatly comforted'. Next, 'I beseech you that you should make haste with your army both by sea and land', for Hepburn, Prior of St. Andrews, had now been besieging the castle of St. Andrews for twenty-three days, 'which I would that your navy would revenge . . . I have sent my husband to break the siege if he may'. She also described her almost constant dilemma — lack of funds: 'I am at great expenses — every day £1,000 in wages, and my money is near hand wasted . . . for I can get no answer of my rents, as I showed you before'. Her adversaries, she continued, hoped for Albany's coming 'which I beseech you to let [hinder] in any wise; for if he . . . come before your army, I doubt that some of my party will incline to him for dread'. Despite all these perils, she ended on a firm note: 'I shall keep this castle with my children till I hear from you'.

But Henry did not send the promised help. His policy towards Scotland depended on his relations with France, and during 1514 these had constantly shifted from war to truce, from peace to alliance. Princess Mary's marriage to King Louis, like others of its kind, was intended to establish a firm and lasting friendship between the two nations. Hence it would now be exceedingly impolitic for English troops to be sent to Scotland. Also, though Henry still hoped to prevent Albany's coming, he now had to hide his distrust of the increased French influence in Scotland by pretending that he was concerned for the security of his infant nephews. Their position would be most precarious if they were given into the care of one who might make himself King by getting rid of them. He kept emphasizing this danger in the messages which he sent to his sister by way of the Warden of the Northern Marches. The best way for her to prevent Albany harming her children, Lord Dacre told Margaret, would be for her to slip away from Scotland and bring them to England. In a town near the Border, such as Carlisle or Penrith, they (and her husband, of course) would be safe for the present. Henry would then secretly send them enough military aid to enable them to return north and defeat all their enemies. By this method, Henry would avoid the necessity of openly sending his own troops into Scotland and thereby antagonizing the Scots against England.

Such was the purport of the advice which Dacre regularly sent the Queen through her special envoys, Williamson and Inglis. These two would go to Berwick to consult with the Warden and return to give the Queen his advice and messages from her brother. Margaret expressed deep appreciation for the kind invitation to bring her bairns south of the Border. Nevertheless, she was wary of accepting it. Her brother even hinted that raising her sons in England would do much to endear them to the people and that, if Catherine of Aragon continued to be unable to produce a healthy successor to the crown, the English would be eager to make one of them heir to the throne. Margaret, however, feared that if she took her sons from Scotland, the disgruntled nobles would make Albany their King — an idea which was already current among members of the 'Governor's party'. Those in favour argued that this plan would at once solve the problem of the disputed regency and would give the nation a mature man as ruler, instead of an infant whose minority was causing such turmoil. If their plan succeeded, the young James V would not gain an additional throne, and might well lose the one he already had.

Whether Henry was sincere in his protestations to his sister is debatable. He probably wanted simply to control the young King in order to strengthen his hand in Scotland. However, one thing is clear from these discussions. Margaret was loyal to her son's hereditary right. Her staunch refusal to take the easy way, thereby endangering his future, justifies the faith which James IV had shown in her when he left her as Regent and guardian of his son. She carefully hid from her brother the fact that she had made the decision not to come south. Instead of refusing outright to fall in with his plans (which would certainly have provoked the Tudor wrath), she made excuses for her inability to do as he urged. She wrote that she would love nothing better than to come to England, as was indeed true:

> I would be gladder to do [this] than to make me the greatest lady of the world. Yet it comforts mine heart to hear your fraternal desire; but it is impossible to be performed by any manner of fashion that I, my husband, or his uncle can devise; considering what watch and spies there is daily where I am, and I dare disclose my counsel to none other but God. If I were such a woman that might go with my bairn in mine arm, I trow I should not be long from you, whose presence I desire most of any man.

Meanwhile, could he not at least send money, if not an army? This request was also phrased very diplomatically:

> I trust, dear brother, to defend me from mine enemies, if I had sufficient expenses to [until] the coming of your help: but I am so super-extended that I doubt that poverty shall cause me to consent to some of their minds which I shall never do without your counsel, as long as I have a groat to spend. Wherefore I pray you to send me some money, as you think necessary, for it is not your honour that I or my children should want.

Others too heard of her dire financial straits. Lord Fleming, writing from Paris (where he now represented the interests of the 'Governor's party') told a Scottish official on the Borders in December 1514: [The Queen has written to England and to the Pope complaining that] 'her bairns and dowry is taken from her and that she dies for hunger and has laid her jewells in *wed*' [security for loans]. He went on to say that the English King was therefore threatening to invade Scotland and planned to make young James King of England (if Henry's succession failed) and the little Alexander King of Scots. 'Therefore', he ended with this warning: 'I pray you ye cause to *gar* [keep] the bairns well'. So Margaret had been telling the truth when she wrote to her brother that all her movements were watched. She was not, alas, 'such a woman that might go with my bairn in mine arm', for her bairn was the King of Scots.

CHAPTER 8

SURRENDER (1514–1515)

The rugged castle of St. Andrews, perched above the rocky coast, had withstood many sieges and witnessed many bloody scenes prior to 1514, when Gavin Douglas strove to hold the old fortress against his rivals for the primacy of Scotland. Angus and his Douglas followers made a valiant but futile effort to come to his rescue and raise the siege. However, the hoped-for assistance from Angus's brother-in-law, Henry of England, failed to come, either by land or by sea. Eventually the stark choice was surrender, or starve. Gavin wisely chose to yield, as perhaps he realized that without the support of people, Pope, nobility, or even of his fellow clergymen, he would have had a difficult career as Archbishop.

The impasse over this important church post was thus broken, and the archbishopric went to the Pope's candidate, Forman, Bishop of Moray. A clever diplomat, Forman had helped to persuade James IV to aid France in 1513, and by doing so had attained a see in France, yet he had managed at the same time to keep the friendship of Pope Leo X, through whose influence he obtained the prized position in St. Andrews. Forman's previous see of Moray now went to John Hepburn. Gavin Douglas also received some compensation by being made Bishop of Dunkeld, although he received this office primarily because the Queen had persuaded her royal brother secretly to intercede with the Pope on behalf of her husband's uncle.

As the controversy over this issue subsided Margaret felt free to leave her fortress of Stirling, which by now was in need of the usual cleaning between visits, and moved to Perth. Here she called Parliament to meet on March 12th 1515. However, the two sides again failed to agree on anything except peace with England. Louis and Henry had, eight months earlier, settled on terms in which Scotland could be included. Louis himself had died in December 1514, having enjoyed his new bride, Mary Tudor, for less than four months. In fact, some gossip held that marriage to a girl who was not yet twenty had proved fatal to the ailing and prematurely decrepit monarch. His successor, King Francis I, was himself only twenty when he ascended the throne and his reign began somewhat uncertainly. For the time being he followed the course of his predecessor in foreign affairs. Hence the peace with England continued, and there seemed no reason for Scotland to maintain a state of war, alone and deserted by its 'auld ally'.

Henry had tried to persuade Francis I to keep the Duke of Albany away from Scotland, but the Scots themselves were becoming more and more anxious for his arrival. In a letter of January 21st 1515, Gavin Douglas described the need for someone to take a firm hand in government: the people were becoming 'so weary of witnessing scenes of extortion, robbery, and petty warfare, that they would be glad to live under the great Turk, if by so doing they could have justice!' At last, late in May 1515, the Lord Governor arrived. Coming by way of the west coast to elude the war vessels Henry had sent to try to prevent his coming, he landed at Dumbarton Castle on the Firth of Clyde. In the fleet accompanying him were several of the ships James IV had lent to Louis. The *Great Michael*, however, was not among them. The Duke had sold this ship to Louis on behalf of Scotland. Later he persuaded the Scottish Council to agree to the sale, from which he himself had received some profit, as proved by later historical investigation. Margaret sighed regretfully when she heard of the fate of the vessel, recalling the high hopes James had had for it and the happy hours she and her husband had spent on board. How far away those carefree days seemed! But she had no leisure now to reminisce. All her energy must be husbanded for the ordeals ahead. In preparation for Albany's coming, she moved from Holyrood Palace to Edinburgh Castle. This would appear a gracious gesture on her part as it would give the Duke the more regal residence. Besides, the great fortress overlooking the town would give her and her family more security.

She dressed carefully for her first meeting with the Lord Governor, in a gown of her favourite red velvet, with a gold and ruby pendant at her throat. Despite her understandable antagonism for the man now being groomed to take her position, she found herself pleased by his appearance and his manner. Above average height but somewhat stout, he had a florid face and iron grey hair. His dress was rich without being overly ornate; his manners showed the gentleman born, polished and courtly. He bowed low to her curtsy and addressed her in French, apologizing for the fact that he knew no Scots. She at once answered him in his own language, waving away the interpreter. What a triumph that she could speak his tongue even though he was ignorant of hers! They exchanged the usual banalities. He expressed sympathy for the death of James IV, but wished her a happy future with her new husband, whom he congratulated on having acquired so lovely a bride. He thanked her for the welcome he had received in Scotland, especially the elaborate displays with which he had been entertained on arrival in Edinburgh. Reassured by this conciliatory speech, Margaret replied with becoming graciousness. She hoped his voyage had not been too tedious and that his quarters at Holyrood were comfortable. Lastly, she invited him to call upon her for any assistance he might need for the enjoyment of his stay in Scotland.

Aside from this hint that she looked upon his arrival as merely a visit rather than a permanent residence in her country, she made no reference to the topic uppermost in both their minds, their rivalry for the regency.

Unfortunately, before this important subject could be brought up other matters had arisen causing friction. First the Council was angered by rumours that Margaret's brother, as uncle to the young King, was claiming to be both his rightful protector and Lord Governor of his kingdom. These allegations were said to have been made in Rome, and the Scottish lords wrote to the Pope vigorously denying them and stating that the Duke of Albany now held both these titles, and was acknowledged by the Queen. They added 'that the said King of England nor none other his predecessors was never protector nor governor of the realm of Scotland . . . nor will [they] never admit and accept him to the same, in no time to come'.

Then, in an even more embarrassing incident, Margaret's efforts to acquire the bishopric of Dunkeld for her husband's uncle came to light. Accused of having received the see through English influence, Gavin Douglas publicly denied this fact before the Council and the Duke. The latter then sent for Margaret and asked Gavin to repeat his statement in her presence. After the Bishop had reiterated his vehement denial of the use of English influence to acquire his appointment, Albany asked Margaret whether this was true. She replied that it was. In so doing she may have bolstered her conscience with the reflection that she had indeed used the legal method of requesting papal consent and this with the full knowledge of the Council. To her dismay, a few days later evidence was produced proving that she had prevaricated. Sometime previously the Duke had come into possession of several letters which confirmed her efforts to gain the bishopric through Henry's influence with the Pope. They also proved that since Gavin himself knew all this, he also had deliberately lied. Despite his efforts to establish his innocence by emphasizing Margaret's use of open and legal, as well as covert and disapproved, methods, he was declared guilty of law-breaking and imprisoned in the same castle of St. Andrews which he had tried unsuccessfully to hold against siege the previous year.

As if this was not bad enough, Margaret was now afflicted with still more problems brought on by her in-laws. Ever since she had elevated Angus to the position of co-regent with herself, his maternal grandfather, Lord Drummond, had openly gloried in the power thus acquired by his family, adding to the bitter resentment of the rival families. On one occasion the elderly Justice General had even gone so far as to strike the Lyon King of Arms in public, because the latter had failed to address Margaret as Queen Regent, calling her only 'My Lady Queen, mother to His Grace, our King'. Now, trying belatedly to ingratiate himself with the dominant party, he swore to serve the Lord Governor and apologized for his past actions in support of his granddaughter-in-law. Despite this virtual desertion of her failing cause, he was nevertheless attacked by those opposition nobles whose triumphant side he was now espousing. Accused of plotting secretly against the Duke, he was removed from the governorship of Stirling Castle and placed in the custody of Lord Fleming at Leith, where he was held incommunicado until his trial for treason.

Margaret was distraught. Not only was Lord Drummond her husband's kinsman, but he had become for her a kind of father-figure, symbolizing her deep affection for her own father, Henry VII. Although Drummond had apparently deserted her cause in taking the oath to the Duke, she was still sure of his underlying loyalty to her. On news of his fall from grace, she left the castle and hastened down the steep, muddy road, now known as the Royal Mile, to Holyrood Palace. She was permitted to see the Governor, but found him stern behind a façade of outward affability. Unmoved by all her tears, he refused her pleas on behalf of the elderly Drummond. In utter dejection she decided to leave the capital and return to her castle of Stirling. The children were there, and she wanted to be with them lest they too might now be wrested from her, a danger of which Lord Dacre had continued to remind her.

Meanwhile the Lord Governor ordered a memorial service for King James IV. Such a ceremony was long overdue. None had been performed previously because of the national emergency and on account of the series of problems which had followed his death. Some kept hoping that he was still alive and would surely return. Others felt that at least his body should have been returned to Scotland for proper burial. However, his interment had taken place, not in Edinburgh, but at the monastery of Richmond in England. His tomb there, incidentally, was broken into by Protestant extremists during the reign of King Edward VI. The corpse, still in its leaden casing, was thrown aside in a storage room. A workman even severed the head from the body and took it home with him as a grisly souvenir. Fortunately, he later returned it, so that it could be re-interred, along with the body, at St. Michael's Church in London. Whether this corpse was actually that of the Scottish monarch is still a matter of dispute. In fact, shortly after Albany arrived in Scotland, a servant of Lord Home offered to show him the body of King James, which he said was hidden on the premises of Home Castle. By this time, of course, many rumours had arisen concerning the possible treachery of Lord Home at Flodden and his subsequent capture and murder of the King. As late as the nineteenth century there was a revival of these stories when a skeleton was found in the moat of Home Castle, with an iron chain around its waist. Whether this was possibly the real corpse of King James, or another one put there by the above-mentioned servant of Lord Home in order to implicate his master in such a charge, is now impossible to prove. At any rate, the Duke of Albany obviously did not believe the man because he refused his offer to show him the evidence, in spite of the fact that at the time Albany was trying to have Home convicted of treason.

Although there is some doubt about the whereabouts of James's corpse, it was fitting that at last there was a public service in his memory. The people of Scotland were grateful to the Duke for having this service, which was held in St. Giles' Church in the middle of July 1515. Over a hundred beautifully painted banners decorated the old church, hanging above the heads of the Governor and his party as they formed a procession going up to the high altar for the requiem. Whether or not the Queen also took part in this ceremony is unknown. At that time she was in the midst of so many woes and beset with so many problems that she may have envied her former husband's departure from the cares of this mortal world.

On July 12th Parliament unanimously confirmed the regency of Albany. Even Angus now supported him in this position and although this waiver of his wife's claims appears pusillanimous, it was certainly the only sensible course. Opposition in the face of such overpowering odds would have been futile and probably would have brought about his own imprisonment, which would have been an additional burden and sorrow to her. On the other hand, as long as he remained free, there was the chance that he might be able to assist her. His grandfather, Lord Drummond, was soon brought to trial. The treason charge against him was dropped for lack of evidence, but the other offence of which he was accused, that of striking the Lyon King of arms, was one of which he was unquestionably guilty, having done so in full public view. He was spared execution through the mercy of Parliament, but the elderly nobleman was sentenced to imprisonment and lost all his estates.

The final blow to Margaret was the news that reached her in Stirling that Parliament had decreed that her children were no longer to be under her supervision as their *tutrix*. Instead of replacing her with another tutor (such as the Duke himself), the Council named eight noblemen, of whom the Queen was to choose four, to act jointly as guardians to the little Princes. When a delegation from the Council came to Stirling to convey this message, Margaret had with her only her husband and a small number of servants to defend the castle. Yet she refused to yield. An eye-witness described what happened in a letter to Lord Dacre:

> '. . . And when she saw the lords within three yards of the gates, she bade them stand, and demanded the cause of their coming . . .'. They told her they had come from the Duke and Parliament to demand 'deliverance of the King and his brother'. Without hesitation, she defied them: 'And then she caused the portcullis be letten down, and made answer, saying that the castle was her own feoffment, given to her by the King her late husband . . . and that her said late husband had made her *protectrix*, and given her authority to have the keeping and government of her said children, wherefore she could in no wise deliver them to any person'.

Knowing, nevertheless, that such defiance would soon prove futile in the face of overpowering odds, she then played for time by demanding a 'respite of six days to give her farther answer. And then the Earl of Angus said and showed openly it was his will and mind that the King and his brother should be delivered, according to the decree of Parliament, and thereupon desired to have an instrument raised, for fear of losing his life and lands'.

Again her husband's behaviour smacked of cowardice as he deserted her cause. It was obvious that Angus had neither the stalwart courage nor, more importantly, the royal blood of a Tudor. He knew full well that the opposition lords would not hesitate to declare him guilty of treason and would gladly mete out to him all the penalties, including execution, which they certainly would not dare to inflict on the sister of King Henry VIII. Hence, again, on the grounds of political necessity he must be excused from a charge of cowardice and given credit instead for having the good sense to hold on to his life and lands in order to give real help to his beleaguered wife. As soon as the messengers had left and the way was clear, he slipped away from the castle and hurried to his own estates to collect men and material with which to return to the rescue.

While he was gone, Margaret prayed for the help she had so long been urging her brother to send to her. It did not come. Henry had reached a gentlemen's understanding with King Francis I: so long as the latter sent no troops to strengthen Albany against England, neither would English troops be sent north of the Border. Therefore, since his sister simply refused to bring her family to him for the shelter he had generously offered, she would just have to fend for herself.

Consequently, at the end of the six days' period of grace, Margaret found herself obliged to yield. She temporized, nevertheless, trying to salvage what she could from the wreckage of her original position. In her formal reply she stated that she wished to remain *tutrix* to her children, as stipulated in the will of James IV, thus reminding the lords that their action was in breach of this most sacred command of their dead sovereign. But, to show her complete willingness to co-operate with them and to allay any false suspicions they might harbour (such as the rumoured plot to spirit away the little Princes to her brother's court), she would agree to have the children supervised by four outstanding and respected leaders of her choice. Of course, there was also the proviso that she would always expect the free access to her bairns that any mother ought to have. Her four choices for tutors were the Earl of Angus, Lord Home (Lord Chamberlain and provost of Edinburgh), Earl *Marischal* Keith and Sir Robert Lauder, laird of Bass. Since she had personally selected these men, it was clear they must all be favourable to her cause — the first so obviously that there was no likehood of his being acceptable to the other side. Lord Home had originally tried to ingratiate himself with Albany on his arrival in Scotland, but having failed to advance as he had hoped in this way, he had since veered to the Queen's party. That he had definitely chosen her side was soon proved, when he refused to carry out Albany's order to arrest George Douglas, Angus's brother, as a suspected traitor. Instead of obeying this order, Home precipitately fled from the capital to Newark, where he soon contacted Lord Dacre. Meanwhile George Douglas fled to Bunkle Castle, near Berwick.

Margaret realized it was unlikely that the men she had selected would become her sons' guardians, but she still hoped her reply would have a softening effect on the Duke. She was sadly disillusioned, therefore, when, instead of continuing their exchange of messages (which would have given her more time to collect her forces and to make new plans), the Governor simply sent an armed force to take the children from her. Troops, under the command of Lord Borthwick, aided by the Earls of Lennox and Cassilis, soon arrived in front of the castle. The Queen refused to relinquish her sons or even to permit these leaders to enter the castle. Instead she had the draw-bridge raised and the portcullis lowered. Atop its lofty precipice, her castle appeared invulnerable to direct attack; a prolonged siege might be a different story. If only Henry would send help!

Lord Dacre did his best to alert his sovereign to his sister's desperate situation, urging Henry to use his influence with Francis I. As Albany's master, the French King could order the Duke to accept a fair offer of compromise. Otherwise, there was no telling what evil might await Henry's nephews. Evidently, Lord Dacre fully believed the worst of the Franco-Scot.

By this time, Mary Tudor, the young widow of Louis XII, had left France as the happy bride of Charles Brandon, Duke of Suffolk. They had even taken with them a number of jewels which Francis I claimed as the property, not of Louis's widow, but of the French crown. English influence in France had waned considerably in consequence and Henry's pressure on Francis was unlikely to succeed. In any case, the extreme slowness of communications would mean that any such plan would be far too late to do any good in the present crisis. Margaret was therefore left on her own to defend her rights and her sons.

Yet she was not entirely alone as there was still the hope that Angus could raise a force for her rescue. Albany now sent Angus an impossible command, namely to assist the Governor's forces to besiege Stirling. Young Archibald was therefore forced to choose: he could either refuse obedience to lawful authority, or join in an attack on his own wife. To his lasting credit, in this instance at least, he accepted the risks to himself and proved loyal to Margaret. This loyalty would be a consolation to her during the bleak months of their coming separation. Unfortunately, it was of no avail in the immediate emergency.

Angus tried to carry out a plan which had been devised by Lord Dacre. The latter was still determined to take the Princes south to England and was convinced that in her desperation Margaret would now agree to this suggestion, rather than be faced with separation from her children. In order to carry out the English Warden's plan, Angus and Lord Home's brother galloped to Stirling at the head of sixty horsemen. The inadequacy of this tiny force became apparent the moment they approached the castle and found it besieged by nearly ten times their number.

Instead of attempting to combat such insuperable odds, Archibald Douglas, with his younger brother George, found an entrance to the fortress which was not being guarded by the Duke's men. Creeping up to it, they gained admittance. Margaret greeted them with joy, throwing herself with tears of thanksgiving into the arms of her husband. They sat down together and tried to devise a plan of action. It would be far too dangerous, she felt, to try to take the little Princes through the unwatched gate. If they should be apprehended, such an attempt would give the Governor's party definite proof that they were plotting to carry the children off to England. This would of course lay Angus open to charges of treason and in all probability lead to his conviction and ultimately to the punishment meted out for such a crime.

Instead, they agreed, Angus would leave alone. Later, if actual fighting seemed about to occur, Margaret would take the young King with a 'crown on his brow and the sceptre in his hand' out on the battlements. Surely the sight of their infant monarch would arouse the loyalty of the soldiers and they would find themselves unable to assault him and his mother. This spirited scenario greatly appealed to Margaret. It was not so attractive to her husband, who feared the men would think more of their own fate if they disobeyed their orders than of respect for their young King. But because he could think of no plausible alternative, he acquiesced. Leaving George Douglas to support Margaret during his absence, the Earl then slipped out the way he had entered so that he could seek Lord Dacre's advice and — hopefully — assistance in the form of English troops and supplies. As he was leaving the vicinity of the castle, Angus was detected by some of Borthwick's men. A brief skirmish took place, in which sixteen of the Douglas men were killed. The rest were able to escape, including Lord Home's brother and the Earl himself, to the intense relief of his wife, who had witnessed the encounter from a tower window.

For several days after this interview with her husband, the Queen held out some hope of rescue. But instead of the longed-for English troops, a formidable army including a train of artillery came marching across the plain from the direction of Edinburgh. When she heard that one of the guns was the famous Mons Meg, Margaret gave up her plans for armed resistance. Against the projectiles of this well-known cannon and the others like it, the walls of the old castle would not stand intact for long. Moreover, she had no one left to fight for her. At the first news of the approach of the Duke of Albany with this new force, her brave masculine protector, George Douglas, had fled in a panic, 'followed by the subalterns and the men'. As a result the Queen was left to guard the entire precincts with only a handful of women. She did not panic. In the face of danger she was always at her best. Showing every ounce of her Tudor determination, she stood firm.

The original plan in the event of such a crisis was discarded. Margaret knew better than to expect Albany's men to disobey his orders with the Duke himself in command, and the sight of his young sovereign on the battlements would hardly affect this Frenchman. But she thought of an alternative scheme with just as much dramatic effect and more likelihood of success.

At her order the drawbridge was lowered and the portcullis raised. As the Duke and his party passed in through the high stone gateway, he was confronted by an appealing group. Queen Margaret stood at the entrance, holding three-year-old James V by the hand. Beside her stood the nursemaid with the infant Alexander in her arms. The womanly appeal of the Queen mother was enhanced because she was once again pregnant, a fact which was obvious despite the billowing skirts worn at that time. With great dignity, she handed the keys of the castle to her little boy and bade him give them to the Lord Governor. James stepped forward manfully holding up the heavy brass keys to Albany, who, bowing low to his little sovereign and his mother, received these tokens of submission with graciousness. As she then led the way into the great hall, Margaret felt a great sense of relief. True, she had had to surrender, but she had carefully noted the effect which the little scene she had just enacted had had upon the new Regent, and she felt confident that her instincts in planning it had been correct. John Stuart was a gentleman; he would prove generous to a lady in distress.

Sure enough, later when she pleaded most humbly for herself, her children and her husband, he responded by promising his protection to her and her *enfants*. To ensure their safety he now ordered a guard of a hundred and forty to stay behind him at Stirling. As leaders of this force he appointed Lord Fleming, Lord Borthwick and Lord Keith. His inclusion of Keith, the Earl *Marischal*, was generous, since she had herself indicated her reliance on this nobleman by choosing him as one of the four guardians of her sons. However, in response to her plea for her husband, the Regent refused to make any guarantee for traitors. Much as she wished to contest this, she managed to refrain from doing so at that moment. Later, when tension had eased and she again brought up the subject, the Duke proved more lenient. He forgave Angus for having disobeyed him rather than carry out the order to join the forces besieging his own wife, but he insisted on obtaining a promise from both Margaret and Archibald not to call for aid from England.

Thus a truce seemed to have been established between the Queen and her rival. Although she had failed to remain Regent or even legal *tutrix* to her sons, she felt that the men appointed to be their guardians were trustworthy. Also the Duke had assured her she should have access to her bairns whenever she wished. In this manner, her most pressing worries were eased. Moreover, Albany had promised to get Parliament to see that henceforth her rents were paid so that she should no longer be in such difficult financial straits. She now felt more confident of her ability to deal with this Franco-Scot. Henceforth she would rely on one of her preferred maxims: charm, and above all an appeal to his chivalry, are more effective weapons against a man than force.

CHAPTER 9

ESCAPE (1515)

He would 'kill some six or seven dozens of Scots at a breakfast, wash his hands, and say to his wife: "Fie upon this quiet life, I want work"'. These lines describing the ruthless energy of Shakespeare's Hotspur have also been applied to Lord Dacre. Stationed as he was near Berwick, on the very threshold of Scotland, the English Warden of the Borders was inevitably kept busy by the guerilla warfare which was endemic to this troubled region. Which side was more culpable in this ferocious warfare is impossible to prove. Lawless groups both north and south of the frontier made their entire livelihood from stealing what other men grew. Once a raid came from one direction, another was sure to follow in retaliation from the other, causing a vicious circle of rapine that kept the entire region desolate. This state of affairs was profitable to the Warden, for it was in time of conflict that his talents made him particularly valuable to his sovereign. Hence, when things appeared to stagnate and peace threatened to envelop the area, it behoved him to stir things up.

Moreover, he was encouraged in this sort of activity by his superiors. In fact, one of their earliest complaints about him seems to have been that he was not vigorous enough in harrying the Scots. Any squeamishness he may have felt at first for this brutal business was suppressed, however, and he soon gained the reputation of being the most ruthless ravager of the Scottish Borders.

In addition to meting out swift vengeance for Scottish raids into England, he occasionally attacked his northern neighbours for other reasons. Here again, he was encouraged by his superiors in Westminster. England's aim was to keep Scotland divided and therefore weak. One method which has already been mentioned was the bribery of nobles in influential posts, especially those living close to the English border. That Dacre employed this device is amply proved by his correspondence with Wolsey and other high officials, as well as by the royal accounts. Another method was to stimulate feuds among the Scottish noblemen in order to break them up into quarrelling factions. This was never a difficult task; constant bickering among the lords was more or less the usual state of affairs, except when a strong and popular ruler like James IV was on the throne. So successful was Lord Dacre in these divisive tactics that he boasted to Wolsey that he was the King's 'fiddling stick to hold Scotland in cumber and business'.

King Henry was alarmed by Albany's early popularity in Scotland because this might strengthen the 'Auld Alliance'. Therefore, as soon as the Duke had arrived, 'the fiddling stick' received instructions to concentrate his attention on the nobles. Dacre quickly found several prospective renegades among the Border lords who were his neighbours and in some instances his kinsmen as well. One of these was Lord Home, Chamberlain of Scotland, who had at first seemed to Margaret to be her chief enemy because of his early support for Albany, but who had changed sides after the Duke, having risen to power, had favoured a rival. Under Dacre's clever prodding, Home changed from being originally a strong advocate of Albany, to being his opponent, and finally becoming an outright rebel abainst the Duke's authority. This last step occurred after Home's brother had helped Angus in his attempt to rescue the Queen and her sons from Stirling.

Angus, another protégé of the Warden, would naturally oppose the Duke for having ousted the Queen and himself from their joint regency. Also, as noted previously, when Margaret refused to yield to the Governor's demands, her husband felt obliged to disobey Albany's orders to help keep food from her and her supporters besieged in Stirling Castle.

When he learned of the Queen's eventual surrender to the Duke, Dacre was predictably upset. This capitulation ruined his main aim of persuading her to bring the young King and his brother, the Duke of Ross, to England. Her apparent submission to Albany's regency and her acquiescence in the Council's guardianship of her children worried both the Warden and Henry, who feared his sister might supinely accept the francophile Regent's control of Scotland. Both Henry and Dacre were completely wrong in accepting Margaret's apparent acquiescence in the new arrangements at face value. She had yielded out of necessity to vastly superior forces and in doing so had simply made the best of a very bad situation. By appealing to the Duke's chivalry, she had at least assured temporary security for her husband and her own right of access to her children. However, her surrender did not mean that she was satisfied with the new *status quo*. With pragmatism typical of the Tudors, she was now bending to necessity, but as soon as the opportunity arose, she would return to the pursuit of her real objectives.

As time passed, additional difficulties arose which made her submission even more distasteful to her. She found that her movements were circumscribed and she could no longer come and go at her own volition. She was soon forced to leave Stirling for

Edinburgh, where she could be watched more closely by the Governor. This move deprived her of her own particular stronghold, her dower castle, and much worse, separated her from her children to whom she was as devoted as any affectionate mother. Little Alexander, now over a year old, was her special joy. She thought him even more precocious than his older brother and eagerly talked about him to outsiders with whom she came in contact. Even while she had been besieged in Stirling Castle, she had forgotten her problems long enough to write to her brother about her little boys, who were, she thanked God, 'richt lifelike' [right lively]. So it was particularly galling to be deprived of their company now when, having lost the regency, she had little public business to absorb her time. Her access to the little Princes turned out to be not so ready as she had hoped when the Duke originally promised it to her. She could journey from Edinburgh to see them only when it was convenient for Albany and the Council to arrange a suitable escort to and from Stirling — an escort which appeared to her ominously like a guard.

Another unpleasant aspect of her new status was the loss of privacy in her correspondence, all of which was now read by the Regent. Frequently he even dictated to her what she must say in the letters to her brother. Such strictures explain her apparent satisfaction with the new agreement between herself and Albany. Its terms included an indenture signed by herself and her husband on August 14th 1515, in which they swore under oath to observe the peace and not to call in foreign (meaning English) aid. When Henry remonstrated against their having agreed to these demands, his sister replied that both she and Angus had voluntarily made this pledge to the Duke because they were content with the new arrangements. Even though three noblemen had replaced themselves as guardians for her children, she continued, she still might see them whenever she wished. This cheerful letter of August 20th was signed, 'Margaret R', a signature which sent a message in itself. For, according to a plan that she had described to Henry the previous year, she would sign herself in this formal way in any letter that she was being forced to write. Only when she wrote without supervision would she include her usual closing phrase, 'Your loving sister'.

Of course, Albany soon became aware of this little stratagem and forced her to end all her letters to Henry with 'Your loving sister'. On August 24th Dacre learned from informants in Edinburgh that the Duke had compelled the Queen to write to her brother and also to the French King and the Pope, assuring each of them that she was content. However, the Warden of the North was able to intercept the French messenger carrying all these dictated letters, which were then forwarded at once to Wolsey. After this episode the statement which was reiterated by the Duke in his letters to Dacre, Henry, and others that 'the Queen is quite content' received no credence from his correspondents.

Dacre himself responded to Albany's letter by listing all the reasons why the Queen obviously could not be 'quite content', although she dared not object to the arrangements knowing that her husband, who was merely 'a subject of that realm', would certainly be punished. In fact, several of his relatives (Gavin Douglas and Lord Drummond) had already been imprisoned. Another grievance was that 'she hath but small profits . . . of such revenues and mansion houses as she should have by reason of her dower' because the Duke's promise to see that these revenues were paid had not been fulfilled. Worst of all was the fact 'that her children are out of her keeping', a grievance that she would have written about herself, 'if she were in a place where she might and durst speak' without endangering Angus.

Meanwhile another item was added to the list of Margaret's injuries. She was forced to sign a document acknowledging the Regent to be guardian of her sons. Now she was permitted to see them even less frequently than previously, and was herself treated with more severity after the Duke found out that she had had his French messenger intercepted. He learned all that her secret messenger had told Lord Dacre on that occasion, for the Warden was by no means alone in running an espionage system.

As a result, even though Margaret still felt that the Duke was basically a gentleman and could not believe that he was planning to usurp her sons' rights to the crown, as Dacre kept insisting, she was infuriated by the treatment she was receiving. As her situation grew more unpleasant she began to yield more and more to the suggestions which the Warden kept urging upon her. Having successfully won over Home and Angus, Lord Dacre now turned the full force of his persuasion on to the Queen. On September 7th he sent her a plan, a copy of which was dispatched to King Henry. If this scheme proved successful, 'as we trust verily it shall, to the great disturbance of all Scotland', Dacre asked whether he should next plan to keep her and Angus in England, and if so, where? The scheme had the same purpose as his original plans before the Duke's arrival the previous year: that Margaret and her family should cross the English border and seek refuge with her brother.

Margaret was still reluctant to leave Scotland, but this solution appeared to be her only hope of escape from an increasingly intolerable situation. Albany remained so popular with both lords

and people that his regency threatened to last until James V came of
age. The detested French connection would be strengthened; the
ties with England eliminated. Furthermore, she would be kept from
seeing her children and would continue to live in a state bordering
on penury, since her dowry was unpaid. Her husband would also be
without influence, as he kept reminding her. (Angus, having been
won over to the Warden's schemes, now helped to persuade his wife
to agree with them.) Moreover, there was no time for her to ponder
the pros and cons. She was now nearly seven months pregnant.
Soon she would be too incapacitated to make any sort of move.
Finally, in desperation, she appealed to Lord Dacre, who began to
appear as her sole hope for relief.

His first response was to remind her that her calamitous
cirumstances were the result of her own refusal to take his advice
before. 'Madam, all these premises the King my master, and his
most honourable council hath at all times heretofore supposed this
great trouble and danger would ensue unto you, unless you would
have followed counsel, which you would in no wise do in time
convenient . . .'. Her refusal had led, therefore, not only to her own
'extreme danger, but also to the utter destruction of the King and
Prince, your sons, my master's nephews'.

After this unnecessary recrimination, he outlined his own wise
plans for her next move, which this time she would do well to
follow. In urging these schemes Dacre was now seconded by
Thomas Magnus, King Henry's chaplain, whom Henry had sent
north to work with Dacre regarding all relations with Scotland and
in particular in straightening out Margaret's affairs — to England's
advantage, of course. Most of the letters to Queen Margaret and to
the English King and Council were therefore signed by both Dacre
and Magnus. However, in spite of what Dacre always told Margaret
to the contrary, the plans were obviously the Warden's own
invention, even though they were endorsed by his royal master.

Dacre wrote: 'With all the politic ways and wisdom' she could
muster, Margaret must leave Edinburgh for Blackadder Castle (a
fortress situated in the Marches close to Berwick, then in the hands
of Lord Home's brother, William). The Warden would meet her
there and would see to it that she was cared for at the 'time of your
lying down'. For her 'sure conveying' he had devised 'with the help
of your friends and mine, to convey you into the March, from
within a mile of Edinburgh, whither, with good wisdom, ye may
resort without any danger'. Her husband, he added, might come
with her or stay with the Duke, as he preferred. 'Howbeit, mine
opinion is plain that, for his most surety and for further practice
hereafter to follow, that he go into his said country'. By this, Dacre

intended the Douglas estates close to Berwick, where Angus would have his own retainers and strongholds, and from where he could flee to Berwick in an emergency.

This secret message, together with some English money for her immediate needs (such as the bribery of servants to connive in her escape), reached Margaret on September 1st. She sent a faithful messenger, Robin Carr, to take her answer to the Warden; afterwards, Robin was to deliver a message personally to her brother. She told Henry that she was beginning to suspect the Warden and his friend, Lord Home, of intercepting some letters intended for her, as well as some of hers to others. In these messages to the Warden and to Henry she now expressed complete willingness to comply with their plans, providing a few alterations were made which would make her escape easier.

First she would ask the Duke's permission to leave Edinburgh for Linlithgow. In her letter to Henry, dated August 20th, she had already mentioned that she planned to go in a few weeks to her favourite palace for her *accouchement*. Since Albany had of course already read this letter, he would accept without question her reason for now wanting to leave the capital. Once at Linlithgow, however, she would follow the Warden's itinerary and hasten by night, accompanied by only her husband and a few loyal attendants, to a rendezvous with the Chamberlain between there and Blackadder. If some unexpected problem prevented her from escaping that night, Home could cover the true purpose of his trip by making it appear a typical Border raid, an activity which he frequently engaged in, even against the inhabitants of his own country. In order to do this he could 'just burn some town of the Duke's and some other ruffling and so depart into his country again till another night'! Fortunately for the principals in this scheme, and for the proposed innocent victims living in 'some town of the Duke's', nothing prevented the Queen and her attendants from going to meet Lord Home.

Margaret moved to Linlithgow on September 11th, accompanied by Angus and by the usual cortège of carts laden with furniture and clothing, as well as a layette for the expected infant. She herself rode in a litter, the more to emphasize to the Governor that she was ailing and had reached a stage of pregnancy at which it was difficult for her to travel. However, the salubrious airs of her favourite domicile must have worked miracles, for only two days after her arrival there, she was able to ride on horseback over a far more lengthy and difficult route. This second journey was carefully concealed from the eyes of all except those few trusted attendants who accompanied her. At midnight on September 14th, she and these servants, escorted by her husband, his brother and several 'hardy and well-striking fellows' whom she had requested as a bodyguard, stole quietly out of a little-used side entry of the palace and mounted the horses held ready outside the walls. The darkness was intensified by a cloudy sky, while a thick fog rising from the lake helped to cover their movements. As they rode down the hill and along the road past the sleeping village, a chill wind blew gusts of fine rain into their faces. Margaret, pushing back the hood with which she had been concealing her face, took a deep breath of this bracing air — it was the wind of freedom!

She was extremely anxious to go first to Stirling to rescue her bairns, but Angus opposed this idea as being too dangerous. By adding at least twenty miles to their total journey, it would seriously delay them even if they should be so fortunate as to get in and out of the castle by means of the secret entrance. The children were guarded too. It was therefore likely that an attempt to kidnap them would result in the capture of the entire party. For the Queen this would mean a return to captivity; for Angus it could mean death for treason. He promised faithfully that once Margaret herself was safe in England, he would personally make another secret journey to retrieve her little boys — this was in fact another stage of Lord Dacre's plan.

Margaret concurred with this decision, although with great reluctance. It had been some weeks since she had seen her children and she had heard that little Alexander was ailing. But the very real danger of her husband's execution if they were apprehended was an argument strong enough to override her maternal instincts. So they continued their ride into the marshes which, at that period, lay to the east of Edinburgh. Here they met Lord Home at the planned rendezvous. He had intended to lead them next to Blackadder Castle. However, the Queen was growing weary. She had been braced at the start of the journey by the heady excitement of escaping, but the twenty-mile ride had so jolted her that she needed immediate rest. No, she reassured her anxious husband, it was not the onset of labour pains; her right hip was in fact aching from the unaccustomed exercise. If she could just go somewhere and lie down she would be all right.

A refuge close by was immediately chosen: Tantallon, Angus's own castle. As they rode down to the coast, moonlight was beginning to break through the clouds. The mists were blown aside and revealed the red stone walls of this mighty fortress, its towers sharply outlined against the sky. Margaret felt a great sense of relief, for she knew Tantallon had withstood many a siege. Perched high above the rocky coast, it could be provisioned by sea, while the enemy pounded in vain against its landward battlements.

At Angus's imperious summons the drawbridge was lowered and the portcullis raised. The entire party clattered across the moat and into the broad courtyard. The weary Queen was lifted down and borne into the great hall. A fire, burning low in the stone hearth, was at once replenished and blazed sufficiently to make a small oasis of warmth on one side of the vast, chilly room. She reclined beside the fire on pillows in the only chair the house afforded, while servants rushed to bring her a hot posset. Other servants hastened to make up the bed in the lord's chamber and to warm the dank covers with pans of hot coals. The Earl's castle had not been prepared for its royal visitor, nor had it quite the amenities of Linlithgow. Nevertheless, while she stretched her aching limbs and sipped the steaming brew, Margaret felt buoyed by a sense of triumph. She was free!

News of the Queen's flight reached Edinburgh late in the morning of September 14th. The Regent could not believe his ears. That a lady, so close to the time of her 'lying in', whom only three days before he had himself seen being carried in a litter from which she seemed barely able to raise herself to bid him adieu, that this lady so obviously *enceinte* should then have ridden horseback nearly thirty miles — '*C'est impossible!*' he cried. In a perfect fury at finding himself so tricked, he tore off the jewelled velvet cap from his head and cast it into the blazing fire, to the horror of the servants standing nearby.

Then, in a calmer mood, he hastened to try to recapture his flown prey. A body of horsemen galloped to Tantallon, only to find that the Queen and her party had already left for Blackadder. This castle, held by the Chamberlain's brother, William Home, refused to yield up its guest to the Governor's men. The Chamberlain and his brother were charged with treason, but their stronghold was capable of withstanding a lengthy siege and they gave no indication of surrendering. While Albany prepared larger forces with which to subdue the defiant Chamberlain, the Duke also made every effort to recoup his losses by diplomacy. Messengers were soon beating a path back and forth between Holyrood and Blackadder, bearing one offer after another from the Regent to the Queen.

Since she seemed unconvinced by his own frantic promises, Albany asked the French ambassador, du Plains, to reason with the Queen as a disinterested third party. Du Plains assured her that the Duke was honourable and trustworthy, and that it was not he but the Estates who had taken away her guardianship of her sons. He also reiterated the Regent's promises that if she were to return he would immediately see that her dower revenues were paid, her castle of Stirling was restored to her, and her husband's relatives were liberated. Even if she preferred to wait where she was until after her confinement, which was surely imminent, he would still guarantee to fulfil these promises. If, meanwhile, her husband and his brother would act as hostages to ensure her keeping her part of the bargain, he would grant each of them a free pardon for all their previous misdemeanours.

Margaret rejected these efforts at reconciliation, reminding the Duke that he had made her promises before which he had failed to keep. How could she be sure he would fulfil those which he was now making? In reality, however, she was probably less obdurate than these letters indicate. The original exhilaration of having success-fully outwitted the Duke had begun to wear off and she may have begun to wonder just what would be the eventual outcome of her ecapade. She was concerned that her husband had been declared an outlaw as the result of his abetting her escape and she was deeply worried by the possibility of a lasting separation from her children. Surely if she returned, Albany would feel honour-bound to keep his part of the bargain and, after all, the restoration of her children, her dower rights, and her husband's security were the very things she wanted. If only she could be sure.

The satisfaction of Margaret's wishes, her reconciliation with the Regent and restoration of tranquillity in Scotland were, however, the very last things desired by the English Warden of the North, profiting as he did from turmoil in those regions. Peace would be even less advantageous to Dacre's friend and protégé, Lord Home. He would surely suffer the fate of a traitor if harmony was restored. These two — the English Warden and the Scottish Chamberlain — had collaborated in bringing about the Queen's escape from Albany. They now continued to work together to prevent her return. Thus the unfortunate lady sensed that she had escaped from one captor only to fall into the hands of others, more ruthless than the chivalrous Duke of Albany.

She had not wanted to come to Blackadder, preferring to remain at Tantallon, her husband's stronghold. But at the time of her arrival, Tantallon was not adequately furnished for a prolonged occupancy, especially by a person of her prestige and demands, nor was it provisioned for a possible siege. Blackadder Castle, on the other hand, had been prepared with everything needful for her coming. Therefore, she had had to acquiesce in the plans already made for her and, once behind the doors of Blackadder, she was firmly in the hands of the Homes. The Warden of the North had also chosen this hideaway for her because of its proximity to the Borders; he could visit her frequently and keep a close watch on her movements. Moreover, just as in Edinburgh her letters had been censored by the Duke, here they were not only opened, but secretly tampered with by Lord Dacre. When he felt that a message from Albany was so conciliatory as to appeal to Margaret, he would insert a phrase that would be sure to antagonize its recipient. Similarly, he doctored her return letters to the Regent. Far from being ashamed of such underhand tactics, he boasted of them in his own letters to Wolsey and Henry. For he knew they were almost as anxious as he was to keep her from any form of settlement with the Franco-Scottish Regent.

Another means of preventing the Queen's reconciliation with Albany was Dacre's complete misrepresentation to her of some of the Duke's actions. For some time the Regent had been preparing an attack on the Chamberlain's strongholds. The latter was a declared outlaw, accused of treason against James IV as well as against the present government of Scotland. He had openly consorted with the English Warden of the North and had conducted raids against his fellow Scots from his base on both sides of the border. So the Regent's determination to capture this criminal and bring him to justice was certainly understandable. But when Albany assembled an army of 40,000 to attack all Home's strongholds, Dacre told Margaret that the sole purpose of this great expedition was to capture her and her supporters and that the Regent's immediate goal was Blackadder Castle, her present refuge. The Queen, Dacre advised, would do well to leave at once. The Duke's effort to subdue her by force, added the cunning Warden, proved how specious were his smooth promises of better treatment if she would only return to Edinburgh. Margaret swallowed the bait. Once again she fled precipitately — this time straight to Berwick, the gateway to England, where, she reasoned, she would be out of reach of the Scots.

The Queen, the Earl of Angus and their attendants made the journey to Berwick without incident. The sight of the strong stone walls of this northernmost English fortress raised Margaret's spirits. Alas, her joy on reaching her homeland evaporated when the guardian at the gates refused to lower the drawbridge. Captain Ughtred, Governor of Berwick, although he wished to admit the lady and her party, could not do so without an express order from headquarters. He would of course send a messenger post-haste to Westminster to obtain the requisite permit. Meanwhile, he regretted exceedingly the inconvenience this delay was causing her, but his orders were explicit. Without permission from the authorities in London, no one from Scotland could enter, not even its Queen, the sister of the King of England.

Exhausted, Margaret shook with sobs of anger and frustration as together with her little party she recrossed the River Tweed. Where should she go? Whom could she turn to? She was almost tempted to ride straight back to Edinburgh. It would serve Lord Dacre right for having persuaded her into this whole wretched scheme if she now became reconciled with Albany; Dacre had not even made proper provisions for her to enter his own border town. However, it would gall her pride too much to yield to Albany from necessity, instead of holding out for the strict assurance of achieving her goals. How humiliating it would be to return to the Scots capital, having been refused admission to her brother's own kingdom! She would never do that.

There was another refuge where she could go, one that even the vengeful Duke would not attack — that blessed sanctuary available to all those in need — the Church. The Priory of Coldstream was not far distant. The unhappy Queen was welcomed. The Prioress opened the hospitable doors to the weary refugees and here, once again, Margaret lay down to rest and to try to reassemble her shattered plans.

At least she had gained one advantage by her second flight. In leaving Blackadder she had not only avoided possible capture by the Duke, but had escaped the control of the Homes and, for the time being at least, of Lord Dacre. Now, at last on her own, she could try to come to terms with the Regent. The very next day she dispatched a messenger requesting Albany to send her his terms in order to persuade her to remain in Scotland. She asked for du Plains, the French ambassador, to bring her these conditions. If they were reasonable, she would return to Edinburgh; otherwise, she would still feel compelled to seek aid from her brother by going to England.

Albany was delighted by this evidence that Margaret would indeed listen to reason. He called an emergency session of the Council, which yielded to his insistence that they should now make the necessary concessions to the Queen. Together with this offer he included his own promise to protect her and 'to do to her all that accorded to be done upon reason'. He would 'shew her all the humanities that he can, so that she will return and come to Scotland, and be a good Scotswoman, as accords her to do, for the great love she should have to her son the King, his realm and lieges'. Furthermore, he would 'offer to her any place she likes best to lie in to, and protest that if she does in the contrary, whatever happens, therethrough, that it may impute to her and not to him, nor to the realm of Scotland'.

Bearing these conciliatory messages, the French ambassador

hastened to Coldstream, happy in the belief that he was to be the instrument of ending the wretched quarrel that had so torn the kingdom of Scotland. To his dismay, he arrived at the door of the priory only to learn that the Queen was no longer there. She had left, he was told, that very day to go into England. Her brother had sent for her, assuring her of a safe refuge and a warm welcome in her homeland, as well as promising any assistance necessary to restore her to her lost position as Regent of Scotland and *tutrix* to her sons. Lord Dacre had brought her these messages and had insisted that she leave with him at once.

Du Plains was utterly dumbfounded. He asked where they had gone and was told, to Morpeth Castle, one of Lord Dacre's residences across the border. The Frenchman eagerly offered to follow them there, but was refused. He persisted as long as he could, but finally had to accept the only recourse left to him, to communicate with Margaret by letter.

The ambassador had been tricked. When he was arriving at the front door of the priory, the wily Dacre was just in the act of conducting the Queen out by an exit at the rear. The Warden had learned of Margaret's refuge and had sent post-haste to London for the requisite orders to admit her into England and for the soothing messages of welcome with which he might persuade her to come south. Determined at all cost to keep her from any reconciliation with the Regent, he had hastened to Coldstream in time to prevent her from receiving du Plains. The King's 'fiddling stick' had again succeeded in keeping Scotland dancing to England's tune.

CHAPTER 10

THE ROYAL FUGITIVE
(1515–1516)

As she rode with Lord Dacre away from Coldstream, Margaret was strangely depressed in spirit. She had wanted to stay a little longer at the priory, for she wished to receive du Plains's expected visit. In spite of the Warden's assurance that he had learned otherwise, she still felt that the French ambassador would come, as the Duke's messenger had indicated he would. Surely the message he would bring would be news that the Regent would grant at least some of her requests. If he offered to restore her right to live in the same household as her little boys that would now satisfy her. Let the Council choose whom they would to be their tutors; as for the regency, she hardly cared for that at the moment. Indeed it would be a relief to let someone else handle the reins of government. Now that she was leaving Coldstream, the hope of returning to Edinburgh seemed more remote than ever, despite all Lord Dacre's promises.

She had been excited when the Warden had come rushing in that morning to bring those generous promises from England. It was so good to hear again from home, to be reassured that King Henry loved her and wanted to welcome her back to London. She should come in time for Christmas and they would all celebrate Yule together. These happy visions warmed her and made her eager to accept this kind invitation, forgetful momentarily of her pressing problems here in Scotland.

She had nevertheless argued that before leaving she must first see du Plains. Dacre had responded quickly, suspiciously quickly, that du Plains was not coming. Dacre knew this for a certainty, he said, because the Regent had already sent him a message to let him know that he was bringing up his army against the rebellious Angus and Home, and would take the Queen back to Edinburgh by force. Dacre's inclusion of Angus in the list of Albany's intended victims clinched his hold upon Margaret. She realized the danger to her husband, for Angus had broken his promise, taken under oath before the Regent only six weeks earlier, to live peaceably by the law of Scotland and never to seek outside help. Angus himself was even more forcibly struck by this argument and added his vote for immediate departure.

The Warden of the North had artfully woven a few threads of truth into the web of falsehoods with which he thus convinced Margaret. The Duke had indeed sent him a message that he was bringing his armies south; his purpose was not, however, to seize Margaret and Angus, but to capture the rebel Lord Home. Albany informed Lord Dacre of these intentions in order to ensure that this military movement would not be misinterpreted by the English as an attack upon their soil.

Du Plains also wrote the next day to Anthony Ughtred, the Captain of Berwick, to assure him of the Regent's true purpose in moving troops into his vicinity, namely to capture that arrogant rebel, the Scottish Chamberlain. Du Plains also told Ughtred that Lord Dacre would try to misrepresent Albany's purpose and therefore oppose these troops, 'because of the great affection that he has for the Chamberlain of Scotland . . . whose welfare he is more interested in than that of the King, his master, or of his sister, the Queen of Scotland'. Du Plans continued to tell the Captain of Berwick about the journey he himself had just made to Coldstream to make peace between the Regent and the Queen. He also explained how Dacre, fearing she would accede to the Duke's reasonable conditions which might bring peace and hence endanger his dear friend Home, had whisked Margaret away from Scotland, 'not wishing to permit me to speak to her . . .'. 'I hope to God that someday all this will be clearly known [to the world]', the frustrated French ambassador added bitterly. Unfortunately, Lord Dacre's double-dealing was not clearly exposed for many years, and far too late to benefit Albany, Margaret, or Scotland.

Meanwhile Margaret had more immediate problems. To the vague feeling of uneasiness that had troubled her since leaving Coldstream was now added a sudden searing pain. Lord Dacre expressed sympathy, but surely it could not be . . . was there not yet a month until her time? She retorted sharply it should have been longer than that, but, thanks to the constant jogging about on horseback in order to comply with his plans, it had come early. And, certainly she was sure — this was one symptom she knew well from experience. She could not be mistaken. The Warden was very perturbed. Morpeth Castle, where he had planned to take her, was still over twenty miles distant. 'How soon must she lie down?' The need for immediate action was plain, for as she answered, her words were punctuated by a little scream as another pain shot through her.

Lord Dacre was a warrior, hardened to all the brutality of frontier fighting, but he was also a man and this sort of scene was one he could not endure. They would find shelter at Harbottle, a castle just across the border. Here the unhappy Queen was faced with another disappointment: Henry's permit for entering his kingdom was for her only. No Scots might accompany her, not even her husband — a stricture the Warden had unaccountably neglected to mention earlier. In reply to her indignant demand for an explanation, Dacre offered the lame excuse that Angus's exclusion was merely an oversight and he promised that when it had been set straight, Angus too would be admitted into England. Meanwhile, in the face of her coming ordeal, Margaret had now to part from her husband. She would be forced to rely solely on the Warden of the North, a necessity that the latter himself was soon to regret.

Harbottle Castle was by no means prepared to receive a Queen as visitor. But even the shelter of such a border fortress was welcome to Margaret at this juncture. Once again she was able to stretch her weary limbs upon a bed which had been hastily made up and warmed for her occupancy. The pains she had been suffering now began to subside and she realized that again it was chiefly her hip that was aching. Her hour had apparently not yet come. It was in fact almost a week later that the true labour pains began. She had a long and difficult delivery, but at last on the morning of October 7th 1515, a squalling infant crowned with a wealth of red-gold hair entered the world; a 'cristen sowle being a yong lady', as the Queen announced later to the Duke of Albany. This 'yong lady' grew up as Lady Margaret Douglas. Never a Queen herself, she nevertheless became grandmother to a King. Her son, Lord Darnley, eventually married Margaret's granddaughter, Mary Queen of Scots, and their child, James VI of Scotland, became James I of England. Yet at the time of Lady Margaret's birth, Lord Dacre was so unimpressed that he waited eleven days before bothering to send the news of her arrival to her uncle, Henry VIII. 'We could not ascertain your highness of the same till this time unless we should have sent up a post purposely for the Queen's said deliverance, which we thought was not greatly requisite [unless] there had been further matter touching your causes to have been sent up unto your highness'.

Perhaps there was some excuse for the Warden's tardiness in sending this announcement. The 'fare young lady', whose entrance into the world Dacre reported to King Henry, caused her mother to become most severely ill. For a time her life was despaired of, and even as she slowly recovered from the birth itself she continued to suffer excruciating pains in her hip. This sciatica, as it has been diagnosed, doubtless had been aggravated, if not actually caused, by the many horseback journeys the expectant mother had had to take at a time when she normally would have simply 'taken to her room'. Margaret was never the sort to suffer in silence, so that her screams of pain, whenever she had to be moved in the bed, echoed through the dismal stone walls of the castle, shattering the nerves of all those at Harbottle. Lord Dacre felt obliged to stay in close attendance while his sovereign's sister was so desperately ill, but it was not the sort of duty he enjoyed. Raiding the Borders would be a pleasant respite.

Moreover, he was unable to provide more than the minimum necessities for the Queen at Harbottle. More elegant quarters had been prepared for her at his own residence of Morpeth, but in her state of health, moving her was out of the question. The layette that Henry and his wife, Catherine, had sent for the new infant was delayed by the difficulties of transport in that troubled area, so the 'fare young lady' was swathed in very ordinary infant attire, by no means the sort that her mother desired for her. She kept complaining about the beautiful layette she had had to leave at Linlithgow, as well as the other comforts available there, and bitterly blamed the Warden for her present miserable circumstances. He must have begun to wonder whether his efforts to remove her from the Regent's influence had really been worth his while. In so far as saving his friend the Chamberlain from disaster was concerned, his intervention had apparently been unnecessary. The Duke had successfully reduced Lord Home's strongholds and eventually had captured the Chamberlain himself, but Albany then proved unexpectedly generous. Instead of pressing the charges of treason to the ultimate sentence of death, he simply imprisoned Home and his fellow rebels, permitting the Chamberlain himself to be held captive by his own relative, the Earl of Arran.

By this remarkable example of clemency the Regent hoped to encourage the Queen to come back to Edinburgh. At Harbottle she had received the letter du Plains sent her when he was unable to see her in Coldstream. This letter urged her to return to Scotland and her children. She replied promptly on October 6th that there was nothing she would rather do, 'if all things might come to good concord'. Unfortunately, Lady Margaret's arrival the very next day interrupted this promising correspondence, which the Queen was too ill to attend to for some time. Her next letter, dated October 10th, was evidently written by Lord Dacre. It arrogantly demanded the entire re-establishment of her regency, guardianship of the Princes, a right which it stated was guaranteed by the Pope himself, and the reinstatement of her husband's relatives. The Council replied in a similarly brusque tone, denying that she had any right to these offices. They seemed particularly indignant at use of papal authority as basis for her guardianship: 'And as to the Pope's confirmation of the said office, your grace must . . . know that the realm of Scotland has ever been, since the first inhabitation of it, in temporality subject to Almighty God, not recognizing none other superior in earth'.

Next came an equally frigid letter from the Duke, threatening to punish all her followers as rebels unless she listened to reason. Simultaneously, however, he sent a trusted servant, 'Messire Jacques Ay' (James Hay, Abbot of Dundrennan), who secretly brought her a much more conciliatory message. It promised to restore Gavin Douglas to freedom and to a good benefice, and to permit her on her return to resume guardianship of the Princes, so long as she promised not to take them out of Scotland. He begged her to 'think well of this and to have confidence in me that I desire the welfare of the King, his brother, his Realm, and of you . . . Rid yourself of the evil counsel of those who for their own evil aims, like to see trouble and debate between these two Realms'. Unfortunately, the Queen was then helpless to evade the control of these 'evil counsellors', even if in her desperate illness she could have exerted her mental faculties enough to make any important decisions. She simply replied by gratefully accepting the offer to release and reinstate Gavin Douglas.

Meanwhile her husband had been endeavouring to carry out the promise he had made to Margaret during their flight from Linlithgow: to rescue the children from Stirling. In fact, this was another of the plots originated by the Warden of the North and entrusted to Angus and Lord Home. The latter, whom Albany had placed in the custody of cousin, Lord Arran, now persuaded his kinsman-gaoler to join in Dacre's new scheme, and the two fled from Edinburgh to meet with Angus in the Borders. There the three men signed a bond promising each other to work together to overthrow Albany and to free the little Princes from his guardianship. The Duke, however, learned of their plans and at once had the trio charged with treason. This threat ended the conspiracy. Arran promptly surrendered and, being of royal blood, obtained a pardon. His two confederates remained at large, but had to give up their plot to kidnap the young King and his brother as the Regent had been put on his guard.

Of all these activities Margaret was blessedly unaware, being still confined to her bed. She improved very slowly, but by the end of November her doctors cautiously agreed that it might be possible for her to be moved a short distance. Harbottle's discomforts, they felt, might be partly responsible for her continued loss of appetite. So from the rough frontier fortress she was taken by easy stages to Morpeth. Sir Christopher Garneys, whom King Henry had sent from London to keep him directly informed of his sister's welfare, wrote a complete account of this move: 'She was so feeble that she could not bear horses [to be harnessed] in the litter, but Dacre caused his servants to carry it from Harbottle into Morpeth'. So, although the total distance was less than thirty miles, the trip took a week, with rests of a couple of days at two stopping places. These stops were probably necessary for the men bearing the litter on their shoulders as well as for the Queen, who cried out with pain every time her bed was even slightly shaken. 'I think her one of the lowest brought ladies, with her great pain of sickness, that I have seen and scape', wrote Sir Christopher. She had 'such a pain in her right leg', that she could not endure to sit up while her bed is a-making . . . it would pity any man's heart to hear the shrieks and cries her grace giveth, when she is removed or turned'.

The writer was obviously a very kindly gentleman in his outspoken sympathy for the suffering Queen; her host, Lord Dacre, was beginning to feel sorry for himself. He had gone to great expense to prepare his home for her visit. The great hall was hung 'with the newest device of tapestry, and with all other manner of things thereunto belonging'. The other chambers were also furnished far more elegantly than those of most barons and 'his cupboard all of gilt plate, with a great cup of fine gold with the cup of assay, and all the lord's board, with the board's end served all with silver vessels . . .'. Yet all this magnificence was lost upon his royal guest, who lay moaning in the carved-oak four-poster of the lord's own bed-chamber which he had vacated for her use. Nor could she partake of the sumptuous viands with which he had stocked his larder, 'lacking no manner of good victual and wild fowl . . . that can be gotten for money'.

So the Warden of the North ordered his cooks to prepare all the special delicacies which were considered proper fare for invalids: 'cullis', a broth made of water in which meat had been boiled; and 'mortress', a sort of hash made of various kinds of meat, beaten together; 'almond milk . . . and pottages . . .'. She sent them all back to the kitchen, despite her physicians' urging that she must eat or she would never become strong enough to travel to London. 'Please, God, let her start eating!' was the silent prayer of her weary host, as week after week passed and his sovereign's sister stayed on and on.

Lord Dacre sent for new physicians, specialists in diseases of the joint who might speed the recovery of her painful hip. She refused to see them and insisted on keeping only the two she had had since the beginning of her illness. The 'intolerable ache in her right leg, nigh to her body' continued. Finally, Dacre wrote to her brother to ask him to send his own physician and his surgeon. She had agreed to see them, 'trusting much the better, by their good comfort and counsel, to have the sooner recovery of her great infirmity and sickness'. Dacre revealed his own feelings in the matter when he wrote, 'we beseech your highness for the speedy sending hither of the said physician and surgeon, which will greatly be to your said dear sister's comfort', to say nothing of the relief it would be to her long-suffering host.

Not only did the Warden have the problems of dealing with his invalid guest, but also the expense of maintaining a continual open-house for the nobility of all the surrounding countryside. The English flocked to pay their respects to the sister of their King. Then, as soon as King Henry lifted the ban against Scots crossing the border, nobles came from the north with their wives, to honour their ailing Queen mother. Naturally all these important guests had to be fed, and the more distant ones, given lodging for the night as well. Morpeth Castle began to resemble an inn.

It was Henry who, perhaps at the suggestion of his wife, hit upon the key to his sister's recovery: new clothes. He had originally hoped that she could join them in London for Yuletide. Now that her long illness had made that impossible, he quickly dispatched a pack-horse train laden with elegant fabrics as his New Year's present to her. Nothing he could have devised would have delighted her more. As soon as she heard of their arrival, she demanded to see the wonderful goods. Sir Christopher Garneys, having presented the clothes to her in his sovereign's name, wrote to the donor to describe the occasion: 'Her grace was borne in a chair out of her bed-chamber into the great chamber, to the intent that her grace would see all such stuff as your highness had sent her by me to be laid abroad'. And what beautiful 'stuff' it was: cloth of gold, cloth of silver, rich velvets in purple, green and red, trimming materials of gilt fringe, ermine fur and gold and tinsel braid. At once the Queen sent for dressmakers. They must start to make her some gowns of the beautiful new material straight away. One would be made out of cloth of gold; one of cloth of 'tynsen'; and another of red velvet trimmed with ermine. In addition, she required 'in all haste a gown of purple velvet lined with cloth of gold', with sleeves slashed to show the beautiful lining, and skirt front turned back to display it; plus 'three gowns more and three kirtles of satin'. Margaret still screamed with pain when her servants moved her in bed, yet despite her suffering, 'she hath a wonderful love for apparel'. When the new dresses were completed, she could not of course try them on, but she 'liked the fashion so well' that she would send for them to 'have them held before her once or twice a day to look at'. And all this in spite of the fact that she already had 'within the castle twenty-two gowns of cloth of gold and silks', and had sent to Edinburgh for those that she had left behind there. Sir Christopher marvelled, but he was, after all, just a man.

It was not only the lovely clothes, however, that overjoyed the Queen. Rather, it was the evidence that her brother loved her, as all the world could now see. She bade all the nobility who came to pay their respects to come and see the magnificent gifts that had been sent from London. 'So, my Lord', she would exult, 'here ye may see that the King my brother hath not forgotten me, and that he would not I should die for lack of clothes'.

Of the Scottish visitors who came to Morpeth when they were permitted to enter England, the first was of course Angus, accompanied by some other Scottish noblemen. Seeing her husband once again, unscathed by the weeks spent in hiding and flight to avoid capture by Albany, was a great relief and joy to Margaret. She happily introduced him to their little daughter, of whom he appeared as fond and proud as any new father. One of the noblemen who accompanied the Earl of Angus to Morpeth was his great friend, Lord Home, together with his wife. It must have been especially gratifying to the Queen to be able to show off her new finery to this lady, who was none other than Lady Bothwell, the former mistress of James IV.

The reunion with Angus and their shared pride in baby Margaret helped the Queen to survive the truly crushing blow she had recently received. Alexander, her favourite child, was dead. News of his decease as the result of a brief illness had reached Morpeth just before Christmas, but had been kept hidden as long as possible from his mother. She was then so ill that it was feared she might die from the added shock of this tragedy. She did indeed suffer a relapse when she finally learned of her loss, which was especially heart-breaking because of the long time during which she had been separated from him. Nor did Lord Dacre help matters by insistently hinting that it was the Duke of Albany who had caused his death so that he himself could ascend the throne. Margaret refused to believe that Albany could be guilty of such a crime. For one thing, why would he remove the little Duke of Ross rather than the young King himself? In response, the Warden implied that this would be the next step in the plans of the wicked Regent. Though the Queen did not accept these accusations, she did become concerned over the health of her elder son and was more anxious than ever to be reunited with him.

Therefore, when she at last began to recuperate slowly and to regain some independence of mind and spirit, she was more willing to come to a satisfactory truce with the Regent. The latter managed to smuggle a personal message in to her without it being intercepted by Dacre. Responding to the conciliatory tone of his message, she admitted in her reply that the Duke had promised to redress her grievances by 'many goodly and pleasant words'. However, she insisted, that he show his goodwill to carry out these promises by performing friendly deeds, such as setting free Gavin Douglas, the Bishop of Dunkeld. He also should send an *embassade* to King Henry to settle the entire question of her future status in her son's kingdom and to establish a lasting peace between Scotland and England. So far only a truce had been effected, which was to last until the following Whitsuntide.

Even though Lord Dacre doctored her letter so as to render it less appealing to its recipient, it did have at least one of the effects she wished. Gavin Douglas was set free, to her intense gratification. It looked for a time as though she and the Regent might arrive at a true reconciliation. The Warden was determined to prevent such a solution; he had not spent all that money, to say nothing of suffering the lengthy visit of a demanding woman, simply to let her go back to Scotland on friendly terms with the francophile Duke. In a letter to Henry, written on March 15th 1516, he emphasized his suspicion that Margaret might accept some of the offers which, he said, Albany had been making: to free Lord Drummond as well as Gavin Douglas, to restore the property of 'all her adherents', and to guarantee 'all the service and pleasure he might do her'. She had responded to these offers by writing personally to the Duke, 'hoping to have part of her pleasure'. However, Dacre had 'penned her letters, in such wise as the Duke would not consent' to them, in order 'to prevent any renewal of friendship between them'. To illustrate his work, he sent Henry a copy of Margaret's last letter to Albany, and included his own insertions. He urged the King to do all he could to hasten his sister's 'going southwards', because 'the daily messages from Scotland trouble her mind and put her in study what is best to do. Nothing comforts her so much as when your highness writes to her'. He also assured Henry that 'she, as a great wise woman persevereth and resteth upon this, that she will do nothing without the consent of your highness'.

This letter and others written during this period were composed jointly by Lord Dacre and Thomas Magnus, Archdeacon of the East Riding of Yorkshire and chaplain to the King. The latter had come to Morpeth to assist Dacre in looking after Margaret and in making sure that she fell in with the wishes of the King and Wolsey, the chief architect of England's foreign policy throughout the period.

At the same time that Dacre and Magnus wrote the above letter, they informed the King that they had sent the Duke of Albany a book of the Queen's formal complaints against the Regent, plus a list of the 'attemptats . . . committed on the *partie* [part] of Scotland to the King our Sovereign lord's subjects of England . . . to the violation of the comprehension [truce] . . .'. Although signed by Margaret, the tone as well as the substance of the book of grievances indicates that most of it was dictated or inserted by the Warden, because it is far more truculent than her own letters to the Duke.

The book of complaints includes her usual charges against Albany: depriving her of the government of her children during their minority; taking them from her and putting her out of Stirling Castle, which was her 'conjunct feoffment paid for by the King my father'; imprisoning her friends; and forcing her to write letters telling the Pope, and the French and English Kings 'that she had voluntarily resigned the office of *tutrix*'. It also blamed the Regent for reducing her to such poverty that she was virtually forced to escape and seek help from abroad. Hence, it claimed, he was responsible for all the suffering she had undergone during her subsequent flight by pursuing her with an army of 10,000 men from one place of refuge to another. 'Being at that time great with child, she was forced to seek refuge in England, where she delivered . . . fourteen days before her time, and fell into such extreme sickness that her life was despaired of by all'. Meanwhile, the Duke 'acts in all points like a King, and appropriates the revenues of the crown, so that it is much to be suspected he will destroy the young King, now that her son, the young Duke, is dead, most probably through his means'.

To this exaggerated survey of Margaret's alleged wrongs was added the Regent's treatment of her husband and his friend, the Chamberlain: 'He withholds from her husband Angus the castles of Tantallon and Bothwell; has procured in Parliament the attaining them and seizing their castles'. Finally, to complete this list of actions showing Albany's inhumanity, a melodramatic account of his treatment of 'an ancient, good and worshipful gentlewoman called Lady Home, mother to the said Lord Home' was added. Because she had visited Margaret at Coldstream, the Duke 'caused a Frenchman called Messire de la Bawty [Bastie] suddenly to take her from out her house in furious and cruel manner, and . . . conveyed her upon a trotting horse, to her extreme peril and pain to the castle of Dunbar . . .'. Here he had kept the poor old lady imprisoned for six weeks without attendants, and with nothing to eat or drink, but 'brown stoore brede and watter', — all of which had severely impaired her health.

To this incredible account of the wrongs suffered by the Queen and her adherents, Dacre and Magnus added an even longer catalogue of the Scottish breaches of the truce with England. When this joint 'book of wrongs' reached Edinburgh, the natural reaction was one of angry repudiation of all the charges made in it. The subsequent debate to a large extent nullified the advances which the Duke and Margaret had made towards a reconciliation. Indeed, the incident now developed into an intense propaganda campaign to convince all the courts of Europe that the Duke was a brutal monster, unfit to reign over Scotland even on a temporary basis. Such a war of words was conducted chiefly through diplomatic correspondence in the sixteenth century. Unlike the modern news media this method did not therefore reach the entire population, which only heard such news through the spread of rumours, but it was effective amongst the ruling circles of each country, and at that time these were the important persons to influence.

Albany himself realized the importance of their opinion, as is shown by the letters he forced Margaret to write to the Kings of France and England, and to the Pope, immediately after her surrender to him at Stirling, stating that she was 'quite content'. As soon as she had escaped his control, however, she began a counter-campaign, by telling these same important individuals her opposite version of affairs. She was aided and abetted by Lord Dacre and Magnus, and it was then that the 'book of wrongs' was probably compiled.

The effect of these letters on opinion in courtly circles is well illustrated by the Venetian news-letters of this period. These accounts were written to the Doge or to the Council of Ten in Venice by their representatives in London and summarized the course of events in England.

On September 20th 1515, the Doge was informed that 'the disturbances in Scotland are raging more than ever. Albany laid siege to Stirling; the Queen fled, leaving in his hands the royal infants; he overtook her, fleeing towards the kingdom with her royal wardrobe; seized her goods, leaving her nothing but the garments she had on and two attendants. The whole blame of this cruelty will be laid upon Francis'. King Francis I of France was the one Henry most wished to influence by this propaganda, so that he would remove his protégé, Albany, from Scotland.

A few days later the same correspondent told his compatriots in Venice that he had recently met Cardinal Wolsey who 'spoke with great vehemence' against the Scottish Regent, '. . . such a thing had never been done as offer violence to a Queen and her children'. Because of this outrage, the King was now threatening to invade France, though Wolsey had tried to calm him by saying. that Albany, rather than King Francis, was to blame.

A similar threat of war was mentioned in a letter from a French representative in London to a member of the ruling class in France. Wolsey had told this correspondent that if 'the Duke of Albany does not abstain from and make reparation for the injuries to Margaret and her children, Henry would make him do so. . . . He is determined to assist his sister to obtain what is due her'.

In December, the war alarm was still being sounded. According to the Venetian news-letter of December 24th 1515, England planned to attack Scotland the following year, where Albany was now all-powerful, 'having expelled the Queen and kept her two sons'. Worse news followed. In January 1516, the Venetian Council of Ten learned from their London informant that 'King Henry has affairs of Scotland very much at heart. Queen Margaret is grievously ill, having been prematurely delivered of an infant, who had subsequently died, that she was expelled [from] the kingdom by Albany, who had exiled some of her friends and put others to death; that one of her children was dead, and if the other died the kingdom would fall to the Duke. All this he [the King] uttered very passionately, throwing the blame on Francis'.

On February 6th, the Venetian emissary was quite adamant: 'There will evidently be war between England and Scotland'. The culprit responsible for it was of course the man then acting as Regent of Scotland, the wicked and heartless Duke of Albany.

The 'villain' of these often fictitious accounts tried in vain to secure a hearing for his side of the whole controversy. He replied personally to each of the potentates who wrote to upbraid him for his brutal behaviour. They were not convinced. Jean du Plains tried to set the record straight, assuring Wolsey that Albany had been unanimously chosen by the Scots as their Regent, that he had 'treated the Queen better than she ever has been before, as she'd confess if she told the truth', and that the Scottish Council had put three 'ancient lords' in charge of the two young Princes, whom Lord Home and the Queen had treacherously attempted to kidnap from Stirling. Some day, he promised, he would himself prove all this to Wolsey by documentary evidence. All du Plains' efforts were to no avail. Neither Cardinal nor King wished to believe anything good about the man who had supplanted Margaret as Regent. John Stuart, Duke of Albany, was already stereotyped as a ruthless monster who had seized the property and the babies of a defenceless woman — a Queen at that — driven her from her home, connived in the death of her younger son, and soon no doubt would eliminate the King, his brother, so as to make himself ruler in his place. A new Richard III was in the making. As a matter of fact, Sir Thomas More had written his famous history of the last Yorkist monarch two years earlier and, though this book was not published until 1543, the tale it told was already quite familiar to the general public, who were informed by means of rumour which the Tudors had done nothing to dispel. Consequently, it was easy for the English to picture their Princess Margaret as a much-wronged Queen who had suffered at the hands of another ruthless tyrant.

Meanwhile, the victim of all the wicked Duke's machinations became strong enough to start her journey to London. The litter and horses sent by King Henry to carry his sister in as much comfort as possible, arrived at Morpeth late on April 7th 1516. She set out the next day with her baby daughter, her servants and an escort led by Lord Dacre and several other noblemen.

To her dismay, her husband did not number among the party, although King Henry had sent him a special invitation to accompany her on her visit to the English court. Without a word to her or to anyone else, he and Lord Home had slipped away from Morpeth Castle and returned to Scotland. Dacre, writing angrily about this to his sovereign, said he had followed them the next day and tried to persuade them to come back to England. He remonstrated with the 'Earl of Anguysshe and the Lord Chamberlain' for having broken their sworn promise to remain loyal to the interests of the Queen and the English party. But the sanctity of an oath apparently meant little to them. The immediate restoration of their property, which they hoped to gain by appealing to the clemency of the Duke of Albany, was more important. 'The Queen, your said sister', wrote the Warden, 'takes the same right heavily, making great moan and lamentation. Albeit, remembering your great kindness and goodness done unto her at all times, she pondereth her grief less and full discreetly saith, whatsoever ensue hereafter, she will refuse all the world, and ... come unto your grace, for ... without your said help the King, her son, and she are likely to be destroyed'.

So it was with a little less than the expected delight that she began her long-postponed trip south. As she left the Scottish border behind, she could not help contrasting this journey with the one she had made north nearly thirteen years before. She had then been accompanied by over a thousand people all in holiday attire and spirits; now she had a retinue of fewer than a hundred, including sevants and men-at-arms; then she had been *en route* to meet her eager betrothed; now that husband had long been dead and his successor was not even bothering to accompany her; then she had been filled with the self-importance of a new Queen, eagerly awaited by her people; now she was leaving a nation that seemed no longer even to want her. These dreary reflections matched the weather, which was damp and chilly. Squalls of misty rain blew in from the coast, penetrating the litter in spite of the curtains. The dull ache in her hip was less painful than the one in her heart.

At each town where the Queen stopped for the night, the leading dignitaries would come forth to escort her to her resting place, but this time there were no street decorations or pageants, and only sparse crowds came out to welcome the King's sister. One night was spent in Newcastle and one in Durham. Shortly after leaving Durham, she was met by the Earl of Northumberland who accompanied her to York. The gallant Percy, whom she recalled from her previous passage through this area, had aged perceptibly during the thirteen-year interval. Though he still rode a splendid steed, he did not put it through the 'gambades' which had so impressed Somerset Herald. The middle-aged Earl now suffered from rheumatism and preferred to ride with as little jarring as possible. He sympathized with Margaret over her recent bout of sciatica. Cold and damp weather, he told her, were very bad for any aching joints. As they conversed, the twenty-five-year-old Queen felt that she too must be ageing, and her depression deepened.

However, in York she was wonderfully surprised, for who should come bursting into her quarters just as she prepared to retire, but Angus! He had received permission from Albany to cross the Border to catch up with her. With him was his uncle, the Bishop of Dunkeld, who had been liberated from captivity just as Albany had promised. As she joyously embraced her handsome husband, Margaret felt her own youth returning. The whole journey now assumed a new brightness; they would have a wonderful time together in London — almost like a second honeymoon, and better than the first which had been so quickly interrupted by the pressure of events in Scotland. Angus dashed these happy plans by explaining that he still could not accompany her. He must go back, he explained, to regain his confiscated estates. He would also look after her interests in Scotland during her absence, by seeing to it that her tenants paid her their rents. Then, as she was still not satisfied, he promised to join her later in London. He would accompany the diplomatic envoys Albany would soon send to renew the truce with England.

Although much disappointed, Margaret agreed to this plan, not knowing that in actual fact this embassy had already left Scotland and would reach London long before she did. Angus was deceiving her in more than this. Looking after his estates was only one motive for his return to Scotland; he also wished to continue seeing Lady Jane Stewart of Traquair to whom he had been betrothed before his grandfather had persuaded him to marry the Queen instead. Ever since Margaret's flight from Linlithgow — perhaps even before this — he had visited Lady Jane regularly, so regularly in fact that she was now expecting his child.

He felt he could keep this liaison from his wife while she continued to be absent from Scotland, and hopefully this situation would last still longer. But above all, he did not want her to find out while she was in London, where she could expose his double-dealing to her powerful brother. So, as she left York the next day, Margaret knew only that her husband had to go home temporarily on business. Yet he still cared for her, she kept reminding herself and cared enough to ride all the way to York to see her once more and to reassure her that he loved her very deeply. He had hurried off from Morpeth before, as he had explained, only because Lord Home had persuaded him he must. Then he had realized that he could not leave her without even bidding her farewell. She fought down the nagging doubts and turned her thoughts to the trip she was now making. She was going home.

TUDOR FAMILY REUNION (1516)

"Dereste broder, as hartly as I can I recommend me onto you, and let you wit that yesternyght I cam hyther, soo being comforted of you in my jornay in many and sondry wywes that, lovying be to our Lorde God, I am in ryght good heal [health], and as joyous of my sayd Jorney towarde you as ony woman may be in commyng to her broder, . . . and am moost desirous now to com to your presens and to have sight of your person in whom next God, is myn oonly trust and confydens . . .'.

This letter, addressed 'Unto my dereste broder the King's grace', was dated 'At Stony Stretford the xxvij day of Apryll', and signed 'Zowr loveng suster Margaret'. From this it is clear that although her journey south lacked the ceremony and entertainment of her progress to Edinburgh in 1503, it had the advantage of being far more speedy. As her little retinue had moved down from York, the weather had steadily improved. Cheered by the greenness of the country and the new spring blossoms, Margaret was also in far better health and spirits than when she had set out from Morpeth. She gratefully breathed the air which was fragrant with the scent of hawthorn and lilac, and basked in the warm sunshine as she leaned back in her litter. Despite the constant jolting of the long journey, her hip now hardly troubled her, and she responded with real enthusiasm to the welcome extended to her by the gentry who entertained her. Sir Thomas Lovell, Household Treasurer to Henry VIII, opened the doors of his beautiful mansion in Enfield to her and her companions on May 1st. They rested two nights there.

On May 3rd the Queen moved on to Tottenham where, at the home of Sir William Compton, she was finally met by the King. She could hardly believe that the chubby little boy whom she had left in 1503 had grown into such a magnificent man. At twenty-five, Henry was six feet tall, with a muscular physique not yet marred by the corpulence of his middle years. His complexion was nearly as rosy, and his blue eyes as sparkling as she remembered them. He had recently grown a beard which was neatly trimmed and matched the red-gold of his hair, also cropped in the close cut now fashionable in France. The flat velvet cap tilted over the side of his head was of dark green velvet edged with white egret feathers. His short coat, also of dark green velvet, had enormously wide shoulders and sleeves slashed to show a lining of yellow satin. The doublet beneath, likewise of yellow satin, was covered with embroidery of green glistening with gems, and his tights were of yellow velvet.

He, on his part, was also pleasantly surprised by his sister's appearance. He had feared she would show the ravages of her recent illness, but her loss of weight was becoming to one with a natural tendency to over-plumpness; the drawn look of her face had now been replaced by eager smiles of anticipation and her eyes were shining with the joy of this reunion. She was dressed as elegantly as he, in one of the gowns made from his gift fabrics — purple velvet lined and slashed with cloth of gold. Her head was covered with a three-cornered scarf of cloth of gold pinned into a coif with a great gold and ruby clasp.

After a brief rest and some refreshment, they left for London. Queen Catherine had sent a beautiful white horse as gift to her sister-in-law. Delighted with this present, Margaret declared she no longer needed to use the litter. Instead she was placed on this steed, on a pillion behind Sir Thomas Parr. She was soon riding through Cheapside beside her handsome brother and at the head of a glittering cavalcade of nobility. Great crowds turned out, as they always did to see the King, but this time their cheers were also for the Queen of Scots, for whom much sympathy was expressed. Rumours of the dreadful treatment which she had undergone at the hands of the 'brutal' Franco-Scottish Duke of Albany were widespread. Margaret responded graciously to their applause, exuding the typical charm of the Tudors towards the commoners.

She was taken to Baynard's Castle, which was to be her temporary residence in London. This building, not far from St. Paul's Cathedral, overlooked the River Thames and had frequently been occupied by royalty. Here she found everything prepared for her stay: fresh rushes on the floors, tapestries on the walls, a well-stocked larder, and servants to attend to her needs. She expressed her appreciation to her brother for all his thoughtfulness. He soon left her so that she might rest uninterrupted for a few days, before starting to enjoy the many festivities planned for her visit.

He also told her that the Scottish ambassadors, who had reached London several weeks earlier, were anxiously awaiting her arrival, for Henry had refused to start negotiations with them, or even to see them, until she also could participate in the discussions. He thus showed his appreciation for her waiting to get his advice before answering the letter she had received earlier from this embassy. So, after she had had time to relax for a few days, the King and she discussed their joint policy towards Scotland. It was now apparent that Francis I was planning a new foray into Italy, a move which was opposed by the Emperor, with whom England had just allied again. Francis might arouse the Scots under the leadership of Albany to invade England should Henry help the Emperor. Hence, Henry was more than ever determined to break the Duke's control over the northern kingdom. He persuaded his sister that this was also an essential step if her guardianship of the young King was to be restored. Henry had learned that the boy was becoming sickly; they should be prepared in the event of his death. Margaret refused even to consider such a dread possibility and she still could not believe that the chivalrous Albany would plot to kill her little boy. She agreed to do all she could to force the Duke to relinquish his control of Scotland and her son. Indeed, she warmly recommended this policy in a meeting of the English Council.

As a result, the Scottish ambassadors were presented with a catalogue of her grievances which was almost identical to the one Dacre and Magnus had sent to the Regent from Morpeth. Refusing to accept these as valid, the Scots were vehemently opposed to the English demand for the removal of the francophile Regent. Consequently all that the meeting achieved was an extension of the existing truce between the two realms until the following November. The Scottish Parliament, meeting a month later, took the same stand on all these issues. They strongly reaffirmed their trust in the Regent and denied that he had any sinister designs on securing the throne for himself, as Henry had strongly implied.

Du Plains, who had gone to London with the Scottish embassy, again complained that Margaret's antagonism to Albany was the result of the bad advice she had been given, first by Lord Dacre, and now by Wolsey and his master. Unable to win a hearing from her, he did nevertheless manage to secure a small olive-branch from Henry to take back to the Regent. The King privately assured the Duke that he would give him a permit to travel to France via England should he desire to visit his wife. Albany certainly did wish to visit France, since he had not seen his duchess for over a year and missed her sorely. Furthermore, he genuinely wanted to establish peace with England and he might hope to achieve this by a personal visit to Westminster. For a time efforts were made to arrange this summit meeting between Duke and King. Since Margaret's future status in Scotland was one of the most important subjects to be discussed at this meeting, she was extremely anxious that it should take place, though, as she confessed in a letter to Wolsey, she feared that it was too much to hope for. As it turned out, she was right.

Margaret gave her support to most of her brother's foreign projects, but there was one which she refused even to consider. It was Wolsey's idea that she should become the wife of the Emperor

Maximilian. Even before her arrival in London, the Venetian news-letter had contained this interesting rumour. While admitting that the Scottish Queen had some months ago married a 'Scottish Earl, an extremely handsome youth, by whom she had a daughter', the Venetians dismissed this fact as a trivial impediment. The letter continued to describe how 'authorities here, pretending Scotland was under the ban of excommunication at the time, maintain the marriage was null. The report is it has been dissolved and the Queen betrothed to the Emperor'. A few days later, a correspondent told the Duchess of Savoy that Wolsey had said 'he would willingly renounce the hat [of Cardinal] or lose a finger of his right hand, if he could effect a marriage between her and the Emperor'.

Whether or not Henry and Wolsey pressed this possibility is dubious; Margaret was probably more valuable to them as a focal point of English control of Scotland, than as a symbol of the new alliance with the Empire. In any case, it is certain that the possibility of becoming Empress did not attract her. For one thing, the annulment of her marriage would bastardize her daughter; likewise, moving to the continent would separate her from her son; a third point was that Maximilian was now quite elderly and unattractive. There was one more consideration, Angus. Margaret had been severely hurt by his failure to come south with the Scottish envoys, and had realized that he had been lying when he made her that promise, but she still loved him. She was forced to admit this to herself, but not to her brother. At their first meeting Henry had asked her about her husband. When she told him, he had snorted, 'Done like a Scot!' and had henceforth treated the Earl with contempt. But, although Margaret acknowledged that Angus was not all she had first thought, she was not willing to discard him. Of course, she did not know then about Lady Jane Stewart.

While she awaited the outcome of the various diplomatic negotiations that were to affect her future, Margaret thoroughly enjoyed the present. After all the trials she had undergone since Flodden, it seemed utterly blissful once again to be able to relax and enjoy court life. During this part of his reign, in the interim between the wars on the continent and the trauma of the divorce case and religious controversy, Henry's court was at its most brilliant. Tournaments, masques, banquets and other gala events were planned almost every week; hunting took place by day, and music and dancing by night. Yet, the Queen of Scots' visit provided an excuse for a special round of merry-making.

From May 19th to 21st, tourneys were held at Greenwich. The King, his best friend, the Duke of Suffolk, and two other nobles were the challengers. On the first day they wore magnificent costumes of blue velvet embroidered in gold with a design of honeysuckle, as did their eighteen 'knights waiters on horseback'. A dozen foot attendants were garbed in blue satin, while the more lowly participants, guards, armourers, trumpeters and 'honest persons of the stable', appeared in damask of the same colour. Their horses were as gorgeously apparelled as the knights and were 'trappered' in cloth of gold, with harness to match. It took 37 yards of white velvet to make a 'trapper for the King's spare horse, set with rich bells and a border of cloth of gold, a steel saddle, headstall, reins, etc.'. On the second day the King's coat was made of '388 ounces of damask gold, costing £90, 3s, 8d. . . . A long tassel for the horses' throats, and fringes for the stirrups were made of 211 ounces of Venetian gold, costing £49, 3s, 8d.'. These examples from the King's account book show that no expense was spared to provide a fine spectacle. To no one's surprise, the challengers were the winners in this contest, and the outstanding victor was the King himself.

Margaret was enthroned above the lists as guest of honour. The pageantry vividly recalled the many tournaments she had witnessed in Scotland during the reign of James IV. Her present situation was a pale reflection of those early golden days. As she thanked her brother for the splendid entertainment and congratulated him on his prowess in the lists, she found herself remembering the brilliant pageant her first husband had arranged in honour of her favourite lady-in-waiting, Black Ellen. James and Henry were much alike in many ways, and especially in their athletic skill, their enthusiasm for sports and their admiration for the knightly virtues. If they had met in person, might they have become firm friends, or would international disputes still have driven them into opposite camps? Deceitful, scheming Louis and his French Queen, would no doubt still have driven James into war against England. Margaret managed to refrain from putting these thoughts into words. Her brother resented criticism from anyone and, since he had made peace with Louis, he expected his family to cease holding grudges against him. After all, Louis had been briefly both his ally and brother-in-law as their sister Mary's first husband.

Another joyous reunion for Margaret was the meeting with her younger sister, who had been only seven when Margaret left for Scotland in 1503. Even more than Henry and other Tudors, Mary had improved with maturity. Always pretty, she was now a real beauty. At twenty, she was slim, graceful and golden-haired, the personification of the fairy-tale princess; moreover, she was as sweet and charming as she was beautiful. Like Margaret, the French Queen, as she was now called, was back home after her foreign marriage, but, more fortunate than her older sister, Mary was now going to remain at home permanently as the wife of Charles Brandon, Duke of Suffolk.

Though deeply in love with this nobleman, she would hear no evil spoken of her first husband, who had been kindly and most considerate to his youthful bride. Margaret could not imagine how the lovely but fastidious Mary could have agreed to marry a stooped and gouty old man of fifty-two, who, it was said, dribbled when he spoke because he had lost most of his teeth. In response to Margaret's persistent queries, Mary told her interested older sister about the French marriage and its sequel.

She admitted that she had indeed abhorred the scheme. It was not Louis's decrepitude that appalled her, but rather the fact that she would have to leave Charles Brandon whom she had secretly loved since childhood. His father had been killed fighting at Bosworth for Henry VII, and the orphaned Charles had afterwards been reared with Henry's own children. Charles had become a boon companion to young Prince Henry, with whom he rode, hunted and jousted. Consequently, after Henry became King and Charles and Mary fell in love, they hoped he might countenance their union in spite of the difference in their rank. But the French marriage scheme of 1514 had dashed their hopes. Nevertheless, Mary had pleaded with her brother to spare her this diplomatic marriage. She had finally succeeded in getting his promise that in return for her agreeing to marry Louis with at least outward acquiescence, he would let her choose her own second husband. Louis was universally deemed likely to die very soon, being so elderly and in such poor health. So the wedding had taken place, and Mary, true to her word, was sweet and loving to her unattractive spouse. Moreover, she added, she found this an easy task because the French King was such a kindly gentleman, who did everything for his eighteen-year-old bride.

In honour of their marriage he had ordered the most magnificent ceremonies and entertainments that even the luxurious French court had ever witnessed. He insisted, too, on participating in all the activities, disregarding the warnings of his physicians, who had cautioned him that he would only survive if he maintained a strict regimen of diet and rest. Instead, he went riding and hawking with his pretty bride and stayed up for all the festivities that continued until late each night. In response to Mary's solicitous pleas that he obey his doctors, he would simply assure her that marriage to her had renewed his own youth.

At first this seemed true, and the morning after their first night as husband and wife, Louis gleefully boasted to his gentlemen-of-the-bedchamber that he had succeeded in 'crossing the river three times'. He therefore felt encouraged that he would at last beget a son of his own to succeed him to the throne and prevent the accession of the heir apparent, his nephew, Francis, whom he detested. In appreciation for her loving co-operation in this aim, Louis gave Mary some new and magnificent jewel every morning.

All Louis's determination, however, could not undo the ravages of the years upon his health. Soon he was forced to curtail his unwonted activities and eventually to admit that he was too ill even to rise from bed. Day by day he grew weaker, despite the frantic medications of his physicians and the gentle nursing of his wife; finally, on January 1st 1515, less than three months after his wedding, Louis died.

Her husband's death brought Mary new problems. Immediately after his burial, she had to leave the court and live in seclusion for six months, according to the French custom for royal widows, but during this interim she was visited frequently by Louis's nephew and successor as King. Francis was already married and his wife, Queen Claude, was pregnant, but he had become infatuated with his uncle's beautiful wife. He made her the most outrageous propositions and also tried to persuade her to agree to a new diplomatic match which would benefit France. He would give her no rest from these importunities until Mary, in desperation, confided to him that she was already irrevocably in love. By doing so she was throwing herself entirely upon Francis's mercy, relying on his chivalry as a belted knight to protect both her and Charles Brandon. This dangerous gamble succeeded. Francis's masculine pride would not let him force his attentions on one whose heart was firmly bound to another. Hence, since he could neither win her for himself nor use her hand in marriage as a diplomatic prize, he would help her to marry an unimportant nobleman, thereby preventing King Henry from marrying her to one of France's enemies, such as the grandson of Maximilian, Charles of Hapsburg, Prince of Castille.

Gaining King Francis's help, however, did not resolve all Mary's difficulties. She had yet to persuade Charles Brandon himself to marry her before she returned to England. As a young courtier, the Duke of Suffolk had come to Paris to deliver Henry's condolences on Louis's death and his congratulations to the new French monarch. The latter, true to his word, at once sent Brandon to see Mary. But it was she who had to do the courting, begging Suffolk, with many tears, to wed her at once. For she feared (with good reason) that her brother might be tempted to overlook his pledge to her and include her in some new diplomatic match. Once back in England, she might find it impossible to marry the man of her choice. Mary could of course understand her lover's reluctance to oppose her powerful brother. Unlike her, he might easily be charged with treason and face execution if the King became really angry.

King Francis helped her to overcome the scruples of her uncertain suitor by promising to intercede with the English King on behalf of the lovers. Bolstered by these promises and softened by Mary's tears, the Duke of Suffolk finally agreed to the scheme. The two were secretly married in Paris, as they subsequently confessed in letters to Wolsey and his master. True to the young Duke's fears, the monarch appeared to be extremely angry, since, before Charles had left England, Henry had made him promise not to use the opportunity to marry the French Queen before returning to Britain. The reason for this was that Wolsey and Henry had plans, even as Mary and Francis had surmised, to marry his pretty sister to either Maximilian, or to his grandson, Charles of Hapsburg.

Eventually, however, Henry forgave them, after they promised to give him all Mary's dowry from her marriage, together with the jewels which Louis had given her. The silver and gold plate and the jewellery alone amounted to over 100,000 crowns, so that Henry had gained a small fortune from this bargain. It meant that henceforth Mary and Brandon would be plagued with impecuniosity and would be chronically in debt to her royal brother. Nevertheless, Mary felt triumphant; she had finally won her long and difficult struggle to marry the man of her choice.

This account of Mary's past took place during one of many tête-à-têtes between the two sisters, who now saw each other frequently. For, although the young Duke and Duchess of Suffolk had several country estates, they spent most of their time at court. The King wanted the company of his best friend Charles for hunting and tilting, and his sister Mary added lustre to his court. She was his favourite dancing partner, since his wife, Catherine, was usually incapacitated by pregnancy and at thirty-three had lost her trim figure and the prettiness she had had as a young girl. Nevertheless, in 1516 Catherine still appeared to be his well-loved wife, especially since she had at last borne a child healthy enough to give promise of growing to maturity. Even though this baby was a girl, her survival encouraged the royal couple to hope that more healthy babies would follow, including the all-important son who would be King after his father.

The three queens spent many happy hours conversing in Catherine's pleasant apartments in Greenwich Palace. Margaret recounted all the details of her recent tribulations to her attentive listeners. They expressed sympathy for her and outrage at those who had caused her sufferings. Catherine described Henry's fury when he first learned of Albany's treatment of his sister. Blaming most of it on England's traditional foes, the French, Henry had threatened to invade France once again unless King Francis at once recalled the Duke from Scotland. As a result of these threats, Francis had sent a special envoy to London to try to prevent such a conflict. This envoy, a man named Bapaume, had made every effort to appease the angry monarch. He had also appealed to the Duke of Suffolk to recall the debt of gratitude which he owed Francis for the help he had recently given Suffolk and Mary, and to do all he could to dissuade his angry brother-in-law from a conflict with France.

Both Suffolk and Wolsey had told Bapaume that the surest way for Francis to avoid war was to remove the Duke of Albany, who had so shamefully abused Henry's sister, the Queen of Scots. If her rights were not restored to her promptly, her brother was determined to see to it that she regained them. Bapaume next asked Mary if she would grant him a favour. She had met the Duke of Albany while she was living in Paris, and Bapaune asked her if she would now write to him personally concerning his treatment of her sister. Mary did so immediately and received a gracious reply from the Duke. He assured her that he meant only the best, and tried to mitigate the effects on Queen Margaret of the decisions made by the Scottish Council and Parliament. It was they, not he, he emphasized, who had voted to remove her from the regency and from the guardianship of her sons. He also promised to treat her with all deference and kindness if she would only return to Edinburgh.

Margaret was curious to know what her sister had thought of the Duke when she knew him in France. However, Mary had apparently only been slightly acquainted with him. She did admit that he had a reputation as a very courteous gentleman, and she had been quite amazed when she heard of his cavalier treatment of Margaret.

In addition to these affairs of state, in which all three women had great personal interest, they also spent much time talking of feminine matters more related to every-day living, such as fashion, furnishings and children. Mary described the latest styles in Paris, which had also begun to appear in England. Skirts (or 'gowns') were still high-waisted, but fuller than hitherto and magnificent with heavy embroidery. The bodice of the kirtle (an under-dress to which the skirt was fastened with laces) was now stiffer and had a square neckline cut low enough to display the embroidered top of the chemise. A ribbon was laced through this ruffled edging which could be drawn tight to cover the bosom completely, or loosened to expose more of it. Similarly, the neckline of men's doublets was often squared off and cut to show the edge of the under-shirt, which was also threaded with a drawstring. Men's coats (or 'gowns') worn over the doublet, hung loose from the shoulders and open at the front, exposing the hose and the padded codpiece beneath. Colours for both men's and women's wear were still vivid and were used in strong contrasts for effect. For example, the slashing or slitting of velvet sleeves permitted the satin lining of a contrasting shade to be pulled through. The materials used by both sexes were so lavish that Parliament had recently passed laws forbidding the use of some of the most expensive, especially cloth of gold and heavily embroidered velvets. Obviously this stricture did not apply to members of the court, and in practice had little effect on those of the lower classes who were wealthy enough to afford such fabrics.

The luxury of her brother's palaces, as well as that of her sister Mary's new town house, Suffolk House, impressed Margaret. The tapestries on the walls seemed more vivid than those in Scotland, and many more of the windows were paned with glass, but the innovation that added particular comfort was the 'stool-house' which was now attached to each living-quarter. This invention was a far cry from the water-closet (not destined to come into use until the end of Queen Elizabeth I's reign), but it was such an improvement over the foul-smelling *garderobe* that the Scots Queen determined to have one installed at Linlithgow as soon she returned.

While Mary was showing her sister through the library in Suffolk House, Margaret spied a familiar object — the Book of Hours which King James had given her so long ago. She had sent this lovely volume to Mary as a wedding gift when she married Louis XII, since at that time Margaret was far too short of money to buy a suitable present. Noticing her sister's apparent pleasure in seeing the book again, Mary offered to return it to her, but Margaret insisted that Mary keep it. After all, it now brought her only sad memories of vanished happiness. She closed the cover firmly and turned her thoughts to the present reunion with her own family.

Each of the three Queens had recently given birth and therefore their children naturally formed a favourite topic of conversation. Lady Margaret Douglas was the eldest of the new arrivals and was seven months old on arrival in London. Little Princess Mary Tudor (named after her aunt) was born on February 15th 1516, while the French Queen's first-born (baptized Henry after his famous uncle) had arrived on March 11th of that year. Margaret, as the mother of two living children, took precedence in giving advice on child care, especially on the important subject of the wet-nurse, who was considered by physicians and laity alike to be the root of all infant disorders. Hence, if a baby had colic, his wet-nurse was purged or bled. If the nurse's milk proved insufficient for her little charge, the way to increase her supply was to dose her with powdered earthworms. If this medication proved unsuccessful, she should be put on a diet of stewed goats' udders. A wet-nurse was able to earn excellent wages and prestige, but obviously her position had considerable drawbacks as well as benefits.

Frequently Catherine would send word to the royal nursery and the infants themselves would be brought to the Queen's apartment. The three women could then enjoy their company. Sometimes the King himself would burst into their midst and join in the frolic with the children. He would catch up little Margaret Douglas, who was old enough to be handled with some abandon, and toss her until she squealed with joy. Then he would chuck his tiny namesake under the chin, and finally lift up his own small daughter and stride proudly about the room with her. Watching his enjoyment of these infants, Margaret prayed he might have his wish for plenty of offspring of his own; his wife's prayers were even more fervent.

As the monarch strode about the apartment, he was of course the centre of attention for all Catherine's ladies — just like a bunch of hens when a cock enters the henhouse, thought his older sister amusedly. She noticed one maid of honour looking up at him from her deep curtsy as he passed her, and then pressing close to him to look down at the baby in his arms. It seemed to Margaret that Henry stayed an unusually long time beside her. She was a remarkably pretty little thing, not more than sixteen or seventeen, called Bess Blount. Later Margaret asked her younger sister about Bess. Mary reluctantly admitted that their brother did seem attracted to this girl, who had first appeared in court two years earlier. However, Mary refused to believe the rumours now circulating in the court that the King had made her his mistress. Mary was quite loyal to her brother and very much devoted to her sister-in-law, Catherine, to whom she had become very close after the early death of her mother and the departure of her older sister to Scotland.

Musing on her brother's attraction for women, Margaret began wondering about her own husband. Surely there could be no question of his faithfulness to her, yet his letters were so brief and so infrequent. What was his present situation? Was he still outlawed by the Regent? Her anxiety on this score was indicated in a letter she wrote to Wolsey in September 1516: 'I pray you my lord as soon as any body comes out of Scotland that you will send me word, for I think long since I hear tidings . . .'.

From Wolsey, who had informants in and near Scotland, she learned that Albany had proved quite merciful. The Earl of Angus, after surrendering to the Duke, had been allowed to retain his liberty. Moreover, he had even been promised the full restoration of his property. Lord Home had also been forgiven for the second time, but apparently refused to learn from the failure of his previous attempts to rebel against the Governor. Once again he plotted and escaped and once again he was followed to the Borders by the Duke's forces, who finally captured him, his brother William, and a number of followers. This time Albany lost patience and agreed with Parliament and the Council that this persistent troublemaker must be punished. Lord Home and his brother William were found guilty of treason and executed.

Margaret shed no tears for the Chamberlain, though she was sorry for his mother who had visited her while she was ill at Coldstream and had consequently suffered imprisonment for a time. She was very grateful that Angus had apparently learned to stay out of trouble. She still loved him deeply, and refused to believe what Lord Dacre told Wolsey — that her husband was appropriating the rents he collected from her tenants as her agent for his own use. This accusation was made by the three commissioners who were sent by Lord Dacre into Scotland to recover the Queen's personal property left there and to collect the income which was due from her dower lands. The Regent and the Council had agreed that all her own goods (jewellery, clothing and furniture) should be restored to her. Their promise was kept, and such jewellery as she had left at Linlithgow or Tantallon was now forwarded to London; her clothing had already been sent. But the rents from her lands still proved impossible to retrieve. A number of important nobles had used her absence as an opportunity to seize the moneys, and they disdained even to answer the summons issued by the Queen's commissioners. Angus was among those accused of having appropriated the income from some of her estates, though he vehemently denied the charge. His wife wished to believe him, but she could not help wondering, especially since months passed without receiving the moneys due her. Of £14,334 she should have received, her commissioners were able to collect a mere £114.

Throughout her visit to England she was therefore almost entirely dependent upon her brother. From the 'King's Book of Payments', he appears to have been most generous in defraying her expenses. In addition to paying for her entire trip south, he had provided her with a residence: first Baynard's Castle, and later the more elegant palace in Scotland Yard, where previous Scottish rulers had stayed. Her carver, Sir Thomas Boleyn, her chaplain

Master Hall, her gentlemen ushers, the grooms of her chamber, the yeomen ushers, the yeomen of the cellar and the four yeomen of the guard who attended her all received remuneration from the King. Salaries to her women servants were not listed individually, but she probably paid them out of the money paid directly 'to the Queen of Scots'. This totalled over £1,000 during her stay in London, an amount that becomes all the more impressive when compared to the total of all government expenditure: £130,779 in 1516 and £78,887 in 1517. During the same period Henry was also supporting the Duke and Duchess of Suffolk. He had demanded to receive all the income which Mary received as former French Queen, but he permitted them to be constantly delinquent in this regard. They were therefore for ever in debt to him — in 1516 he lent them a further £6,000 — but this situation caused them little noticeable hardship. In addition to five country estates, they owned several London residences, yet they spent most of their time at court, where they also had apartments. It is evident that Henry VIII was generous as a brother — provided his sisters followed his dictates.

The liberality of the King towards his relatives and his lavish expenditure on himself were accepted as normal and proper by the general population so long as this was met by his own income; calling Parliament to request taxes was an emergency measure which could only be taken over matters of great urgency, usually war. Otherwise all government costs were borne by the ruler himself. He must 'live of his own', a phrase which meant that not only his personal expenses and those of his family and household, but the entire civil and foreign service systems, even the armed forces on land and sea, were paid by the King. His income came from his royal estates, which had been greatly augmented by Henry VII, from the feudal dues still demanded from all vassals, from court fees and fines, and from a few specific import and export duties. Hence, when he spent vast sums on magnificent garments for himself and members of his family, on luxurious furnishings for his residences or for building new palaces, the general reaction was one of approval. This splendour was a reflection of the great wealth and power of their ruler, and did credit to the nation as a whole.

Notwithstanding her brother's open-handedness, Margaret hesitated to keep asking him for additional sums although she felt the need. Instead she appealed to Wolsey to procure them for her. On December 26th she wrote 'To my Lorde Kardenall' asking for 'som monne' to buy the customary New Year's gifts for her servants. 'I must give part of rewards and other needful things both for the King my brother's honour and mine'. According to the King's account book, Wolsey did not fail her either then or on other later occasions when she wrote similar pleas. She promised to repay these loans as soon as she received the moneys due to her from Scotland, though she added that she much regretted having to put the King 'to so great cost and charges'.

The Christmas season for which the Scottish Queen had requested a loan was one which was celebrated by King Henry in most royal style. The banquets were even more elaborate than usual, with many novelties introduced by the cooks and bakers, such as cakes and jellies made in the shapes of various animals or of castles. The music during and after the meals was always excellent, quite superior to that available at the French court, as Mary commented, because Henry himself took such an interest in it. He had recently induced a new organist to come to England from Venice, where he had played at St. Mark's Cathedral. He had brought his own 'excellent instrument at great expense' and delighted his listeners with its beautiful tone. The children of the Chapel Royal, directed by Master Cornyshe, sang carols, and adult minstrels also played and sang. The King enjoyed playing the organ himself, and did so quite well, in addition to playing other instruments such as the lute, virginals and recorders. He had written a number of musical compositions, including both religious motets and secular ballads, which he sang to his own accompaniment or to that of his Italian musicians.

Some of the evenings were enlivened by dramatic performances by the court players, as well as by masques in which members of the court would take part incognito. The most elaborate of these witnessed by the Scottish Queen was the revel prepared for Epiphany night. This pageant, called 'the Gardyn de Esperans', was a 'garden' of brilliant artificial flowers, surrounded by a golden fence, all drawn into the hall to the sound of minstrelsy. Master Cornish, now Master of the Revels, garbed 'like a stranger in a gown of red sarcenet with a coat of arms, his horse trappered with blue sarcenet', came forward to explain 'the intent of the revels'. Then six knights and six ladies, dressed 'in purple and cut works on white sarcenet and green embroidered with yellow satin', and with their heads capped with gold, came forth from the gorgeous garden and danced before the company.

After this display the spectators joined in the dancing, led by the King and Queen. Margaret noticed that the favourite bass dance had now become far more energetic than in its original form, with leaps and skips to punctuate the turns. No doubt these innovations had developed partly from the King's preference for this livelier style. It reminded her of the way he, as a little boy, had danced with her before their parents and friends at Prince Arthur's wedding.

She asked Henry if he recalled that day. He laughed and admitted that he had done it partly to catch the notice of his elder brother's pretty Spanish bride. Catherine's face lit up at this compliment from her husband, but her smile faded as he, having brought her back to her dais, led out his next partner, Bess Blount.

Margaret watched the King with this maid of honour and felt certain that court gossip was right in declaring that she was now definitely his mistress. Bess was certainly very pretty and slim and graceful in executing the newer, more difficult steps. Catherine, by contrast, looked old and faded, her once petite figure thickened by the many attempts at child-bearing.

The most beautiful lady in the hall, however, was as always the French Queen, now dancing with the Duke of Suffolk. As Margaret watched her younger sister, so radiant beside her tall handsome husband, she could not help feeling a pang of envy. How fortunate Mary was to be so happily married to the man she loved and to be living with him here at home, where she was universally adored and unfailingly cared for! How bleak by contrast was her own fate, married, it was true, to the man she had chosen, but he had not come with her and seldom even wrote to her. What kind of future could she look forward to? She must soon leave this happy court and return to the cold and forbidding North, where her welcome was anything but certain — from the Council, from the Governor, or even from her husband.

CHAPTER 12

BACK TO THE COLD NORTH COUNTRY (1517–1518)

The old adage that 'absence makes the heart grow fonder' has proved false at least as often as true. Certainly, the Queen's departure from Scotland failed to increase either her affection for her northern realm, or that of the Scottish nobles for her. Nevertheless, her duty was clear: she must return — and soon. It was delightful to relax amid the comforts and pleasures of her brother's court, but it was becoming embarrassing to be forced to depend on his generosity, especially since Henry definitely wanted his sister to maintain his interests in Scotland. Moreover, she had two other strong incentives for returning: her husband and her son.

As to the former, she was much concerned by his continued refusal to join her in London. She had tried to excuse him in her own mind by blaming Albany for preventing him from making the journey. The Duke, however, responded to her request to permit Angus to leave Scotland by telling her that he had already granted him leave, but that apparently the Earl did not find it convenient to take it. This revelation forced her to the humiliating conclusion that the only way to rejoin the man she loved was to go to him.

Her son was now five years old and she had not seen him for over a year. Would he even remember her? With all of a mother's love she yearned to be near him, even if she could not regain guardianship over him. This had been one of her major reasons for leaving Scotland originally. Unfortunately, her absence had had no softening effect on the intransigence of the Scottish Council or Parliament. They resolutely refused to consider restoring her either to the regency or to the position of *tutrix* to the King. Their reasons are understandable: whoever controlled the King held the keys to government. No matter how young he was, he symbolized authority: all proclamations were made in his name, all laws promulgated. Whether or not his mother would herself abuse the position of *tutrix* to his majesty was not the only question. She was married to the head of the Douglases, one of the most powerful, ambitious and distrusted families in Scotland. To permit the wife of Angus to control the monarch was tantamount to putting the Earl himself in virtual command of the government. Even without this handicap, there was the Queen's tie to England, the hereditary foe. Would she not manipulate her young son's policies for the benefit of King Henry VIII, rather than that of Scotland?

Consequently, the Scots refused to consider the main requests which Wolsey and Henry made through successive embassies to Edinburgh; talks with the Scottish representatives sent to London by the Duke of Albany to try to arrange a peace were equally abortive. Once he had established a firm settlement with England, Albany would feel that he had accomplished King Francis's mission and could therefore return to France. He longed to do this, not only because his beloved wife was ill and needed him, but because he much preferred life in France to that in Scotland. His acceptance of the regency had been a means to accomplish his King's desire to maintain France's influence over its 'auld ally'. Personally he found the job anything but a joy. No sooner had he settled one dispute among the nobles than another would erupt. He had finally quashed the rebellion of the Homes, but then Lennox became a problem and had at last to be imprisoned. In disgust, the Regent told the English herald that he 'had had so much trouble he wished he had broken both his legs before he set foot in Scotland'.

Obviously the Duke was not in fact responsible for preventing settlement with England. However, in order to achieve the peace agreement he desired, he must somehow reconcile the opposing views of the Scottish Council and the English King concerning the terms for Queen Margaret's return to her realm. Henry's original demands that his sister be reinstated both as Regent and as *tutrix* became less insistent. He continued to demand, however, that she be permitted to re-enter Scotland whenever she chose to do so, and that definite provision be made to pay the revenues due to her. Both Albany and the nobles stated that they were fully willing to grant these demands, but they refused to incorporate them into the formal prolongation of the truce between the two nations. They reasoned that to do so would give the English King the excuse to invade whenever he wished on the grounds that some whim of his sister had not been granted. The Duke tried to make up for the omission of these clauses from the formal terms of the truce by promising most solemnly to protect her rights. He swore an oath on a 'piece of the Holy Cross and on divers other relics which he [wore] in a tablet of gold hanging about his neck'. Both he and the Council members promised the English ambassadors that they would welcome the Queen into the realm and 'do her as great honour, pleasure, and service, and in all her causes be as diligent as they would be to the King their sovereign lord . . .'.

The members of the Council would go forth to meet her on her return, they added, and render her all the homage due her. She might bring twenty-four English attendants, male and female, plus as many Scots as she wished, so long 'as they be not rebels'. The limit on the number of her English attendants was, of course, to prevent her from trying to import a virtual army with her. On the question of her dower rights, unfortunately, nothing specific was agreed. Lord Dacre was anxious to arrange for the truce to be prolonged immediately, rather than to wait months for the Scottish Parliament to meet in order to deal with the Queen's 'conjunct enfeoffment'. Therefore, the collection of her revenues was left to the border-commissioners. The latter had already proved incapable of collecting Margaret's rents during her year's stay in London, and therefore this arrangement did not augur well for after her return.

Her concern over this matter caused Margaret to beg her brother to make any permanent peace treaty with Scotland, or even a further prolongation of the truce, contingent on the satisfaction of her claims. While staying with her brother and his court at Windsor she made Henry promise to make it clear that any such agreement was the result of her influence. Only if the Scottish nobles felt that her good will was essential for the maintenance of good relations with England, would they see to it that her income was paid and was not 'intrometted' [appropriated] by their own coterie. All she had to rely on, as she pointed out to Henry, were promises: that she was to live in Scotland with a suite befitting her station; and that she should receive all the profits from her dower lands and from any personal property, none of which had yet been forwarded to her.

These guarantees were included with the permission to return to Scotland which was granted to her on April 17th 1517 by her son, the King, who also sent her a formal safe conduct for re-entering his realm. This document stated 'that, for the right singular and natural affection moving us to desire the sight and presence of the right high and right excellent Princess, our dearest mother, the Queen of Scotland . . . we . . . with the advice and counsel of our cousin, tutor and governor, John Duke of Albany, and with the consent of the three estates of our realm, have granted . . . that it be lawful to our dearest mother to come into this our realm, freely and peaceably with her train'. In accepting this very formal invitation from her five-year-old son, Margaret had to promise 'under my God and faith to do . . . both toward Monseigneur the Governor and Council as much as should be done'.

The same day that she received this safe conduct Margaret learned the disturbing news that little James was no longer residing in Stirling. Since this castle was part of the Queen's 'conjunct feoffment' which, she had been promised, would now be returned to her, the Council evidently feared she might gain too much control over the child if he remained there. They remembered that she (or Angus) had previously tried to take him to England. To prevent any such possibility, they now had him moved to Edinburgh Castle, where he was lodged in David's Tower. Here the three noblemen charged with his supervision were to take turns residing with him and commanding the entry of that great tower; in addition, twelve men-at-arms guarded his chamber door each night, with one sentinel posted outside 'on the trees before the little gate' and yet another at the head of the tower. None might enter the King's apartments without a pass issued directly by Sir Patrick Crichton, Governor of Edinburgh Castle.

With all these precautions for his security, Margaret could not share Lord Dacre's fears that Albany might harm the King, now that they resided in the same town. Instead she feared that these new arrangements would make it difficult for anyone to see him, including his mother, even though it was specified that she might do so without hindrance as long as she followed all the prescribed rules for visiting him.

In spite of her anxiety over these developments which were to be so important for her future, Margaret spent the remainder of her visit engaged in the varied activities of the English court. On Shrove Tuesday she attended a play directed by Master Cornyshe, the versatile director of the Royal Chapel choir and of the King's Revels. She also took part personally in a real life drama later in the spring of 1517. On May 1st the London apprentices responded to rumours that cheap imports from the continent were endangering their livelihood by staging a demonstration against foreign merchants. The resulting riot caused much violence and destruction of property. The participants in the outbreak — 278 in all — were swiftly captured and sentenced to be hanged. Many of the culprits were only thirteen or fourteen years old, but being a teenager brought no immunity from the law in the sixteenth century. Thirteen of the ringleaders paid the full penalty for their crime two days after the 'Evil May Day' insurrection. In order to exhibit their bodies to as many spectators as possible, the officials had ten gallows built on platforms which could be moved on wheels from one part of the city to another.

Then, feeling that this example had had the desired effect of discouraging future rebellions, Chancellor Wolsey decided to change tactics. He would now present the King in the guise of a stern but merciful potentate. On May 7th the rest of the boys were to be hanged. However, just before the time for the fatal signal,

Queen Catherine, along with her sister Queens, Mary and Margaret, rushed forward and threw themselves before King Henry, sobbing and pleading for the condemned youths. The monarch proved merciful. The offenders' lives were spared. Unfortunately, since the gallows had been scattered around the metropolis, the messengers arrived at one of them too late. The over-zealous hangman had already dispatched one of his victims. Another boy, kicking desperately in the air, was cut down just in time to be revived with the news that he had been spared by the generosity of good King Hal and the pleas of the three Queens.

Ten days later, the preparations were completed for the Queen of Scots' departure. In addition to providing the necessary funds for her trip, her brother and Wolsey had made arrangements for every detail of the journey. The royal steward, George, Earl of Shrewsbury, and his countess were to lead Margaret's retinue. At each stage of the progress, local officials had been ordered to welcome and entertain her. Some of these notables received this royal mandate with marked lack of enthusiasm. The Earl of Northumberland and his wife, Lady Percy, were requested to conduct the Queen from York to Newborough. The Earl wrote at once to Shrewsbury, asking him to persuade the King to excuse Lady Percy from this trip since 'she is not in case to ride'. He himself would, of course, accompany the King's sister to Newborough, but planned to meet her after she had left York. He hoped the orders did not mean that he must also accompany her into York, since the King had put him to much expense lately. (Apparently, Percy 'the Magnificent' was at last learning to economize.)

In addition to these plans for Margaret's entertainment on her way to Scotland, Henry saw to it that his sister was equipped in keeping with her station and as befitted a member of the Tudor family. Her horses' harness, saddles and pillions were made of white damask cloth of gold, crimson cloth of gold and black velvet, with similar materials for five of her ladies and three of her gentlemen attendants. The King also gave her as parting gifts two golden cups and some other valuables. As she bade him farewell, Margaret was reminded of her parting from Henry VII when she first set out for Scotland in 1503. Was this the last time she would see her brother, or his wife, or her sister? Small wonder that her heart was heavy as, with her infant daughter and her little company of attendants, she left her old home.

Ten days after their departure, the Earl of Shrewsbury wrote to give Wolsey a brief account of their progress. The Queen had been 'often diseased' during the first few days of the trip, but was now well. As the party crossed the country, the lords and gentry of the shires had 'done their duty towards her'. He was enclosing several letters that Margaret was anxious to have conveyed at once to Wolsey and the King, hoping if possible to receive an answer by the time they reached Durham.

Margaret wrote to her brother to enclose the letter she had just received from the Duke of Albany telling her that he was leaving at once for France and would not therefore be on hand to greet her when she arrived in Edinburgh. This news pleased her and she thanked Henry who, she was sure, had engineered the Duke's removal in order to pave the way for her own return to power. Through diplomatic pressure the English had indeed finally persuaded Francis to recall the Regent and also to pledge secretly to keep him out of Scotland — for a time at least.

In his letter to the Queen, Albany wrote that he hoped peace with England could be extended beyond the current deadline of Saint Andrew's Day, but Margaret hastened to remind her brother that he had promised her 'when I vent to Vendsor thys last tyme' that peace should be established only in return for the Scots' fair treatment of her. Nevertheless, she concluded, he should do 'as your grace thynkes best', so long as she be notified in advance of any agreement 'soo that I may have the thanke of Scotlande'.

On June 15th 1517, the Queen of Scots re-entered the realm from which she had fled more than a year earlier. Recollecting vividly her difficulties during that flight, she became most apprehensive about this return. Archdeacon Magnus, one of King Henry's representatives who accompanied Margaret on the journey, was doubtless correct in believing that she would much prefer to remain in England. As he reported in a letter to Wolsey the next day, she had kept inventing excuses to delay her re-entry into the northern kingdom. 'Her grace considereth now the honour of England and the poverty and wretchedness of Scotland, which she did not affore, but in her opinion esteemed Scotland equal with England'. The sojourn in her brother's luxurious court had shown by contrast how stark were the conditions in Edinburgh. The Scottish court had indeed been lively during the brilliant reign of James IV, but had lost all semblance of this splendour since Flodden.

Yet more important by far than the physical contrast between London and Edinburgh was the contrast of intangibles. England under Henry and Wolsey seemed so stable and secure; Scotland, under its child King and turbulent nobles, was so restless and uncertain. And, in trying to restore stability to her son's regime, so much depended upon her, his mother. She felt as if a great weight, which for a year had been lifted from her shoulders, had now fallen back, crushing her. Small wonder that tears kept welling up in her eyes as, at the head of her small retinue, she again crossed the fateful Borders.

Lamberton Kirk, just north of Berwick, was the meeting place for the English and Scots. Here, where in 1503 Princess Margaret had first been welcomed by the huge vanguard of her future subjects, the Queen now was met by her son's subjects. Though now there was nothing of the splendour of that earlier entry, some 3,000 soldiers, mostly borderers, came to meet her and guard her passage through the Borders to the capital. They were led by the Sieur de la Bastie, now Warden of the Scottish Marches and chief deputy of the Duke of Albany, who had sailed for France the preceding week. With de la Bastie came a group of nobles, including the Earl of Angus.

Seeing him once more, thrilling to the sight of his handsome countenance, and warmed by his embrace, Margaret forgot the doubts that had been nagging her. Suddenly the grey clouds that had been hanging over the hills blew apart. The warm June sun beat down on them, revealing the young green of the bushes, and patches of golden gorse across the barren moors. Happily she watched her husband as he lifted their little daughter in his arms. She laughed as little Margaret pulled away from the scratching beard of her father when he kissed her. She would soon grow to know him, the Queen asssured Angus. After all, she was not yet two years old.

As they rode toward the capital, the Earl proudly told his wife that he, along with three other Earls and the Archbishops of St. Andrews and Glasgow, had been left to govern the country during the absence of the Regent. Apparently Angus had not only made peace with the Duke when he surrendered to him the previous year, but had become one of his trusted subordinates. He had gone to France as one of the Duke's emissaries during the past spring. This, he explained glibly, was why he had been unable to join her in London, as of course he had wished to do. In the joy of her reunion with the man she loved, Margaret readily accepted these explanations. She failed to note that whenever he spoke of the authority which Albany had vested in him, it was his own power that he repeatedly emphasized — power that he did not speak of sharing with his wife, the Queen.

In answer to her question, Angus told her that the Duke planned to remain in France for about five months. In order to ensure obedience to commands that he would issue *in absentia* and in order to prevent any attempted rebellion, Albany had taken as hostages the heirs, or brothers, of every great man in the kingdom. This precaution, Margaret reflected, should help to prevent disorder for a while. On the whole, she was content to let things rest as they were at the moment. She would have all that was essential to her well-being: the company of her husband, access to her son and the income due to her from her estates. The latter would certainly be paid now that her husband was himself one of the authorities. It did not occur to her then that the greatest threat to the preservation of her happiness might in fact be her husband.

Two days later, on June 17th 1517, the Queen entered Edinburgh. Unlike her festive entry into the capital in 1503, the streets were not festooned with flowers and tapestries, nor did the fountains run with wine. Nevertheless, such crowds as did turn out to see her were friendly. The common people still remembered her as the widow of their best-loved ruler, James IV, and as the mother of their King, who now resided in the great tower of the castle perched high above the town.

It was there that Margaret hastened as soon as she had settled in her new quarters. She rode up the steep ascent, followed by several servants carrying the gifts which she had brought from London for her little boy. But when the horses had laboured up the hillside to the gate of the castle, she found that the trip had been in vain. She was not permitted to enter. She remonstrated that the Regent had promised she should be admitted whenever she wished, so long as she abide by the restrictions established by the Council that she should bring no more than four attendants and should leave before nightfall every time she came. She had accepted these restrictions, although she considered them to be absurd. Regardless of her complaints, the reply came back from the new Governor of the Castle that no one could be admitted to the presence of the King without the express permission of the lords of the Council. This had not been granted, so all she could do was to hand over the presents to the young King's servants who would deliver them to his Majesty in David's Tower. It seemed that all the weary miles she had come had been travelled in vain. Sobbing with disappointment, frustration and anger, the Queen mother returned to her own quarters.

Angus promised to use his influence to obtain permission for his wife to visit her son, but he was unsuccessful. Apparently the authority which had recently been given to him by the Regent did not greatly impress the other nobles, especially those entrusted with the direct supervision of young James V. Consequently, it was not on account of her husband's efforts that Margaret finally was permitted to see her little boy. In August a child was taken ill in Edinburgh Castle with a disease called the 'botch'. In order to escape contagion, the King was at once transferred from the hilltop fortress to Craigmillar Castle, three miles outside the town. This stronghold was nearly as impregnable as Edinburgh Castle, but Lord Erskine, who was given charge over the young King there, showed more compassion to the royal mother. Much to her joy, he permitted her to visit her son. She was able to see with her own eyes that he was indeed well and rapidly growing into a handsome boy, as she reported in a letter to her brother on August 7th. At first the child was shy with her, but her warmth and love soon won his affection. In fact, once established, his mother's influence became a major factor in his development, and he looked forward to these stolen visits as eagerly as she.

Unfortunately, some of the Council members, learning of these visits, feared she would encourage him to love not only her but also her native land. The rumour spread that she intended to escape again to England, this time taking with her the boy King. Therefore, as soon as Edinburgh Castle was declared clean enough to eliminate any further danger of the 'botch', and James had returned to his former quarters, a new alarm was raised. The Governor declared that George Douglas, Angus's brother, now a warden in Edinburgh Castle, was plotting to kidnap the King on behalf of Angus and the Queen. Whether or not George was guilty of such a design was not proved, but he lost his position and was imprisoned as result of the accusation.

Realizing that she would never be allowed to see her son while such an hysteria of fear was raging, Margaret sadly gave up the attempt for the time being. She moved temporarily to Ettrick Forest on the Borders. Her residence (called the 'New Work', or Newark) was one of her dower properties that she had seldom visited. She needed to ascertain whether it was being properly administered and to let the tenants know she expected to receive the rents from it, for it should have been her most lucrative estate.

Here, one day early in September, her husband rushed in with breathless excitement to bring news which, he assured her, gave them an opportunity to recoup their position as joint Regents. Having discovered that Albany's commission to him meant nothing to the noblemen in control of the government, Angus was now reverting to his earlier efforts to gain power through his wife and her English connections. In reply to her eager questions, he then told her what had happened. The Sieur de la Bastie, whom the Duke had made Deputy Governor and Warden of the Scottish Marches, had just been assassinated. Apparently the relatives of the former Warden and Chamberlain, Lord Home, had slain the Frenchman in revenge for the Duke's execution of Lord Home. The murder had occurred in the restless Border area. The Sieur de la Bastie had gone forth in pursuit of George Home and his brother, the Laird of

Wedderburn, who had raided the vicinity. They had ambushed and killed the Warden when his horse foundered in a marsh (known thenceforth as Batty's Bog). George Home had cut off the Frenchman's head and galloped away with this trophy to the town of Duns, where he had stuck it on a pole.

Margaret shuddered at this gory recital and wondered how such a deed could benefit Angus and herself. Her husband pointed out that de la Bastie had been left by Albany as his chief representative during his absence in France. Now that the Deputy Governor had been eliminated, why shouldn't Angus (and Margaret, of course) seize the power and restore their former joint regency? The Homes were now in hiding (probably across the border in England), but the Laird of Wedderburn was Angus's brother-in-law. He and George would surely aid them in a *coup d'état* if offered a free pardon and the rewards of high office in a new administration.

The idea of joining forces again with the Homes, especially now that they were once more listed as Scottish outlaws, was not a pleasant one. Yet Margaret, without funds to live on as her rents had not been paid since her return, and with access to her son refused by the nobles, was becoming desperate enough to snatch at any opportunity to regain her former power. She agreed to write to Lord Dacre asking him, on behalf of Wedderburn, to send his brother to see her and Angus. She was sure the English Warden must be helping to hide these fugitives as he had in the case of their late relative, Lord Home.

Dacre's reply virtuously denied any knowledge of these criminals, although he certainly was supporting them at the time and had been doing so for some time (as is proved by his correspondence with Wolsey). Dacre advised Angus to avoid contact with the Laird of Wedderburn and to seek help from other, less disreputable, Scottish friends. If, with their help, he and his wife succeeded in overthrowing Albany's control of Scotland, the English would of course support them. This promise of future good will, after they had established their own authority to govern, was obviously no help at all; the hare-brained scheme was therefore soon abandoned.

A new disappointment awaited the ambitious Earl. Instead of receiving the now-vacant post of Deputy Governor as he hoped, James Hamilton, Earl of Arran, was given the appointment. Margaret had realized this might occur, since Arran was himself of royal blood. She had therefore endeavoured to make Angus and Arran joint Regents. Instead, when Hamilton alone was appointed, Angus was furious. He even stopped attending the Council meetings, until he learned that by absenting himself he would also lose his place on the Council. He returned to the meetings, but continued to quarrel with Arran at every opportunity. This was the beginning of the bitter Hamilton-Douglas feud, which was to plague Scotland even in the time of Margaret's granddaughter, Mary Stuart.

Angus was by now obsessed by power; he would go to any lengths to obtain it. His wife had far more modest aims, namely, reunion with her son and sufficient income to live on in at least a semblance of the style to which she was accustomed. Yet even these quite reasonable wishes seemed beyond her reach. Since Lord Dacre was closer to Scotland than any other English authority, it was to him that she looked first for a redress of her grievances. A letter which she wrote to him several months after her return eloquently expresses the utter hopelessness of her situation: 'I stand in a sore case, an [if] I get not the King's grace my brother's help . . . for such jewels as his grace gave me . . . I am so constrained that I must put it [them] away for money'. In fact, of all the valuable gifts which Henry had given her as she left London, only two gold cups remained. As these too now had to be pawned she offered them to Lord Dacre for, she added, 'I had liever [rather] you had them nor another'.

She had had to dismiss most of her servants, for she could not pay their wages, let alone have enough to live on herself. She was forced to accept charity. 'And had not Robin Barton, comptroller . . . laid out of his own purse 500 pounds Scots I had been fain to live like a poor gentlewoman, and not like the woman I am'; for, she explained, 'since my last coming into Scotland, I have not gotten, of all the lands I have, 400 pounds Scots'. But the most bitter disappointment of all — 'the cause that I came hither most for was the King my son's sake, and I am holden from him like a stranger and not like his mother' — was too much to bear, for 'I have no other comfort here but him'.

Therefore, 'since they will not let me be with my son, nor is not answered of my living . . . I beseech his grace to let me come to be in his realm'. She would let King Henry have all her rents, from which he could then pay her whatever portion he wished — enough at least to cover her own living expenses. Margaret underlined the weakness of her position by writing that, 'his grace knows well that he may get reason of Scotland; and so may not I'. His written response to the lords on her behalf would, she knew, be futile. They would merely reply with 'fair words, but they do to me never the better, and that I have assayed long'.

This was certainly true. She had 'assayed long', going personally day after day before the Council table to present her claims against each individual nobleman, clergyman or commoner who was her creditor. Frequently she obtained favourable decrees, for most of her claims were well justified. Unfortunately, nothing was done by those in authority to force these delinquent creditors to pay. The result was that she became increasingly more destitute. Having to pawn jewellery and other valuables was humiliating for anyone, more especially for a Tudor! Even more frightening was the question of what her next recourse would be; what should she do when all her valuables were gone?

Lord Dacre forwarded her complaints to the English King and Chancellor, assuring them that 'the Queen of Scots . . . verily . . . is marvellous evil entreated, and no promise kept unto her . . .'. He urged that 'the King's Highness send down some quick [capable] man to move the Council of Scotland that she may have her right, without trouble or vexation . . .'. At this juncture Henry and his Cardinal were evidently too preoccupied with other affairs to give immediate attention to the problems of the Scottish Queen. Henry had not even kept the promise made to his sister at Windsor shortly before she left for the north that he would not make any new peace or truce with Scotland without first consulting her. Instead, through Lord Dacre, he had extended the truce once again. Margaret felt that this step had made the Scottish Council feel free to disregard her rights.

On top of all these woes came the final blow. The Queen herself learned what most of those around her had known for some time: Angus was unfaithful. He was living a large part of the time with Lady Jane Stewart of Traquair and with the daughter this woman had borne to him over a year earlier. Margaret's cup of bitterness was full. Small wonder that she now felt about the Scots as she wrote to Lord Dacre: 'There is neither kindness nor truth with them, wherefore I had liever [rather] be dead than that I should live my life amongst them'. Alas for Margaret, she was to have no other choice.

CHAPTER 13

BEWARE THE FALSE DOUGLAS
(1518–1522)

> I said Tantallon's dizzy steep
> Hung o'er the margin of the deep.
> Many a rude tower and rampart there
> Repelled the insult of the air,
> Which, when the tempest vexed the sky,
> Half breeze, half spray, came whistling by.

Ruins of this magnificent stronghold, made famous by Scott, still loom over the cliffs near North Berwick. The red sandstone walls and towers stand out against the sky as one approaches from the landward side. Passing through the great gateway, however, one finds the structure directly over the sea has long since crumbled, although in the time of *Marmion*,

> Above the booming ocean leant
> The far-projecting battlement;
> The billows burst in ceaseless flow
> Upon the precipice below.

Queen Margaret stood on this battlement, on a grim, grey afternoon in late January 1518. A cold, misty rain was falling. Looking down on the rocks far below, wet from the pounding waves, she might well have felt ready to leap into those foaming waters. She had just learned of Angus's unfaithfulness. Was there really any use for her to go on struggling against all her misfortunes? She must now face them completely alone. For the moment her life seemed hopeless.

Her anguished self-pity did not last long. Righteous wrath began to assert itself; fury with the smooth-tongued young gallant who had persuaded her so easily to become his wife and to share with him the high position which she had then held. It was because of him that she had lost the regency and with it all her former consequence. She had been forced to flee the country, only to return a year later and find herself faced with abject poverty, scorned by the nobles of the Council, who mocked her efforts to collect her rightful income. Disgust at their attitude now combined with hatred of her faithless husband. That she, King Henry's daughter, wife of James IV, mother of the present King of Scotland and sister of Henry VIII of England should be treated thus!

Why had Henry not assisted her? Why had he broken his promise not to make peace without consulting her? Resentment rose even against her brother. To whom could she turn? The answer came back, clear and remorseless: she must battle alone against all these hostile, or indifferent forces. Somehow she must regain her old power, since only from a position of strength would she again be treated with respect. Desperation affects each individual differently. With some, abject despair leads to suicide; others lose their minds entirely, and retreat into a world of dreams. To Margaret Tudor despair brought determination; an iron resolve to win back her old position, by any means that came to hand — she little cared what.

And so there developed in her that hardness which has brought denunciation from historians. Her word could not be trusted, they relate. She made promises only to break them. She twisted the truth, and sometimes told outright lies. She was fickle — supporting first one side, then another. All of these accusations are valid. Yet, if she was guilty of these sins, so were those with whom she dealt. Who kept promises made to her? How many times did those in whom she trusted prove false? When could she be sure that the nobleman, high official, or clergyman who appeared as her friend today would not help her foes tomorrow? Granted, Margaret Tudor was not a 'good' woman, but she did not live in a 'good' society. Forced to exist by her own wits among ruthless and selfish barons, she herself acted with ruthless self-interest. She came, moreover, of a family that was pragmatic, not principled. So she too acted in response to the needs of each day, each situation. She did what she felt had to be done, for her young son, the King, and for herself. Only thus could she survive on her own.

Her first action after discovering about Angus's double life was to sever relations with him. He might keep his mistress and her bastard, but not the Queen and her daughter, nor her son, the King of Scots. Angus, incredibly, was shocked by her repudiation of him. He was determined to hold on to the wife whose trust he had abused. Only through this marriage could he hope to achieve the power he sought, and augment his income through access to her dower lands. He had (at the time of her return to Scotland) agreed to let Lord Dacre assign the collection of these revenues to other agents, and had signed a bond to this effect. Now he demanded that she release him from this bond, in effect restoring to him full rights to share her income. When she refused he was furious, and his whole family, led by Gavin Douglas, Bishop of Dunkeld, rallied to his support. Although Gavin owed his own position, even his freedom, entirely to the Queen, he now became one of her bitterest foes. Small wonder that Margaret should evince so little regard for the niceties of honour, or gratitude, surrounded as she was with dishonourable and ungrateful men.

Her refusal to restore the legal right to her property to her errant spouse had no effect. He simply seized her most valuable estate, Newark, where he ensconced himself with his mistress, Lady Jane, and her daughter, and proceeded to force the Queen's tenants to pay their rents to him. Outraged by this behaviour, Margaret turned for redress to Angus's sworn enemy, the acting Regent, Arran. The latter took up her cause and persuaded the Council to issue a legal summons to the Douglas Earl. On his refusal to appear before the Council, he was ordered to leave the area, a command which he likewise ignored. He continued both to collect and spend his wife's rents while she was forced to pawn still more of her valuables.

Margaret now thought of a possible solution for her hopeless financial state: she would surrender all her dower lands (from which she was now obtaining almost no revenue) to the Scottish regency in return for a fixed annual income. Since Arran and the Council members now were in accord with her, they would have agreed to this reasonable proposition. Unfortunately, however, this sensible resolution was vetoed by her brother. Henry did not wish her to become so dependent on the Scottish Council as to cease to need his support altogether, even though it was so spasmodically and grudgingly given. His letter forbidding her to make the arrangement with the regency was one more link in the chain that kept her in the intolerable position of an English pensioner living among Scottish potentates.

In her answer to this fraternal command, written in October 1518, Margaret described to her brother the miseries that she had heretofore divulged only to Lord Dacre. She had, she wrote, refrained from troubling Henry with these complaints earlier, but was now forced to tell him all so that he could understand her desperate plight. She continued to describe her abject penury because of the Council's (and Lord Dacre's) failure to secure the payment of her rents; her need to pawn his (Henry's) gifts of jewellery and plate in order to survive; and the disgraceful treatment which she had suffered from her husband. Of the latter she wrote, 'I am sore troubled with my lord of Angus since my last coming into Scotland, and every day more and more, so that we have not been together this half-year'. She went on to relate how he had illegally seized her estate at Newark, withholding its income from her, and how harshly he and his kindred had treated her when she refused Angus's demand to restore his legal share in her 'conjunct feoffment'. In this recital of wrongs she made no mention of her husband's infidelity. It was still too galling to her pride to put this down in writing; instead, she instructed her trusted messenger to relate all the details to her brother. Angus, she wrote, had injured her 'with much more evil, that I shall cause a servant of mine to shew your grace, which is too long to write'.

Because of her husband's 'evil' treatment of her, Margaret concluded, 'I am so minded that, *an* [if] I may by law of God and to my honour, to part with him, for I wit well he loves me not, as he shews me daily'. Once she had achieved permanent separation from her hated spouse, she promised she would 'never marry, but where you will bid me'. Apparently she hoped Henry would choose an English nobleman for her, rather than another Scot, for she added she would 'never part from your grace, for I will never with my will abide into Scotland'.

Henry was horrified by his sister's letter. To divorce her lawful husband would be a breach of God's law, he declared, an immoral action unworthy of a Tudor. He and Catherine agreed that the way to prevent Margaret from contemplating such a sin was to send a holy man to dissuade her. Friar Bonaventure was therefore at once dispatched to Scotland carrying their letters and messages to the Queen. Margaret was delighted by the letters the friar brought as they showed that her brother and his wife still cared for her. In her reply to her sister-in-law, Margaret thanked Catherine for 'the great compassion you have for our sake, as your well-beloved in God, Friar Bonaventure ... has shown on your behalf, together with full wise and substantial consolations ...'. She did not, however, indicate that she agreed with the chief purpose of the friar's errand: to reconcile the Queen with her errant spouse. Margaret was not so tolerant a wife as her sister-in-law. At this very time Henry was openly rejoicing in the birth of a son — born to him by Bess Blount. Yet from Henry's own point of view, there was no inconsistency between his own overt infidelity to his wife and his condemnation of his sister's wish to divorce her faithless husband.

The conflict that thus developed between Margaret and her brother over her relations with Angus complicated all her future actions. She could only count on English support so long as she remained on good terms with Archibald Douglas, because Lord Dacre, who controlled all English policies towards Scotland, favoured his own relatives, the Douglases, and their close friends and kin, the Homes. If she broke with Angus, then Albany's pro-

French party in Scotland would instead be willing to help her. Angus himself was one of the chief problems in this confused situation. Determined to attain control over Scotland, he wanted to remain the Queen's husband (and the little King's step-father). Yet, at the same time, he refused to relinquish his mistress and her child. Hence any lasting reconciliation between the power-hungry and selfish Earl and his proud and equally determined wife was impossible.

Thus, in the tangled course of events from 1517, when Margaret returned from England, to 1528, when young James at last began to rule, the husband-wife conflict dominated much of the Scottish political scene. It also clarifies the otherwise inexplicable twists and turns that Margaret made, supporting first one side, then the other in the struggle between England and France over the control of Scotland.

It was most unfortunate that throughout this period Henry refused to sanction, or even recognize, his sister's determination to end her unhappy marriage. He persisted in the belief that this union could and should be salvaged. His objection was based only in part on his religious aversion to divorce. This pious attitude was less important than his personal ambition and dynastic aims, as his own marital affairs later proved. Despite his avowal of devotion to the Church, it is clear that Henry, like his sister and most of their family, was motivated by self-interest. From a practical standpoint he wanted Margaret to remain united with Angus in the belief, fostered by Lord Dacre, that the Douglases were England's best pensioners and that support of them strengthened England's hand in the northern kingdom. Viewed from his own vantage-point in London, the joint control of his sister and Angus in Scotland would be the best security against the French. He felt relatively little concern for his sister's personal happiness, comfortably entrusting it to the supervision of his Warden of the North.

In consequence, when Friar Bonaventure returned to London and reported his failure to reunite husband and wife, Henry refused to accept this as final. A more vigorous member of the same order, Friar Henry Chadworth, was dispatched north. After six to eight weeks of strenuous argument with the Queen, he was finally able to report success. This was probably not the result of Chadworth's 'loud and sharp sentences', which Margaret resented, but rather of the actions taken by Angus himself. Coached by Chadworth and Lord Dacre, he now came to her in the guise of a humble suppliant. He pleaded for forgiveness and a second chance, and promised to abandon henceforth 'his light conditions' (meaning his mistress) and to refrain from further seizure of his wife's properties.

Having agreed to rejoin her spouse, Margaret journeyed from Linlithgow to Edinburgh. The capital city was at this time in the control of the Douglases. They had obtained the forced elevation of one of Angus's uncles to the position of provost, driving out the Earl of Arran and his followers in one of the frequent *coups* typical of Scotland in this lawless period. Arran and his company tried to dissuade the Queen from returning to her husband, and warned her that by doing so she would at once forfeit their support. Obviously, it was impossible in these times to be neutral. Despite these warnings from the Hamiltons, Margaret left Linlithgow and was met by Angus who rode out from Edinburgh, accompanied by a group of nobles belonging to his faction and by some 400 horsemen. To the accompaniment of triumphant salvos of cannon and the skirl of bagpipes, she and her husband re-entered the capital city together.

For a while the reconciliation appeared to be a success. Angus wrote to King Henry that, thanks to his sending Friar Chadworth, 'her highness is fully *appleased* to resort and remain with me, her husband and servant, according and conform to all reason and laws, both of God and holy Kirk'. In his gratitude Angus offered to do whatever her brother might demand, even if 'your highness commanded me forthwith to pass on foot to Jerusalem, and fight with the Turks to the death for your cause!'

Unfortunately, it was not in Jerusalem that Henry wished Angus to serve him. (From that distance Margaret might have found him less objectionable as a husband.) Instead, Angus was to represent the interests of his royal brother-in-law in Scotland, and it soon became obvious that the country could not peacefully contain both him and his wife.

Before long Angus was consorting again with Lady Jane Stewart. When he also seized another of the Queen's properties, Margaret at once turned to Lord Dacre. The latter had been one of the chief intermediaries in persuading her to take back her erring spouse, and had vouched for his subsequent good behaviour. Now, however, instead of chiding the Earl for his delinquencies, Dacre urged Wolsey and the King to continue to rely on Angus and the Homes, and described Margaret's complaints against her spouse as exaggerated. Angry and embittered, the Queen once again left the Douglases and rejoined their opponents, Arran and the pro-French party.

Dacre was furious. In a contemptuous letter he scolded his sovereign's sister for stealing away by night from Edinburgh to meet one of her husband's bitterest enemies, Sir James Hamilton. In a letter to Wolsey, the Warden described her flight and gave the impression that she had deserted her husband for the sake of another man. Margaret vigorously denied this unjust allegation, asserting that Hamilton was only one of a whole company of noblemen who had met her as she left the capital, by day, not by night, accompanied by a full retinue of lords and retainers. All of them then escorted her from the capital to Stirling. As she surmised, the misleading account had originated with Gavin Douglas, Bishop of Dunkeld, who during this period frequented the English side of the border and lost no opportunity to besmirch the reputation of his former benefactress. Unfortunately his version was given by Dacre to Wolsey and the King first, and so helped to poison their minds against the Queen.

Finding herself cut off from any hope of English support by the machinations of Angus and his family, Margaret now followed Hamilton's lead. Together with Arran and his party, she began urging the return of the Duke of Albany. This was not the first time she had done so. Early in 1520, she had written to King Francis asking him to permit the Governor's return. She had done so under earnest pressure from the Scottish Council. Unluckily for her, Francis had received her letter on the famous occasion of the 'Field of Cloth of Gold'. This extravaganza was arranged in June 1520 by Wolsey and his master to display, on English-occupied French soil, the power and magnificence of Henry VIII. It was also intended to dramatize the friendship between England and France then being touted in diplomatic circles. In order to carry out his part in this display of mutual confidence, Francis had shown the English King the letter he had just received from the Queen of Scots. Henry and Wolsey had been indignant to learn that Margaret, far from opposing Albany's return to Scotland, was now petitioning for it. Accordingly, Lord Dacre was deputed to demand an explanation from her of this inconsistency.

Margaret had replied by explaining that she had written at the demand of the Scottish Council, a request which was hard for her to refuse at a time when she needed their help to secure the payment of her income. It was all very well, she pointed out, for the English Warden to defy the opinion of the Scottish nobles. She had to live among them and, moreover, since Dacre himself was evidently unable to secure her income, her livelihood depended on their aid. Hence she had had to yield to their pressure and had written to King Francis on behalf of the Duke. She felt sure her request would have no real effect on the course of events, and certainly could cause no harm to her brother or his people.

As a result of her renewed friendliness towards Albany, Margaret had discovered that her own situation had improved. He had written to the Council to ensure that she received her rightful income, and even hinted that if he himself could not return, they might restore her to the regency. So long as she remained completely separate from the feared and hated Douglas family, she might evidently get help from the French Duke. She wrote to him secretly to ask him to use his considerable influence with the Pope in order to acquire the divorce she so wanted. Since Albany himself wanted her to break with the Douglases, he promised to make this effort.

After this episode, and having yielded to Henry's and Dacre's insistence, Margaret had, as related, attempted a genuine reconciliation with her spouse, only to find him once again untrue to his word. Consequently, when she left him the second time, she resolved to accept help from his enemies, who were now her natural allies, and willingly renewed her plea for Albany's return.

The Queen and the Hamiltons were not the only ones who longed for the Duke to come back. The common people as well were exhausted by the lawlessness resulting from the continued struggle for power among the nobles and chieftains. The general feeling of discontent was well expressed by a poem of the period addressed to the absent Governor. These verses, usually ascribed to William Dunbar, end with the refrain: 'For lack of justice this realm is *shent* (ruined), alas!'

The arrival of a French ship, early in 1521, was welcomed with widespread anticipation. Aboard was a representative of the Duke, his good friend, Gonzolles, who promised the Council that Albany himself would soon be coming. Gonzolles's arrival was particularly gratifying to the Queen, for at the Duke's express command, the Council were at once to pay her income out of the royal exchequer. This was the result of an agreement which the Queen had made earlier with Arran's faction. She would give up the right to collect rents from a number of her dower lands in return for a fixed income. Meanwhile the generous Duke had even sent a loan of some funds of his own for her immediate needs.

Of course, news of the Queen's part in Albany's projected return quickly reached the English. Dacre's spy-system was in good working order, and the Warden lost no time in advising Wolsey and his master of the Queen's 'dishonourable' actions. Dacre then wrote to her directly, telling her that she had forfeited all hope of assistance from her brother by thus leaving her lawful spouse and joining the pro-French party. In reply to this harsh rebuke, Margaret told the Warden: 'As to my Lord of Angus, if he had desired my company or my love, he would have shewn him more kindly than he hath done; for now of late, when I came to Edinburgh to him, he took my house without my consent and withholds my living from me'. Then, with reference to the scandalous stories of her method of leaving her husband, she wrote: 'You should not give so lightly credence to evil tales of me as you do while you know the truth . . . and I may think it strange that my lord of Angus may make the King my brother so displeased at me without any faultmaking [by me] as shall be well known . . .'.

In defence of Albany, whom Dacre had accused of misleading her with 'fair words', for his own ends, she wrote: 'I believe not his fair words, but as he hath done to me in deeds; were [it] not [for] the kindness that he hath shewn to me, both of his own monies given to me, and caused the lords to furnish me . . . I would have been constrained to have put away my jewels and cupboard. . . . I must have *good mind* where I find *good deed*'.

While the Queen continued to wait hopefully for the coming of the Governor, Arran and his party made an unsuccessful effort to regain control of the capital. The attempt failed because the Douglases were helped by some of the townspeople who leaned 'from the windows of their houses' and handed them the long spears so familiar to Scottish armies. Arran's half-brother, Patrick Hamilton, was killed by Angus during the fracas, an incident which added yet more bitterness to the lengthy feud between the Douglases and the Hamiltons. The episode, known as 'Cleanse the Causeway', ended in victory for Angus and his supporters, but their success was short-lived. On November 18th 1521, the long-awaited Governor arrived.

Albany's return to Scotland had been facilitated by a new development in European diplomacy. Even at the time of the great demonstration of friendliness between England and France at the 'Field of Cloth of Gold', Wolsey was preparing to rejoin the Hapsburgs against the Valois. Charles V, now Emperor, visited England both before and after the Anglo-French spectacle of 1520. Charles's hints that he would use his influence to get the Cardinal elected to the Papacy were of far greater consequence to the diplomat-cum-churchman than anything Francis might offer. As a result, the hand of five-year-old Mary Tudor, which had recently been promised to the French Dauphin, was instead offered to the twenty-one-year-old Hapsburg ruler. Consequently it was obvious that, in the event of war, England would support the Emperor against Francis. Hence, Albany was again permitted to go to Scotland with secret instructions to use its forces when needed as a diversion against England.

Albany's arrival was greeted with joy by the majority of Scots. They recalled his previous regency as the one fairly peaceful and orderly interlude in the series of tumults that had wracked the country since Flodden. Albany began his new administration by replacing all the magistrates appointed by the Douglas faction with men of his own choosing. He summoned a Parliament which commanded Angus and others of his family, along with their colleagues, the Homes, to answer charges of treason and murder.

Albany commuted the death sentence on Angus and his brother to banishment to France. Margaret herself had urged this leniency after her husband had promised that he would cease opposing their divorce. Meanwhile, the Homes fled to England. So did Gavin Douglas, Bishop of Dunkeld, now branded a traitor as a result of his association and collaboration with the English in the Borders. He was also summoned to Rome by the Pope, and on refusing to go lost his episcopal see. In his flight from Scotland he was assisted by Lord Dacre, although Albany protested against the English Warden's permitting a Scottish rebel to cross the border in violation of the Anglo-Scottish truce.

The truce, Henry declared, would not be renewed as long as the Duke remained in Scotland. He accused Albany of advising Margaret to divorce her husband. Ignoring the Governor's immediate denial of this charge, Wolsey elaborated on the theme. The Bishop of Dunkeld, who had been welcomed into the English court, supplied additional tales of scandalous behaviour which added colour to the accusations against the Duke and the Queen. As is usually true of such false rumours, they were undergirded by a basis of fact. The Queen had unquestionably welcomed the French Governor back to Scotland. He had also shown the utmost regard for her, going in person to see her at Stirling soon after his arrival and escorting her back to Edinburgh. Here, they went together to the castle to visit the nine-year-old King. When they had mounted the steep road to the castle gates, the Captain presented the keys to the Governor. He courteously handed them to Margaret, indicating that these symbols of control were hers to dispose of. She, as graciously, at once returned them to the Duke. They then entered the great gateway together.

Albany hoped by this dramatization of his kindly intentions to clear Henry's mind of all the fears which he had previously voiced concerning the welfare of his sister and nephew under the Duke's regency. He also wrote to the English King emphasizing his regard for the Queen of Scots and her son. All in vain — both Henry and Wolsey preferred to stick to their own version of the situation and to impute to all the French Governor's actions the worst possible motives. He was ingratiating himself with Margaret, they declared, in order to marry her himself. For this purpose he had already applied to the Pope for two divorces: one for himself from his French wife and one for the Queen from Angus. Once these were attained, they concluded, he would marry Margaret, kill her son and ascend the Scottish throne himself.

Henry and Wolsey must be given credit for persistence. They stuck to their main theme — Albany's villainy — regardless of the circumstances. When Margaret was unhappy during his first regime in Scotland, the Duke was seen as a heartless monster driving her from her rightful station beside her son. When she was obviously well treated and happy after his second arrival, it was because the same wolf had now donned sheep's clothing and insinuated himself into her good graces. In both cases his nefarious purpose was the same: to eliminate the rightful King of Scots and make himself ruler. (The *Richard III* plot was too good to abandon!)

In this second assault on the Duke's character, Margaret, instead of appearing as the injured heroine, shared the abuse heaped on him. She was now depicted as a woman so besotted with passion for the gallant Frenchman that she left her lawful husband, and forgot her dignity as Queen by consorting with Albany day and night, neglecting the welfare of her young son, whose very life was threatened by this monster.

As before, Lord Dacre supplied the tales to Wolsey, who repeated them in diplomatic circles. This time they were assisted by the Bishop of Dunkeld who spent his time at the English court tirelessly spreading false stories about Albany and the Queen. No doubt his facility in telling such scandalous accounts rendered him popular among the gossip-hungry courtiers. They could talk more openly about the misdeeds of the Queen of Scots than about the amours of her royal brother.

Henry had by now discarded Bess Blount. After his birth, her son, young Henry Fitzroy, was installed in a suitable residence complete with wet-nurse and other attendants. His mother was married by Wolsey to a pleasant young gentleman whose desire for a royal pension was strong enough to make him very broad-minded about his wife's extramarital affairs. Meanwhile Henry had fallen into the throes of a new passion, for another pretty lady-in-waiting who had caught his eye in France during the 'Field of Cloth of Gold'. This seventeen-year-old beauty was the elder daughter of Sir Thomas Boleyn, former ambassador to France. At the court of Queen Claude she had already made a reputation among the young gallants for being expert in love-making and extremely generous with her favours. Now back in England at Queen Catherine's court, it was Mary Boleyn who furnished the back-stairs gossips with plentiful material. However, it was the affair of the Queen of Scots that reached the headlines of the day.

Actually these new stories about her and Albany had far less impact on diplomatic circles than the previous ones of 1515–1516. The courts of Spain, the Empire and the Italian States were too preoccupied with the war which was brewing to pay much attention to Scottish internal affairs, whereas in France the Duke's reputation was too well established to suffer from the reports sent by Wolsey and Henry to King Francis. The latter did pretend, for the sake of diplomacy, that the Duke had left France without his knowledge and against his wishes, but even this pretence was later dropped as war became a reality.

Unfortunately, in England itself the gossip-mongers had more success. In fact, for generations, the histories of that period continued to portray Margaret as the mistress of the Duke. And even though more recent scholarship has exploded this myth, the Scottish Queen is still portrayed as a nymphomaniac. Not that she was free from stain — her later actions make such a claim impossible — but she was far from being the degraded nincompoop that she is often pictured. She lived, as has been said, in the midst of a ruthless, amoral society, and was herself a product and representative of that environment.

For some time she was completely ignorant of the vicious slanders being circulated against her and the Governor. Thus, she quite unconsciously helped to make them sound plausible by the way in which she now praised the Duke in her letters to Wolsey and her brother. She told them of her joy at finally receiving the sort of treatment a widowed Queen should be given. Albany had given her every possible concession. Above all, he permitted her to see her son whenever she wished and for any length of time, an indulgence which was deeply appreciated by a mother who had for so long been allowed only occasional and very brief visits to her child. Moreover, the Duke promised that when he left on a trip he was planning to make south, young James could stay with his mother at Stirling. Albany had also arranged for her dues to be paid regularly — a great relief to one who had been desperately short of cash for over four years. He always treated her with courtesy, deferring to her rightful position as Queen mother. In her letter to Wolsey and the King, she wrote with artless candour, that 'All the honour and authority that he makes to me, he doth it gladly, and he *haveth* [behaves] himself not in my company as governor, but sober and humblier than any lord of this realm'.

In addition to these glowing reports of affairs in Scotland since the Governor's coming, the Queen sent Henry and Wolsey a list of articles for the proposed peace that she and Albany hoped could soon be established with England. She wished personally to mediate this agreement, emphasizing her own deep commitment to this project by writing in her own hand the eight-page list of articles, plus a complete copy for her brother and a private letter to him, vouching for her own sincerity in the entire transaction. (Quite a contrast to the previous letters between herself and Henry in 1515–1516, when she had tried to warn him that she was being forced to write at the Duke's dictation!)

As Margaret completed the letter to her brother and enclosed the lengthy proposals for peace, she must have felt an unusual sense of satisfaction. For the first time in years she had the chief requisites for her personal contentment: unlimited access to her son and an assured income. She was free from the threat of further injury or humiliation from her faithless husband, now banished to France; she could take her rightful place at the centre of the forthcoming peace negotiations. At the same time her son's realm was becoming increasingly stable under Albany's wise and firm government. It all seemed too good to be true.

Alas, it was! At least, it was too calm a state for Scotland to enjoy under a French Regent so long as Lord Dacre was the English Warden of the Northern Marches. Margaret had made no attempt to propitiate this dour official for her part in supporting the return of the Duke. In fact, after Albany's arrival, she had even written a fairly impudent — and certainly imprudent — letter to the English Warden, exulting in the improved circumstances she now enjoyed. She pointed out that all Dacre's dire warnings against the Duke were unfounded. She at last was getting the dower rights she was entitled to, together with access to her son, perquisites the Warden had completely failed to provide for her throughout the four years since her return from London.

Taunting the harsh Warden for his failures may have relieved the Queen's smouldering sense of injury at his hands, but was bound to come back on her like a boomerang. As a matter of fact, though, even the most tactful approach would not have appeased Dacre. Committed as always to hatred of both French and Scots, and to the benefit of his protégés, the Douglases and the Homes, he had lost no time in alerting Westminster to the dangers threatening England if Albany remained in Scotland. He added new facets to the rumours which he had started concerning the Queen and the Governor. He said his spies had reported to him that these two were now 'consorting' day and night, not caring who saw them. His seeds of bitterness soon bore fruit.

Clarenceux King of Arms was dispatched to Scotland. He arrived in Edinburgh on February 1st and went promptly to visit the Queen in the burgess's house where she was residing. Margaret greeted him joyfully. It was so wonderful to get letters from home. And how prompt a reply! Her brother must have been impressed by her diligence. She felt sure he would explain why Lord Dacre had rebuffed the Governor's overtures for peace by refusing even to extend the truce for four more weeks so that negotiations could take place. Excitedly she opened the letter from Henry.

As she read it, her expression changed from joy to bewilderment, then to abject grief. She burst into a torrent of tears, which were not assuaged by the verbal message then delivered by the King at Arms. Following his Master's explicit instructions, the latter proclaimed that her brother, the King, was much displeased by the news of her shameless conduct with the French Duke, whom she was assisting in his effort to take control of her son's kingdom and lead it against her native land; she must mend her ways, or forever lose the hope of support from him.

It took her some minutes to control her sobs sufficiently to tell Clarenceux that she realized from the letter and the verbal message that her brother was angry with her because of 'seditious and ill reports made and contrived against her by very false persons'. She declared 'to God and all honest creatures', that these reports were utterly false. She then dismissed the King of Arms, after requesting him to return to her residence before departing, so that he could take her written reply back to London.

It took her over a week to recover from the shock she had suffered and to write a reasonably temperate reply. The letter was remarkably restrained considering the provocation to which she had been subjected. Henry had accused her of sending for the Duke, foolishly expecting his coming would benefit her. This, she wrote, had indeed happened. Albany had proved more helpful than any other in establishing her in comfortable circumstances. He treated her with honour and respect. The report Wolsey had made to the English Council 'that she loved the Governor to her dishonour', and had sent for him in order to divorce Angus and marry him, was a complete lie. Obviously, it had been fabricated by the Bishop of Dunkeld. Henry's accusation that she was neglecting the safety of her son, whose life was endangered by the Duke, was also absurd. If she really cared so little for James, as her brother declared, she 'might have spared herself much of the trouble she had undergone'. But Albany intended only the good of the young King, who was still in the hands of the same noblemen who had looked after him continuously since 1515, when she had first lost his guardianship. They were completely trustworthy gentlemen, 'as Clarenceux himself can report'. How could the English King procure 'great security for him'? 'If [Henry] be unreasonable, the world will think he aims at his nephew's destruction'. This interpretation would seem especially likely since Henry now threatened to make war on James's kingdom so long as Albany remained there. 'This country desires peace with England, if it can be got with honour, but will not consent to Albany's removal'. She signed herself, 'Your humbyll sistar, Margaret R'.

The last sentence of her letter was re-echoed by the response of the Chancellor and the Three Estates of Scotland to the message they had received from the English King. They wished for peace, but absolutely refused Henry's demand for the removal of their Governor. It was obvious, they said, that Henry had been misled by the lies of persons interested in fomenting war between the two kingdoms. Albany had accepted the position of Governor and of tutor to the young King from the Scottish Estates. 'He does not meddle with the custody of the King's person, or make any appointment in the household; but defers everything to the ordering of the Estates, who, by the advice of the Queen' had deputed 'some of the most aged and honourable lords continually to wait upon him'. How could Henry possibly believe that this Duke, 'who has been nourished with great honour and had so tender familiarity with Popes and greatest Princes', wanted to harm the young King or 'induce the Queen to leave her husband'? They concluded with a declaration. If Henry persisted in demanding the Duke's removal, they would 'make known to all Christian Princes the necessity they were under, either to deprive the Governor unjustly of the care of their sovereign lawfully belonging to him, or expect to be invaded'.

All these statements thus made in writing were also given orally to the English King of Arms, as he reported to Wolsey on February 15th, just before starting his return trip to London. In addition, he described the reactions of the Queen, the Scottish Parliament and the Governor to his messages. The Queen, who he said was 'marvellously abashed', received the message with tears and heartbroken denials of the accusations; the Lords reacted with 'many grim looks' from 'both high and low', followed, after they had consulted privately, by a complete exoneration of the Governor similar to the written one, summarized above. Albany's response was more openly expressive of his feeling.

He had been appointed, he declared, by the Scots to be their Governor; he would 'risk life and goods' for them and 'would not fail' them. 'As for ... "his damnable abusion of the King's sister, moving her to leave her husband and marry him", ... he swore by the Sacrament . . . and prayed he might break his neck if ever he minded to marry her. He had enough of one wife'. He added a remark that should have made an impact on Henry Tudor. He marvelled, he said, that 'the King should think so ill of his sister, and that the Cardinal, a man of the Church, should say before the King's Council to his secretary, "how he doth keep the same Queen as she were his wife or concubine"'. He also stated that he had treated the Queen well and honourably.

To emphasize this fact, Margaret herself had already called for Clarenceux to meet herself and the Duke together so she could, in the King of Arms' presence, express to Albany her deep gratitude for his treatment of her and her son. She would continue to appreciate this 'as long as he acted honourably'.

During the whole of this episode, the Queen acted with admirable restraint and firmness. She made only one mistake. In her letter to her brother she denied that she had ever sought a divorce. Unhappily for her, Albany later admitted quite freely to the King of Arms that Margaret had written to him requesting his help in obtaining a papal dissolution of her most wretched marriage. Furthermore, the Duke added, while in Rome he had succeeded in attaining a papal bull to this effect. Obviously, there was no close communication between Albany and Margaret, or he would not have so openly revealed her prevarication. On account of this patent falsehood, Margaret damaged her case and so stands today, as she did then, as one whose word cannot be trusted. Yet, honesty in this detail would hardly have strengthened her case with her brother, or the Cardinal, or the English court. They were already too thoroughly convinced of her guilt, and too eager to believe the worst of the Scottish Regent, to accept any other version.

'Truth crushed to earth will rise again'. Sometimes, however, its resurrection takes a very long time.

CHAPTER 14

THE ANGEL OF PEACE
(1522–1523)

By the summer of 1522, war-clouds hung heavily over western Europe as the French forces prepared once again to face those of the Empire. The latter were allied with the English King. The twenty-two-year-old Holy Roman Emperor, Charles of Habsburg, had now been formally betrothed to six-year-old Princess Mary Tudor. Also Wolsey had been assured that Charles would exert his considerable influence to place the Cardinal in the position he most coveted — none other than the papal throne itself. Neither of these factors was, of course, included in the reasons given for Henry's entrance into the war. Instead, when Clarenceux King of Arms delivered the formal declaration to the French court, he listed a series of injuries allegedly committed by Francis I against the English. Among these was the sending of the Duke of Albany to Scotland. This villain had come thither to endanger the life of the young King of Scots and to dishonour his mother, and 'damnably to contract matrimony with her'. In response, of course, the French herald loudly refuted this claim along with all the others that had been made, and predictably none of this oratory had the least effect on the outcome.

The effect on Scotland was to increase the tension with its southern neighbour. Lord Dacre stepped up his raids. More villages were burned, flocks driven off and peasants killed; as a result, there were increased Scottish forays into Northumberland and Westmorland. The Duke of Albany, urged on by Queen Margaret, still strove for a new truce. David Beaton, nephew of the Chancellor, was sent south on a peace mission to London. However, nothing came of it. The English Warden refused even to prevent his borderers from raiding during Beaton's diplomatic visit. Dacre was determined that no peace should be made while Albany remained in Scotland. The Duke was willing to leave in order that pacification might ensue, but the nobles of the Council would not permit him to depart at the behest of the arrogant English.

Armed conflict appeared inevitable. Margaret's heart sank as she saw the preparations in progress. The Duke's call for troops brought forth a goodly array, well equipped with spears and artillery. Yet Margaret recalled only too well the splendid army which James had led to Flodden. Must there always be war between her adopted country and her native land?

One of her anxieties was relieved when Parliament acceded to her request that the young King be moved from Edinburgh to Stirling Castle. Here, in her own fortress, he would be a little farther from the border. She was even permitted to choose his attendants and at last was able to enjoy the opportunity for a small measure of vengeance, by dismissing those who had, five years earlier, denied her requests to visit him. At the same time she rewarded the kindly Lord Erskine by retaining him as her son's permanent guardian. The boy, now ten years old, was handsome and intelligent, his mother's pride and joy. He responded to her affection and was happy to be back with her in the hilltop castle where he had spent a good number of his early years. Her enjoyment of his company was marred only by the nagging worry about the imminent conflict.

Therefore, it was with incredulous delight that in mid-August she received a message from Lord Dacre. She opened his letter with trepidation, expecting one of his usual reprimands for some alleged misdeed. To her amazement, this epistle was deeply respectful, almost obsequious in tone. He wished, he said, to avert war with Scotland (having always been a man devoted to peace whenever possible). In his deep anxiety for an amicable settlement he had hit upon the happy notion that the Queen, being, he was sure, likewise desirous to avoid war, might mediate between the hostile forces of her son and her brother. Would she, for this noble cause, send the Chancellor of Scotland to meet Dacre and arrange an immediate armistice?

Margaret was amazed. Perhaps her prayers to Saint Margaret had really been answered! Perhaps so, but, in addition to saintly intercession, another inducement had had an effect on the doughty Warden. His spies had informed him that the Scottish army was more than five times as large as his own, so that even if the Earl of Shrewsbury arrived in time to assist him, they would together still be outnumbered three to one. Most of the best English troops had been sent to France. Consequently, as in other similar situations, the most effectual deterrent to aggression was an appeal, not to the saints, nor to the opponent's good will, but to his instinct for self-preservation.

Margaret's answer to the Warden showed that she had first consulted with Albany. The latter, she wrote, wanted peace, but demanded to know whether or not Dacre was empowered to conduct negotiations on his own. If he had such authority from the English King, she would be glad to work with him to this end. The

Warden hedged on this. He had no written authorization, he said, but he knew King Henry wanted peace. If the Queen would help to prevent an invasion of England, it would redound to her credit. He would promise to halt his army for the time being. He even assured her in confidence that, although Henry had declared there could be no peace while the Governor remained in Scotland, he would accept the Duke's continued presence if he simply acknowledged the permanent suzerainty of James V.

Margaret and Albany were not yet sure whether they could trust the wily Englishman. They compared his letters with messages which the Duke had received from Captain Ughtred of Berwick. Ughtred wrote that the Warden had full authority to arrange peace. Why, then, did he say he had not?

Dacre's reply to this question was again ambiguous, but finally the Duke agreed to hold off his planned attack for a fortnight until negotiations could take place. Actually the English Warden did not have the official authority to make a truce on his own. If he met with a regular peace commission, he would have to display such credentials. Instead, therefore, he simply rode into the Duke's camp alone, pretending that in his haste he had left his authoritative writ behind. With no apology for this 'oversight', he boldly demanded what displeasure his King had done to Albany that he 'with this great army had come hither to invade his realm'. He also accused the Scottish nobles of assisting in this planned aggression, a charge which proved particularly effective on those lords who were receiving secret pensions from England. Thus, by a combination of threat and persuasion, Dacre succeeded in obtaining an agreement to a month's truce.

In writing an account of this transaction to Wolsey, Dacre apologized for having exceeded his powers to negotiate, but explained how necessary it was in view of the overwhelming strength of the Duke's forces. Had Albany actually invaded, the Warden added, Carlisle and Cumberland could not possibly have withstood their onslaught and 'must have been destroyed'.

Now that the Scots had so foolishly trusted in his word and made the truce, he continued, they had also disbanded their forces. So, if Henry wished him to do so, he could use this opportunity to break the truce without warning and to invade their territory. After all, the King need not feel himself bound to abide by an agreement made in his name by one who had lacked the proper authority to negotiate.

Fortunately Henry and Wolsey preferred to end the hostilities at once. Since the best knights of England had been sent to the continent, peace with the northern kingdom was most welcome. So the King sent his herald to inform the Duke firstly, that he was furious with Lord Dacre for exceeding his authority in creating an 'abstinence' of war; secondly, that he had wanted to vindicate his noble and righteous cause by force of arms; but lastly, at the request of his dear sister, the Queen of Scots, he would nevertheless be content to extend the truce to January 31st. This would allow time for the exchange of ambassadors and for a full discussion of a permanent peace.

In all these messages back and forth between the belligerent parties, emphasis was given to the Queen of Scots as the primary factor in the approaching pacification. From the statements made by the Duke, Lord Dacre, Wolsey and King Henry, it would appear that it was only because of her that peace was finally established. Actually her part was an important one, not because of her powers of persuasion, but because each man could lay the credit (or blame) for his decision to back down from his grim and warlike determination on her intervention. In modern terminology, she made it posssible for each side to 'save face', and in that era of intensely personal decision-making, saving face was even more important than it is today. To state that one was willing to avoid bloodshed merely for humanitarian reasons was considered a paltry excuse, but the plea of a Queen to halt conflict between the forces of her brother and those of her son was a respectable reason. Each brave warrior could claim that his chivalry was touched by her appeal. When his sovereign's sister begged for peace, Lord Dacre was willing to consider negotiating; for the mother of the King of Scots, the Governor would hold back his knights and talk; and at the request of his beloved sister, King Henry would instruct Wolsey to work for a settlement, instead of a continuation of his 'just' war.

Consequently, in a trice Margaret found herself transformed from a scarlet woman, whose unholy passion for the French Duke was the scandal of England, into a heroine, the angel of peace in person. Her brother was grateful to her; Wolsey wrote to commend her laudable efforts; even the dour Warden of the North said she deserved praise. How wonderful! After all these years of suffering and struggle, she had at last emerged in the role for which she had longed — as the bringer of peace between England and Scotland. It was for this purpose that she had left home in 1503, and for this destiny that she had been reared since her earliest remembrance.

As Margaret savoured this unexpected reversal of status, she resisted the desire to rest on her laurels, and instead determined to pursue this admirable course of events. A permanent peace, rather than a mere truce, was what was needed. As time went by and this ending still failed to materialize, she lost patience. Late in September she sent a personal servant to bear to the King her brother, by way of Lord Dacre, an urgent message to cease the delays. 'If matters be not well sped now', the messenger was instructed to tell him, 'it will be worse than ever and all through your [King Henry's] fault'. Dacre would not let the bearer continue to London with any such message. He wrote to Margaret to warn her that if she expressed her views so sharply, she would do more harm than good. His advice was undoubtedly correct. Her brother was not one to brook criticism.

The chief stumbling-block to a lasting peace was Scotland's connection with France. As King Francis's servant, Albany was obliged to include France in any peace between Scotland and England. Yet, with English troops even then in France, firmly committed to the support of Emperor Charles V, Wolsey could not agree to the 'comprehension' of France even in a temporary 'abstinence' from hostilities. Finally, the Duke, anxious to resolve the entire problem, went back to see Francis personally and to discuss the matter with him. He left Scotland in late October, promising that he would return before Assumption Day (August 15th) 1523, or else forfeit his position as Governor. He deputed the Earl of Arran and several other Scottish nobles, including Chancellor Beaton as co-regents to conduct affairs in the interim. The Frenchman, Gonzolles, was to assist them. All swore to remain true to the Duke. To reinforce this loyalty and to strengthen their devotion to the 'Auld Alliance', generous pensions from King Francis were soon sent to these and other influential Scots, including the Queen.

Margaret accepted this gift (she never refused money!), but her loyalty to the Duke was weakening. Once he was gone, her income once more became difficult to collect, and she realized that without his active presence in Scotland to enforce payment, the lords would soon forget their obligation to ensure that she received her just dues. This meant that once again she would have to look to her brother for support. Moreover, it was becoming clear that Albany was one of the chief obstacles to Scotland's achieving the lasting peace with England which Margaret so ardently desired. The Duke had continued to insist that France be included in any Anglo-Scottish agreement after he left the country, and the co-regents whom he had designated had been sufficiently well bribed by Francis to uphold this demand.

Another factor in Margaret's shifting loyalty was a change in the tactics of the English leaders themselves. Instead of their callous indifference or downright hostility to her, which had so hurt and angered the Queen, Wolsey and Henry now showed a tactful solicitude for her. When Clarenceux came to Edinburgh in November 1522, he was instructed to visit the Queen and 'much laud and praise her' on the King's behalf for her great efforts in the quest for a settlement. The King of Arms was then to find out whether she and the lords were still supporting Albany's demands or whether they were really intent on a pacification with England. Clarenceux was next to make a speech to the nobles emphasizing Henry's forbearance in refraining from retaliation against Albany's recent attempt to invade England.

A secret addition to these public propositions was for a permanent alliance between England and Scotland, including an eventual marriage between James V and his cousin, Mary Tudor. (Henry and Wolsey conveniently 'forgot' that this Princess was already betrothed to Charles V.) Margaret was excited over these plans to cement relations permanently between England and Scotland. However, one necessary condition for such an agreement was an equally permanent abrogation of the 'Auld Alliance'. The Scottish lords were still too apprehensive of Henry's real motives to abandon their friendship with France — especially since, following Albany's advice, Francis had just sent them good supplies of arms. Moreover, the Duke himself promised to bring with him on his return the following year enough French troops to ensure victory over the traditional enemy, England.

The Governor's insistence that no lasting Anglo-Scottish accord should be made unless France were comprehended was, of course, dictated by his master, the French King. The latter was at this juncture in a desperate situation, encompassed by his foreign enemies (the Emperor and his allies) and threatened by an internal rebellion led by his rival, the Duc de Bourbon. Francis needed the help of his 'auld ally' to remove the English component of this threat. The Scots could aid him either by persuading England to include France in the peace treaty, or, if that failed, they could divert the attention of the English army by a new invasion of Northumberland and Westmorland.

Realization of Francis's aims made Henry and Wolsey eager for a Scottish alliance, or at least a friendship treaty. When Albany's persuasion (and bribes) prevented this 'peace offensive', more warlike measures were at once directed against the northern kingdom. The breakdown of negotiations provoked Queen Margaret. She was particularly exasperated with the Duke of Albany, whose hand was obviously directing Scottish affairs back into the old routine of support for France and enmity with England. Thus, gratitude for the Duke's previous kindnesses to her now changed to resentment as she watched him frustrate all her hopes for the future.

She was unable at this time to play much active part in affairs. A severe illness completely incapacitated her in December. After some days of high fever which threatened her very life, she broke out into a heavy rash. It was *la petite vérole*, a disease only recently 'imported' into Britain from the continent. Henry himself had suffered with it on his return from France in 1514. He now learned through Lord Dacre that his sister had been grievously ill with the same disease. In a letter dictated the day after Christmas Margaret explained to Wolsey that she had to employ a clerk to write for her because 'my handis and all my body are so full of the small pockis that I might neither write nor sit, nor scantly speak'. However, with typical Tudor resilience, she recovered from this dread disease.

As soon as she regained her health, Margaret resumed her efforts for peace. Since the Governor was now the great obstacle in its way, she began plotting to circumvent his authority. His absence in France gave an opportunity of which she proposed to take advantage. The scheme was to elevate the young King to nominal leadership of his nation. (She would of course be the power behind the throne.) James was not yet quite eleven years old, but mature and capable beyond his years: '. . . of his age I believe there be not in the world a wiser child, nor a better hearted, nor that dare better take upon him, in so far as he may; but he wants nothing but help to bear him forth in his good quarrel'. This was obviously a fond mother speaking. Nevertheless, her plan was not too far-fetched. No matter how young, he was after all the King. Anyone controlling him could speak to the nation with the voice of authority, and those who refused to obey could be declared rebels or traitors.

She confided her plan to Lord Dacre and also to the Earl of Surrey, who had recently been sent north to take charge of operations against Scotland. The latter was the son of Margaret's former acquaintance, who had led her retinue on her journey north in 1503. As a reward for his victory at Flodden, the father had been made Duke of Norfolk. His son, now entitled Earl, was, like his sire, a most capable military man. He was to supersede Lord Dacre as Commander-in-Chief in the north of England. The dour Warden deeply resented the appointment of a superior in the area which he had so long commanded and which he felt he knew better than any other.

One privilege, however, which he was happy to share with Surrey was that of being Margaret's chief correspondent. Most of her letters were now directed to the Earl. Written in a nearly illegible hand and using the Scottish dialect, they were also apt to be lengthy and repetitious. Her theory was that the best way to emphasize an important point was to say it over and over again. If the reader was not convinced by your argument the first time, he would be worn down to the point of agreement when he read it for the third or fourth time. Surrey sighed — but she was his King's sister; moreover, he had been instructed by Wolsey to 'flatter and praise her'. So the new Commander-in-Chief was deferential, even obsequious, in his replies to her requests. Admittedly, he was sometimes pretty vague in his answers as to how, or even whether, he would actually follow her instructions, but he always showed deep appreciation of her intelligence and benevolence. Margaret had hated both his parents, who had tried to make decisions for her, but their son was obviously a gentleman — and so discerning in his judgement of her as 'a noble natural lady and mother to your son, and like a loving sister to your noble brother . . .'.

Margaret then wrote not only to Surrey, but also to Lord Dacre and of course to her brother, outlining her proposals and explaining how they could be carried out. In order to establish her son as King, kindly persuasion should first be used on the nobles, to tempt them to shift their allegiance from France and follow their own rightful King (and his mother) instead of the Duke of Albany. However, the principal persuasion, naturally, would be 'a sober thing of money', in large enough quantities to outbid the pensions which some of these gentlemen already received from King Francis. Would the King and the Cardinal provide such sums?

Then, if these methods failed, force could be applied. An English army could be sent against the capital city itself. This, the Queen urged, should be the objective of an attack, rather than more raids on the Borders. The latter type of warfare, she pointed out, harmed only the poor peasants, whose homes were burned and crops destroyed, whereas the nobles, who were uninjured by these ravages, 'set not by the hurt of poor folks, but laughs at the same'. Surely, she repeated, if suffering of the 'poor folks' actually succeeded in influencing the nobles, it should have done so already. The devastation of the Borders had recommenced when the last truce elapsed. Wolsey himself was soon exulting over its effects in Scotland, and wrote: 'There is left neither house, fortress, village, tree, cattle, corn or other succor for man; insomuch as some of the people which fled from the same, and afterward returned, finding no sustentation, were compelled to come into England, begging for bread, which oftentimes when they eat, they die incontinently for the hunger passed'. The English living in the northern area tried unsuccessfully to prevent the influx of these unwanted refugees, yet could not keep them out. They used such deterrents to immigration as 'imprisonment, cutting off their ears, burning them in the face, or otherwise'. The Cardinal concluded this fearful description with the sanctimonious comment: 'Such is the punishment of Almighty God to those that be the disturbers of good peace, rest and quiet in Christendom'.

Margaret's reiterated pleas to Surrey that this brutal campaign be halted were more perceptive (and compassionate). If, instead, a real attack were launched upon Edinburgh, the leaders themselves would feel the brunt of conflict and hence be persuaded to yield. But a full-scale operation against the capital would take more effort and require more men than attacks on unarmed peasants. Surrey feared that alone he lacked sufficient supplies and manpower, and Dacre refused to support him in such an undertaking without express orders from London. The centre of English government was, like Edinburgh, insulated against direct exposure to danger. From the comfortable perspective of Greenwich, King and Cardinal could view the troubles in Scotland with far less anxiety than Surrey or Margaret. Henry and Wolsey seemed unable go grasp the urgency of her requests, even though she repeated her injunctions for speed time after time. So Surrey was able only to assure her that her brother would provide plentiful money for bribes. She could certainly promise the nobles this; but promises were far less effective than the actual gold which they were already receiving from France. (Perhaps, too, the lords took note of the reluctance with which the English King provided his own sister with funds, and so counted even less on the assurances that he would pay them.)

In spite of her disappointment at this lukewarm assistance from London, the Queen made an all-out effort to win over the Parliament which met at the Tolbooth on August 31st 1523. She reminded the nobles that a fortnight had already elapsed since the deadline for Albany's return, and therefore they were now freed of their oaths to remain true to him. She then read them a letter from King James V himself. In fiery language, he commanded his lords to free him from the control of the false Duke and his French minions. James was determined to become King in his own right.

The nobles knew that the Queen, who read them this letter, had herself dictated it, and they also knew that their boy King adored his mother and supported her in these demands. They knew too that he had an impetuous nature. (He had tried to stab a French guard who refused to open the gate of Stirling Castle at his command.) When, therefore, he finally became ruler, he might well execute vengeance against the lords who now opposed him in his demands. While the issue was still in doubt, a messenger arrived in the person of Albany's French secretary, bringing a letter from the Duke. It stated that Albany was coming at once, and bringing with him a splendid army.

This interruption proved the turning-point in the debate. The Queen tried desperately to convince the nobles that this message was simply 'tidings of the Canongate' [a baseless rumour] — a fiction concocted in order to sway their vote. Her eloquence fell on deaf ears. The French faction won. James would have to stay as before at Stirling. The only concession made was that he would now have permission to leave the castle for hunting and hawking expeditions. Thus they hoped to placate the royal boy, but utterly crush his mother's hopes. Margaret wept all day, and for the moment was quite defeated.

She did not remain downcast long. As she reviewed the situation that evening, a new idea occurred to her. James now could leave the castle to go hunting. Might he not use this opportunity to escape his French retinue, ride to Edinburgh and there confront his nobles himself? Faced by their King in person, they would not dare return him to captivity. Then, together with her, he would form a sympathetic Council, end the French alliance, and establish the peace proffered by his uncle, Henry.

In eager haste, the Queen returned to her writing desk to appeal once again to her brother. He must send promises of real reward and future support to those leading Scots who were most likely to be won over. His flattering words, along with her own persuasion, could tempt them to desert Albany, for, by delaying his coming, he had forfeited their oaths of loyalty, made before he left Scotland. Support of these prominent leaders having been secured, there would be no difficulty with the common people, for they hated the French. But haste was essential. Else the Governor himself would arrive, and once he was there with additional troops none would dare to oppose him. 'Wherefore, dearest brother, it standeth all in your hand now at this time; and if ye will not do it at this time, I promise you I will never write more in this matter, nor your grace will never get so good a time'.

She sent this letter by her most trusted servant, Patrick Sinclair, to the Earl of Surrey, whom she begged to forward it at once to London. She also emphasized over and again the need for haste to Surrey himself. She must get help from England, especially in the form of direct promises from King Henry to the Chancellor, the Earl of Argyll and the Bishop of Aberdeen, 'for these are the greatest men and may do most'. With their support she would consider it safe for her son to come forth. She knew there would be

James V as a young man

(*British Museum*)

no difficulty in persuading James himself, who 'loved not no Frenchmen', but she would not ask her son to act without the assurance of help from the leading men, for 'then I am not sure who will take part with him, and that I think dangerous. Therefore I can do nothing *while* [until] I get answer from you'.

She got an answer, but not the one she had hoped for. Surrey, who was playing for time, while he awaited a specific reply from London, told Margaret that he must follow Wolsey's latest order and destroy Jedburgh and little villages in its vicinity. He had postponed doing this for two months in response to her pleadings to spare them, but now Wolsey insisted that the order be carried out. Surrey advised that she should use this raid as a good opportunity to take the King from Stirling to Edinburgh where he would call on both lords and commons to support him. James could then demand that Surrey stop raiding, and in this case the Earl would certainly comply. The credit for restoring peace would, of course, accrue to the Queen and her son. Surrey continued to suggest that they could next call on their people to drive the French rascals into their favourite refuge, Dunbar Castle.

After Margaret and James had succeeded in these undertakings, Surrey would then 'be ready with men and money and give all the assistance that can be of reason desired'. But even the lavish flattery with which this advice was accompanied could scarcely hide the fact that neither the Earl nor Henry would be of much help until after the difficult job had been accomplished.

Margaret was most distressed to learn of the Earl's determination to destroy more border villages. Once more she begged him to attack the real centre of power, Edinburgh, instead. But Surrey considered this project too risky, and having been reprimanded already by Wolsey for his delays, he finally carried out the raid as ordered. On September 20th he burnt the town of Jedburgh. The famous abbey with its beautiful church was completely gutted. In his report to Wolsey, Surrey boasted that he had succeeded in having it blown up with barrels of gunpowder, in spite of the desperate efforts of its defenders to save it from destruction. How ironic that Surrey's destructive raid was ordered by the Cardinal, who was at that time the Pope's personal Lieutenant in England.

The monks and other refugees who crept back to survey the smoking debris in September 1523 did not know who had commanded this destruction. They simply cursed its immediate perpetrators: the Earl of Surrey and all the other hated English. Their curses were echoed by the lords in Edinburgh, whose attitude toward Henry VIII was hardly improved by this latest evidence of his brutality. His sister would have faced an undoubtedly overpowering task if she had tried to persuade them to ally with England at that point. But it was already too late. At the same time that Surrey was burning Jedburgh in the east, ships from France arrived in the west at Dumbarton, bringing with them the Duke of Albany.

CHAPTER 15

THE FICKLE QUEEN (1523–1524)

'She is right fickle ... therefore counsel the man ye know not to take on hand overmuch of her credence ...'. This statement has often been quoted by historians as a good summary of Queen Margaret's character. It is part of a letter sent in October 1523 to the Earl of Surrey by the Prioress of Coldstream. It could have come equally well from the pen of John Stuart, Duke of Albany. Few people had more cause than he to consider the Scottish Queen fickle. Throughout the entire period of their acquaintance, her relations with him had followed a zigzag course from open hostility to warm collaboration. Thus, in the autumn of 1523 he arrived just in time to foil her latest attempt to overthrow his governorship.

Margaret had felt quite secure from the Duke's retribution in this effort to subvert his authority during his absence. She was relying on Surrey's assurances that King Francis's continental problems would prevent him from subsidizing another expedition to support his allies in Scotland. Yet apparently Francis had decided not only to send Albany, but to arm him sufficiently to lead another attack against England. Thus the French King hoped to weaken his rival, Henry. Margaret was not only chagrined at the collapse of her ambitious schemes for her son and herself, but considerably alarmed. How would the Governor now treat one who had been so industriously plotting against him during his absence? She at once dispatched her trusty messenger, Patrick Sinclair, to beg Surrey to help her escape across the border.

Her proposed flight into England had already been mentioned numerous times in the correspondence between the Queen and the Earl. Before undertaking any schemes for overthrowing the rule of the Governor, Margaret had requested assurance that in the event of failure she could once more flee to her brother. Surrey had at once promised this, though in his letter to Wolsey on the subject he remarked that this would not be easy.

Now her moment of need had arrived. With anxious importunity, Margaret wrote to Surrey asking for assistance in her escape. She enquired whether he was certain that her brother would be 'her kind and loving Prince' in accepting her return? Since she had heard nothing at all on this subject from Henry himself, she was very anxious for reassurance on this point. How should she arrange for the transport of her belongings, for of course she could not carry anything but a few valuables with her in a hurried flight. How many servants would be permitted to cross into England with her? She would not let them remain behind to suffer possible punishment for having helped her.

The Earl replied that he could meet her on the border, and suggested she persuade George Douglas to accompany her. George might be induced to do this for the sake of his brother, her husband, as well as for a £100 bribe which Surrey authorized her to offer him. In the same letter the Earl warned her that she should make sure young James was safe, 'for the French can poison a man that he dies not for a year after'. Perhaps he was thus subtly reminding her that her son was her chief responsibility, hoping that her conscience would prevent her from leaving him. Actually the Queen had no fears for the safety of her boy, who, she was certain, would be as well treated physically as he always had been, whether she was there or not. She had never really believed the propaganda about the Duke's ruthless ambition. Albany was a gentleman, and the retribution she feared for herself was not execution or imprisonment, but further curtailment of her income and separation from her son. She would then have to live once more on the verge of penury and she longed to escape from this fate by returning to her brother's luxurious court. Although this would mean absence from James, it would be only a temporary separation — until Albany left again, or at most until the young King reached maturity. Meanwhile, even if she stayed in Scotland, she would probably be refused access to him anyway, as part of her punishment for resisting the authority of the Governor and plotting against him.

Surrey, however, was less than lukewarm over the prospect of having his King's sister to look after in the midst of his other problems. Earlier, in the hope that her plans might succeed, he had readily encouraged her by promising to help her escape if 'worse came to worst', but now that this emergency had arisen, he sought a way to avoid responsibility. Accordingly, on the very day he sent Margaret the above letter suggesting plans for escape, he also wrote to Wolsey: 'Considering that I see no profit should come of her being here, but great costs and charges . . . methinks . . . more good should come . . . to have her remain in Scotland than to come into England . . . And where £300 or £400 should please her well, being there, peradventure 1000 or 2000 marks should scarcely do so, being here . . .'.

Wolsey could not have agreed more heartily, except that he felt the Queen could survive even more cheaply in Scotland — on £100–200 a year at most. Also she might still be of some use to her brother if she stayed in Scotland, far more than she would be if she moved down to England.

Margaret had obviously now lost her chief value to these gentlemen and hence could expect far less in return for her pains. The Duke's arrival had ruined the possibility of her winning the Scots lords over to England. Nevertheless, she could still play a useful function to the English as an informer behind enemy lines. So Surrey began plying her with questions about the forces which Francis I had sent.

These were formidable, she replied, and consisted of about 80,000 men (probably an exaggerated number), with *barded* [armoured] horses, together with all kinds of artillery, including some 'cannon called *pavasies*, with scythes attached to the wheels'. There was no question about Albany's determination to fight this time. The English Commander had better be fully prepared, she wrote. Also, she continued, there was to be an attack elsewhere in England, to be led by Sir Richard de la Pole, the Yorkist pretender. He had found refuge, after escaping from Henry's clutches in England, at the court of Francis I, who was now equipping him for an attempt to regain the English throne for the White Rose, timed to coincide with Albany's invasion from the north. (This rumoured effort by de la Pole was never actually put into effect. Sir Richard was destined to die in battle in Italy, where he later accompanied the French forces fighting against Charles V.)

Although the Queen thus kept her brother's Commander as well informed as she could, she confessed that she could not discover the Duke's precise plans. He was 'doubtless trying to conceal these' from her. Doubtless he was! He had been told, of course, how she had worked against him during his absence — as a result of which he had already stopped her small French pension. However, he did not take the further measure which she had feared: that of keeping her in close confinement at Stirling. Wolsey, to whom Surrey sent Margaret's secret messages, was more apprehensive of actual danger to the Queen than she was herself. He personally wrote a marginal note on one of her confidential letters that, 'she had need beware what she writeth and speaketh and to whom; for one such letter as this is, intercepted might be her final destruction'.

Nevertheless, the Duke was not the ogre Wolsey liked to depict. He also knew that Margaret was not the only one reporting to the English. Many of the Scottish nobles were in Lord Dacre's or Surrey's pay, as well as numerous spies of less exalted rank. Hence, instead of arresting suspected individuals, the Governor simply had them watched, and took care that no Scots at all had access to his own plans.

Therefore Margaret had to admit that the Duke was not troubling her now. Yet she dreaded his anger after he returned from the coming battle. She knew he had a terrible temper which might easily explode against a royal spy. Surrey himself had heard from others of the Duke's hot temper. In a letter to Wolsey, he wrote that when Albany was thwarted, he would 'take his bonnet suddenly off his head and . . . throw it in the fire and no man dare take it out, but let it be burnt'. In this fashion Albany had incinerated a dozen bonnets the last time he was in Scotland. At the moment, however, Albany felt fully confident of success. The Queen wrote to the English Commander that, although neither she nor anyone else knew where the Governor would attack, he was prepared to do so on either the east or the west — hence Surrey had best be ready in both areas: 'If England ever made them strong against Scotland make them now right strong, and therefore I warn you look upon your weal and honours, for you will be sharply essayed . . .'. The Earl did his best to 'look upon his weal and honours', and, as he informed Wolsey, strengthened the northern fortifications, especially Berwick and the nearby castle of Wark. It was fortunate for him that he did so, for it was at Wark that the crucial test of strength occurred.

Before leaving the capital, the Duke roused the Scots to a pitch of martial enthusiasm by a great oration. Then, hoping to force a battle before the ardour of his followers had cooled, and upon ground of his own choosing, he sent a challenge to Surrey to meet him at once. The Earl recalled Flodden, when he and his father had tried to encourage James IV to fight at a time and place that would benefit them. Hence the English Commander now refused to cross into Scotland or to move his forces from their vantage point. The miserable weather, wet and cold, was freezing the blood of both Scot and Englishman, but Albany sent his French legions forward to capture Wark Castle. As Margaret had told the Earl, the Duke would always place his French 'in the vanguard because he giveth not great trust to ye Scotysmen'. His scepticism proved justified. When the French were driven back in need of reinforcements, the Duke called on the Scots to cross over and join in the the attack. The drenching rain had apparently dampened the enthusiasm engendered by his rally in Edinburgh, in which he had stirred them with a call to 'remember Flodden and avenge their dead fathers slain there'. They did indeed now remember Flodden — only too well. Should they, like their dead fathers, now venture into England all for the benefit of France? No! The leaders refused to order their men across the river into the enemy territory.

The Governor tried to encourage his followers with another

harangue. Since this had to be translated from French into Scots, it may have lacked zest. In any event, it failed to budge them. Stunned by their adamant refusal, their Commander had no choice but to retreat. When they reached Teviotdale, a group of lords came up to Albany demanding that he continue the campaign. In a fury of disgust, the Governor burst out, 'I will give him no battle, for I have no convenient company to do so'! Tearing his bonnet from his head, he flung it into the mud (there being no fire handy to pitch it into!).

It was just as well for the Duke that he did not realize the full extent of his lost opportunity. Surrey confessed to Wolsey afterwards that at the time of battle his troops were so poorly paid and underfed he could not have held them together much longer and must soon have abandoned Wark.

When Albany returned to Edinburgh, Margaret was at Stirling, where she had withdrawn to at the time of the invasion of England. She was determined to remain there with her son, from whom she felt sure she would soon be separated by the vengeful Duke. Her fears proved right and this was the first decision taken when Parliament met on November 18th. Not only was she to leave James's side, but his attendants were now changed to noblemen whom she knew to be her enemies. She was particularly alarmed by the inclusion of Lord Fleming among this group of guardians. He had a sinister reputation, for it was rumoured that he had been the one responsible for the murder of his wife and her two sisters. A man of whom such a crime was even suspected was certainly not fit to act as guardian of the King. Moreover, Fleming's sister had recently become the mistress of the Duke of Albany. Fleming, her brother, might therefore be tempted to advance his own family by making Albany himself King. The Duke was, after all, next in line to the throne after young James.

Margaret was not one to keep such fears to herself. She at once voiced her strenuous opposition to the new arrangement before the lords of the Council. She emphasized her 'great cause of dread and of suspicion toward his [James's] person, seeing them that loves him best ... be put from him, and others put to him that is suspicious'. Furthermore, she assured them, 'I *will* let all Christian Princes wit that I am in great fear and dread touching his person'.

Her boldness and determination at this time were admirable, for she was completely alone in opposition to the Governor. Those members of the Council who secretly symphathized with her were afraid to support her against him. She also confronted Albany in person when three weeks later he came with the principal nobles to Stirling to visit the King. She stated her complete rejection of the new arrangement both to Albany and to the Council that met there.

What crime had she committed, she asked them, to be thus separated from her son? They told her that none of the new atttendants would agree to be guardians of the boy as long as she was with him, for they knew she could influence young James to do anything she wished. She might, they feared, even take him to England.

She retorted that James's previous guardians had not objected to her presence with him and it was extremely suspicious for the newly chosen ones to prevent his mother from being with him. She stuck to her position, refusing to yield to either the Council or the Duke, until she was told that he had sent for 800 French troops to take the King from her castle by force. She then promised to accept their decree. Immediately afterwards, however, she called some of her faithful attendants to witness her signature on a declaration stating that she had been forced by threats to make this promise to the Council, which she therefore now formally revoked.

In addition to being separated from her son, the Queen was suffering from poverty. She called on the Council to pay her income according to the previous agreement, but they said the attacks by her brother's armies on the Borders had eliminated all possibility of collecting rents from these devastated areas. They also refused her request to let her coin her gold and silver plate into money. Her pleas to Surrey and the narration of these woes finally resulted in a gift of 200 angel nobles. This was worth about £100 Scots and even less in English money. Surrey was correct in estimating that the Queen could survive on a very small stipend in Scotland. Was this to be her reward for all the efforts she had made to arrange the Anglo-Scottish alliance? She was almost tempted to accept the offer made by the Duke of a pension of 5,000 crowns from France, in return for her firm agreement to maintain the 'Auld Alliance'.

She wrote to Surrey that had it not been for his money, she would have been forced by necessity to yield to French pressure. Why did she hear nothing from Henry in response to her many anxious pleas? Was he going to desert her, now that she was apparently helpless and he could no longer expect her influence to be of value to him? Margaret began to suspect that Lord Dacre was again tampering with her mail and withholding her brother's letters from her. Dacre had again been appointed Warden of the North, since Surrey had requested to be relieved of this unpleasant duty now that the Franco-Scottish invasion scare was over. He recommended Dacre to be his successor as the most obvious candidate for the post, even though he had many unfortunate characteristics. He was an excellent fighter, said the Earl, but a very poor disciplinarian and apt to be insubordinate himself. All the thieves whom Surrey had

driven from the area would be back before the new Warden had
been in charge a month, Surrey added, but Dacre did know the
country and was sufficiently ruthless to scourge the Scots whenever
necessary.

Hence once again Margaret's old adversary was in charge of her
mail. As she suspected, he did tamper with it, but not in the case of
letters from Henry. The King simply did not bother to write to her.
Her constant complaints bored him, and besides, he was very busy
these days with really serious affairs, a matter of religion. Outraged
by the attack recently made upon Catholicism by a presumptuous
German friar, Henry had felt called upon to defend his 'Mother',
the Church, 'the spouse of Christ'. In order to counter Luther's
heresy, the English monarch had taken up his pen to produce *The
Defence of the Seven Sacraments*. Pope Leo X was so deeply impressed by this magnificent opus that he immediately named its
author, *Fidei Defensor*. That the faith of which Henry was thus
declared to be 'Defender' changed, in a dozen years, from the
Church of Rome to the Church of England was an irony which no
óne in 1521 could have appreciated.

Henry's new title impressed no one more than the ruler to whom
it was given. For some time he became immersed as much in
intellectual affairs, as in military projects or court festivities.
Luther, that 'member of the Devil', responded to *The Defence of the
Seven Sacraments* with a blast of his own pen, in determination to
'bespatter his English majesty with his own mud and his own filth
. . .'. Obviously the verbal war was becoming intense. Henry did not
personally stoop to retaliate to this diatribe, but he asked Sir
Thomas More to do so, using the pseudonym, William Rosse. To
the chagrin of admirers of the man who was later beatified, the
invective he employed in his reply to Luther is as coarse as any used
by the Saxon friar. Both of these learned writers show in their
exchange a remarkable proficiency with four-letter words (or their
Latin equivalents).

While More was thus engaged, he and the King held many
lengthy conversations on the subject and on other topics from
religion to politics and diplomacy. Sir Thomas was, in the 1520s,
the King's most cherished confidant. With such intellectual
business to occupy him, how could Henry find time to reply to his
sister's constant demands? He left that duty to Wolsey, or
sometimes to the Earl of Surrey. Surrey did an excellent job
composing letters in the King's name to the Queen of Scots. More
read aloud to Henry a whole sheaf of the correspondence between
the Earl and Margaret. He afterwards told Wolsey that the King
and himself considered one of the letters that Surrey had written in

his ruler's name to the Queen of Scots, 'one of the best made letters, for words, matter, sentence and couching that ever I read in my life'. If only one of its qualities could have been sincerity, what a difference this would have made to its recipient!

The Scottish Queen, receiving only second-hand answers from her brother, began to realize that once again she would have to accommodate herself with the Duke. At his behest, she began to write new requests for a truce, and included the old stumbling-block, the comprehension of France. After all, she reasoned, it surely would not injure her son's kingdom if its 'auld ally' were also at peace with England.

The Governor was desperately anxious for a truce so that King Francis would permit him to return to France. His wife was grievously ill and, after his humiliation at Wark Castle, he wanted no more of Scotland. Finally, in the spring of 1524, a truce was arranged between the English government and the Duke, without the specific inclusion of France. Margaret was deeply hurt to find out about this agreement only after it had been settled, without having had any part in the negotiations. She wrote to Surrey expressing her bitterness. She hoped he would remind her brother, she said, that her living conditions in Scotland depended entirely on the goodwill of the nobles there. They would have no respect for her unless they believed her welfare to be essential to their own interests. If King Henry gave them advantageous terms in spite of their scornful treatment of his sister, they would pay even less attention to her needs than they already were doing. If, therefore, Henry and Wolsey persisted in ignoring her, she would be forced either to endure poverty and separation from her son as her permanent lot in life, or else she would have to make herself agreeable to the French party. King Francis had offered her a good pension, but she had refused it — so far.

Instead of apologies and additional funds from England, she next received word of a truly dreadful possibility: the return of her hated husband who was heading towards Calais. She heard that King Henry had actually invited him to come to England and planned for Angus to return to Scotland to assume leadership of the anti-French element there. This was the final straw! Margaret had endured her brother's neglect; she had accepted his tacit reneging on earlier promises to receive her back into England; she had suffered the humiliation of being ignored by both parties in the recent peace negotiations. All these slights had not been borne without complaint. Her objection to all these injuries had been registered many times, but with no effect. She had begged for help, she had described over and again her pitiable plight until the tale had grown threadbare. She had even hinted in several recent messages that English neglect might at last force her to turn to the enemy. The rumour of Angus's return was the final threat to her peace of mind and indeed proved to be the turning point. She must show by deeds that she really meant what she said.

An opportunity arose at this very time. The Duke brought her a new offer of a very generous pension from King Francis, if she would promise to support the 'Auld Alliance' and agree to her son's marriage to a French Princess. Also, in case Angus were sent back to Scotland by King Henry, she was offered a haven in France, with a suitable residence and liberal income, until the time of her son's majority. Then she could of course return to Scotland under King James's protection. It was a tempting proposition. Ordinarily she would have at once rejected anything which so smacked of a betrayal of English interests, but she was ready to do almost anything to prevent Angus's return.

She considered the proposal in all its details. First, would it do anything to injure her son? The 'Auld Alliance' now depended on the lords, irrespective of her support, and the marriage to a French Princess was so far in the future that it might never materialize. She had hoped James might marry her little niece Mary Tudor, yet she had discovered that Mary was actually to become the bride of Emperor Charles V, and had already been formally betrothed to him at the very time the English King of Arms had offered her hand to the young King of Scots. Not very straightforward of them! Well, Wolsey and her brother should discover that she also could shift her support. They had better not push her too far — and certainly bringing Angus back to Scotland was too far.

Margaret sent her confidential messenger with several letters to her brother and the Cardinal. She also gave this servant, in strict confidence, a copy of the new bond with Albany, with instructions to find out in London what plans were actually afoot concerning Angus. If it was true that King Henry planned to bring him back into Scotland, then the messenger was to show the copy of the bond as proof of the lengths to which the Queen was prepared to go to prevent this. If he was certain the rumoured return of Angus was false, he should simply return the paper to her without showing it to anyone. Unfortunately, before her messenger could get across the border into England, he was stopped by Lord Dacre, who seized all his dispatches from the Scottish Queen and perused them. He sealed the bond with a signet of Margaret's in his possession, and forwarded it to London as a regular part of her mail to the court there.

Amazed and puzzled by this document, Wolsey demanded an

explanation. Lord Dacre wrote to Margaret, denouncing her betrayal of her brother's interests in such vehement language that the Queen impetuously denied any part in the bond. She had absolutely refused to sign it, she declared, and had sent it to her brother just to let him see how the Duke was trying to win her support for France. Though the Warden remained unconvinced, Wolsey and Henry did not this time blame her, feeling that if she had signed the bond it had been under duress.

Meanwhile, with a truce finally established, the Governor at last received permission from King Francis and the Scottish nobles to return to France. Albany promised to come back to Scotland in three months, but this date was destined to be postponed indefinitely. In fact, when he boarded ship on May 31st 1524 he was leaving the country permanently. In view of the frustrations which he had endured throughout his tenure as Governor, his joy on leaving this thankless job can well be imagined. If it was true that he had thrown a dozen bonnets into the fire on his previous visit to Scotland, he must have incinerated still more during this last tour of duty. The Queen was responsible for a large portion of these burned hats. The Duke had ample cause to agree emphatically with those who decribed Margaret as 'right fickle'. Yet she was by no means alone in possessing this characteristic. There were the nobles, who accepted pensions from both France and England, coolly betraying their own native land with hardly a thought when this appeared profitable.

There are innumerable instances of specific examples of fickleness. There was the Prioress of Coldstream herself, who also branded Margaret as 'right fickle'. The Queen felt immense gratitude to this nun because it was in her abbey that she had found shelter during her flight from the Duke in 1515. Therefore, when Surrey began raiding the border in 1523, Margaret's first message to him was a plea to spare 'a poor abbey of sisters, called Coldstream'. She repeated this intercession in several letters to the Earl and his subordinates. They readily promised to grant this request — and with good reason. This pious Scotswoman was the best spy the English had in Scotland. On ostensibly religious errands, she made many a journey to Edinburgh or Glasgow, from which she sent Dacre or Surrey detailed information concerning Scottish military plans. She included private gossip about the leaders, including the Queen, and told Surrey exactly how Margaret was behaving — or alleged to be behaving — with regard to the Governor and other notables. Margaret trusted her implicitly and personally employed her to send her confidential reports. When finally she discovered the nun's double-dealing, she angrily urged Surrey to burn her priory, unless the mended her ways.

But the Prioress was only one of the many whom the Queen could justly accuse of faithlessness to her. Surrey, as already proved by his letters to Wolsey, had little real intention of keeping his promises to help Margaret to escape into England. Likewise, Wolsey, who had originally ordered the Earl to assure the Queen that she would be welcomed into England, had reneged on the actual performance of this invitation, comfortably agreeing with Surrey that it would be far cheaper to maintain the King's sister in Edinburgh than in London. His reluctance to spend the money necessary to bring her to England and maintain her there of course showed his prudence in budgeting for the King's expenditures. The great fortune left to Henry by his father had long since been spent, and even his far-flung estates and other sources of royal income were barely sufficient for the ordinary expenses of his lavish court. Consequently, in preparation for the outbreak of war, Parliament had had to be called but had proved averse to raising £800,000 through taxation; this being the amount that Wolsey had estimated war would cost. England, he felt, simply must do its part in this conflict in order to keep the promises made to its ally, Emperor Charles. For his sake, as well as for their own prestige, King and Cardinal had to send a well-equipped army into France and then continue adding supplies when these were urgently requested. The Emperor must be satisfied, not only because he was now Princess Mary's fiancé, but also to keep him true to his secret pledge to Wolsey.

Charles had promised to use his tremendous influence with the Vatican to assure the election of the English Cardinal to the papacy as soon as that exalted throne became vacant. Yet, despite all of England's support to the Emperor in this war, the death of Pope Leo X in 1521 was followed by the election, not of the English contestant, but of a Dutchman, Adrian VI. Wolsey consoled himself for this disappointment by the reflection that the new Pope was elderly and ailing, Sure enough, Adrian VI·expired in September 1523. At once Wolsey redoubled his efforts to win the great prize, promising unlimited gold from his monarch's treasury to bribe crucial members of the Sacred College. But he depended chiefly on his personal sponsor, the Emperor, whom he urgently reminded of his promise.

Charles responded by sending Wolsey a copy of the letter he had written to the College of Cardinals on his behalf. It was a magnificent letter of recommendation, and should certainly have had the desired result, except that it arrived in Rome well after the election. The courier carrying it to the Vatican had been detained in

Barcelona, on express secret orders from the Emperor himself. As a result, the new Pope was Giulio de'Medici (henceforth known as Clement VII) who had actually been Charles's real choice all along. Although proof of this duplicity was of course not then available, Wolsey was certain that he had been tricked, and from that moment lost all enthusiasm for the alliance with the Empire. The English troops, then apparently on the road to victory in France, suddenly retreated, to the shocked dismay of their imperial allies. When subsequently England declared itself unable to help the Emperor with the supplies needed for his continued fighting in central Europe, Charles concluded that this alliance was not of much use to him.

Since Charles could no longer benefit from the 1522 agreement with King Henry, he began reconsidering his planned marriage to Princess Mary Tudor. Early in 1524, he decided (because of 'his Cortes' insistence' and not of course for personal reasons) to wed a Portuguese Princess, with a larger dowry and better dynastic prospects within the Iberian Peninsula. Although the excuses for thus jilting his eight-year-old English fiancée were made in plausible diplomatic language, the basic reasons were obvious.

The above instances are only a few examples of the faithlessness exhibited by world leaders of the Renaissance period, and more can be found throughout the pages of diplomatic correspondence. For, even before the dissemination throughout Europe of Machiavelli's most famous book, its cynical advice was widely practised by Princes and potentates of all ranks. Queen Margaret of Scotland may indeed have been 'right fickle', but she lived in treacherous times and dealt with other fickle individuals.

CHAPTER 16

THE DANGEROUS AGE
(1524–1525)

By 1525 both Henry VIII and his sister Margaret were entering the dangerous age. In the sixteenth century, with an average life-span of thirty years, fifty was old, and sixty truly ancient. The traditionally dangerous feature of middle years is a heightened susceptibility to the charms of the opposite sex, an attraction which in some cases overrides all other considerations. Extremely erratic behaviour may then change the whole tenor of life of the individual thus affected. In the case of a monarch, the results can be truly cataclysmic. During his dangerous age, King Henry turned his kingdom upside down; Queen Margaret, during a similar period, influenced her realm less drastically, though her own career was severely damaged.

For both brother and sister, the dangerous tendency was aggravated by unsatisfactory previous marriages. Henry's dissatisfaction resulted from Catherine's inability to produce a healthy male heir; Margaret's love was turned to loathing by Angus's infidelity and seizure of her property. Both Tudors sought the remedy of divorce. In his pursuit of this objective Henry eventually was to sever connections with the Roman Church he had previously 'protected', to make enemies of former continental allies, and to execute old friends and numerous lesser impediments to his will. In her drive for the same objective Margaret was to neglect her straightforward goals of gaining control over Scotland and establishing a lasting alliance between it and England. She incurred her brother's wrath, damaged her reputation at home and abroad, and even risked alienating the one she loved most, her son.

Of course, in both cases, there was a specific spark that set off the train of explosive developments. For Henry it was the black-eyed temptress Anne Boleyn; for his sister it was a young gallant named Harry Stewart. In 1526 Henry began courting Anne, the younger sister of his discarded mistress, Mary; in 1524 Harry Stewart was made head carver in the household of King James V. This youth was of little importance, being simply referred to as Lord Avondale's younger brother. But he had attributes other than powerful family connections: a handsome face, a good physique and agreeable manners. Above all, he knew how to please a woman, and

Margaret, deprived of a close relationship with any man for six years, was now extremely ready to be pleased. At the age of thirty-four she had lost her youthful prettiness; her once pink and white complexion was scarred by smallpox; her short figure had become stout and matronly. She resolutely ignored these flaws; no Tudor ever admitted inferiority of any sort. However, she was more than ever vulnerable to flattery, and when a virile young man eyed her with apparent admiration or complimented her on a becoming gown, she flushed with pleasure. Obviously this young gentleman had good taste and breeding. Surely he deserved a more important position than head carver in the King's household. Soon the court was buzzing with rumours of an affair between the Queen and Lord Avondale's brother.

It was most unfortunate that Henry VIII chose this time to try to restore Margaret's former husband into her good graces. She was not likely to agree to this reconciliation under any circumstances, but certainly her new infatuation increased her determination to break all bonds with her long-hated spouse. She was, according to Edinburgh gossip, already living on terms of unseemly intimacy with the attractive courtier. Nevertheless, like her brother in his later amours, she wished to sanctify this relationship by matrimony, and was now redoubling her efforts to attain the divorce which she had so long been seeking.

She was, therefore, furious when she learned that the rumour which had so upset her a few months previously was true. Her brother had indeed invited Angus to come from France to London, and planned to send him back to Scotland. Why King Henry persisted in this course despite his sister's vehement rejection of any reunion with Angus is difficult to understand. Apparently, the King agreed with Dacre and Wolsey that a mere woman should not be entrusted with such important matters as establishing the new Anglo-Scottish alliance which they were now hoping for. As Wolsey expressed it: 'Albeit the King and I think good that the Queen of Scots is to be used as . . . convenient instrument in this matter . . . it is no folly for a good archer to have two strings to his bow, specially whereas one is made of threads wrought by woman's fingers!'

But by choosing Margaret's hated husband as the other string to their bow, they actually complicated the entire process so much so that it ruined all chances of success. In fact, the return of Angus, and the consequent struggle for power between him and his wife, was to postpone a genuine alliance between Scotland and England for more than an entire generation.

In the early stages there were hopeful indications that this

James V as a boy
Artist unknown

(*Scottish National Portrait Gallery*)

alliance might work out successfully. At the Queen's earnest solicitation, the Douglas Earl was kept in England for the time being, and she alone was permitted to manage the first important step in the new plan to establish young James as King, a project initiated soon after the Duke of Albany left the country. The Queen met with a number of important noblemen who were in favour of England, or at least susceptible to English bribes. Prominent among these was the Earl of Arran, who desired greater power than he had enjoyed under the French Governor. Their effort to win the Chancellor, James Beaton, Archbishop of St. Andrews, to their side was a failure. He would not break the oath he had taken to support the late Governor. Nevertheless, a sufficient number of lords were willing to join, especially after they were provided with the generous pensions now arriving from England. King Henry evidently realized that this time he should give his sister all the support she demanded — and she demanded plenty! Money was sent to her, to her son and to Arran. A guard of two hundred picked fighters was provided to ensure the safety of the young King — all to be salaried by the English King. Margaret felt that the Earl of Arran should be honoured for his part in the affair with the Order of the Garter, and that his son should be given a lucrative English benefice. Winning Scotland for an ally would not be cheap, but, as she reminded her brother, these expenses were less exorbitant than the alternative of financing continued warfare.

With the help of his new English guard and several Scottish officials, young James successfully broke away from his French custodians at Stirling Castle on July 26th 1524. Asserting his determination to assume the powers of monarch at once, he rode with his mother to Edinburgh. The people thronged to greet him, happy to have their own ruler in their midst again. How like his father he was, they exclaimed! Smiling, debonair, already at the age of twelve he looked every inch a King. Away with the hated French! Scotland had its own monarch once more.

The fact that their monarch was now surrounded by an English guard, and that by his side was his English mother was overlooked for the time being. With her, he at once established residence in Holyrood Palace. Here, within a few days, each of the leading nobles was summoned to the presence chamber. Beginning with the Chancellor, every lord in turn was commanded to sign a bond revoking all previous oaths to Albany and instead swearing obedience to his own King. By the clever device of calling on each individual separately to sign this pledge, Margaret prevented disaffected nobles from uniting to overthrow the new regime. Chancellor Beaton, it is true, a little later reneged on his promise to desert the 'Auld Alliance', as did also the Bishop of Aberdeen. Both were temporarily imprisoned for this refusal, a punishment which proved for a time effectual in stopping the majority of the nobles from following their example of defiance to the Queen Regent. Triumphantly, Margaret sent her brother a copy of the bond signed by the leading magnates, along with a letter from his nephew expressing deep gratitude for all the assistance he had received in executing the recent *coup*.

Margaret also wrote personally to thank the English King and his officials for their co-operation. She did not neglect this opportunity to remind them that it was she who had engineered the entire revolution, successfully replacing the previous French government in Scotland with one now pro-English. She wrote to the former Earl of Surrey, now known since his father's death as the Duke of Norfolk. He had again been sent to assume supervision of the Anglo-Scottish borders; and hence was once again favoured with many epistles from the Scottish Queen.

'And now, my lord', she wrote, 'his grace and you may see perfectly what I and my partakers hath done, for the weal of the King my son and for the pleasure of the King's grace my brother; wherein methinks there is both great thanks and reward to be given to them . . . and in special to my lord of Arran . . . Wherefore, my lord, I pray you heartily to remember and inform the King's grace my brother that this is a great act that I and my partakers hath done!' Margaret was never burdened by over-modesty! And although she gave full credit to Arran and her other 'partakers', it was obvious who was now the true power behind the throne of young James V. She personally presided over the Council meetings, signed all state documents, and appointed the officials who were to serve in her son's government.

Unfortunately, her choice of these officials was more often dictated by personal preference than by their ability or other qualifications, and her rapid elevation of her particular favourite caused great dissatisfaction. Harry Stewart was made Lieutenant of the King's bodyguard in place of Patrick Sinclair, who had long been her most trusted messenger and confidant. A short while later, young Stewart also acquired the position of Treasurer to the Queen's household. His rapid advancement at court had the predictable effect of rendering him odious to the other courtiers, who felt far better qualified for such honours than this brash upstart. His influence was shown not only by his acquisition of titles, but by the way in which the Queen seemed to follow his advice in preference to that of older and abler counsellors. The only member of the established nobility to whom she listened was Arran, and his arbitrary temperament made him increasingly unpopular as he too maintained his controlling voice in affairs.

Her preference for Arran was due in part to the assistance he had given her in executing the *coup* of July 24th, and in part to the fact that he apparently shared her deep antipathy for the Earl of Angus, who had killed his brother, Lord Patrick Hamilton, in 1520.

The Douglas Earl himself had meanwhile hurried to the north of England, impatient to return to his own lands and achieve the restoration of his former powers there. After King Henry's promises to help him to attain these ends, as well as to make him England's chief representative in Scotland's affairs, the Earl became extremely resentful when he found himself halted on the very threshold of his native land. Lord Dacre and the Duke of Norfolk had been warned by Wolsey to stop the Earl at Newcastle and then later to send him back to London again. There he must stay until some means could be found to make his return acceptable to his wife. She had been so enraged to learn of her brother's attempt to bring Angus back, that she had threatened to shift her own support and that of her son, whom she completely influenced, back to the Duke of Albany, rather than to complete the plans being made to establish an alliance with England. Albany had been on the point of returning as scheduled from France to Scotland when he learned of the revolution that had overthrown his authority there. King Francis was too deeply enmeshed with problems on the continent to give him any help at this time. Hence, the Duke remained in France, but was soon making lucrative offers to all Scottish leading nobles, hoping to lure back to the 'Auld Alliance' those who were disenchanted with the new regime. Margaret was not the only one who took advantage of this French threat to try to force her wishes upon the English officials.

Angus, increasingly provoked by being detained in London, was ready to seek any means to return to his country. There he intended to regain his estates and establish control of the government. He would do this if possible by re-establishing his conjugal rights over his wife and asserting his powers as her husband and as brother-in-law to the English monarch. If this effort failed, he would try other measures. Finally, if Henry would not fulfil his promise of helping him, he would go to France and offer to lead the pro-French forces against his estranged wife.

Thus, beset by orders and counter-orders from King Henry, and threatened by the defection to the enemy of first the Queen, and then the Earl of Angus, the threesome of Wolsey, Dacre and the Duke of Norfolk found themselves in a dilemma. Dacre, still loyal to his old friend and relative, tried to restore Angus to his desired powers. First, he planned a new *coup* in which Angus should join with Archbishop Beaton, the erstwhile Chancellor, in overthrowing the regency of Queen Margaret and replacing it with one headed by themselves. Wolsey quickly vetoed this suggestion. The Warden next made use of his underground connections across the border to spread rumours against Margaret in order to stir up more dissatisfaction with her government. She learned of this slander through her own spies, and complained bitterly to the Duke of Norfolk 'of my Lord Dacre, that does and says to my hurt; for he says to Scotch folk, that he marvels that they will let any woman have authority and specially of me . . .'. The Duke of Norfolk, suffering once again in his role as chief recipient of the Queen's complaints, applied to Wolsey for a reassignment to some post well removed from this unpleasant border area — in vain.

Instead, Henry VIII next dispatched two envoys to Edinburgh, to try to arrange an accommodation with the new government there, and to report directly to London on conditions in that troubled country. The representatives selected were Archdeacon Thomas Magnus and Roger Radcliff, a courtier of King Henry's own privy chamber. Both gentlemen were skilled in diplomacy, a quality which they were to need in no small measure for this assignment. They arrived in the northern capital on October 29th 1524, and were admitted into Holyrood Palace a few days later. Here they found King James and his mother surrounded by their court. Margaret had carefully stage-managed their reception in order to impress these ambassadors with the magnificence of her newly established regime. The letters presented by the diplomats from Henry to his sister and his nephew were graciously received, as were the gifts sent from London: a jewelled sword for the boy, and a coat of cloth of gold, which he wore all afternoon, expressing much gratitude to his generous uncle. Margaret was equally pleased with a length of cloth of gold, 'right rich' in texture.

The emissaries next delivered the messages from England, particularly a request for ambassadors to be sent at once to arrange for a permanent peace between the two nations, in place of the existing three-month truce. This pacification, it was hoped, would result in a lasting alliance between England and Scotland. In order to seal this union, Magnus told Margaret confidentially, her brother had secretly determined to break off the engagement of his daughter Mary to the Holy Roman Emperor, and instead to bestow her hand upon her cousin, the King of Scots. This honour delighted the Queen, whose dearest wish, she declared, was for a permanent alliance between her native land and her son's kingdom.

This happy scene was interrupted by a knock at the door. The

Queen was told a messenger had come with important news for her. She stepped outside to receive this message, and to her incredulous dismay learned that the Earl of Angus had just entered Scotland. When Margaret returned to the room with a face like a thunder cloud, Magnus and Radcliff quickly ascertained the reason for her change. They tried to mollify her with a carefully tactful explanation: her brother had felt obliged to permit the Earl to re-enter his own country, because he had really no legal grounds to hold him in England. Moreover, Henry had simply given him permission to cross the border. Everything else — his reception and treatment in Edinburgh — would depend entirely upon the Queen. The 'Earl of Anguisshe' — as Magnus always spelled this name — had promised to give her his complete obedience, and to expect no favours from her. Above all, he was to demand no part in the government, for he was certainly not to supersede her as the person responsible for the handling of England's affairs in Scotland.

This explanation was not true to fact. Henry and Wolsey had, indeed, sent Angus back with the promise of allowing him to take over the leadership of affairs in Scotland before Margaret could ruin the chances of peace by her arbitrary government. Wolsey's sources of information in the North had told him that the Queen's regime was causing intense dissatisfaction among nobles and commons alike. Since most of this information had originated with George Douglas and others of the same faction, it was not entirely reliable. Nevertheless, it was true that the Queen's favouring of Arran and Stewart had seriously displeased the other nobles, whereas the population as a whole were unhappy because she had been unable to establish the justice and tranquillity that had characterized Albany's stronger leadership.

The Queen accepted the envoys' explanation of her brother's action with apparent graciousness, and even agreed to seek a way to establish a better relationship between her estranged husband and the Earl of Arran. Feeling that they had succeeded in restoring her good humour, Magnus and Radcliff then retired. The next day they revisited the palace to present some horses to young James, sent him by his royal uncle. To their bewilderment, they found Margaret's attitude had become disdainful. She would now seek new friends, she told them, who would not try to force upon her the company of her unfaithful spouse. On other subjects she appeared reasonable, but on this topic she remained adamant.

They suspected that Harry Stewart, with whom they heard she had spent the night, had influenced her to take this belligerent attitude. Whether the favourite really urged her to adopt this haughty behaviour, or whether it was simply that he agreed with her in her anger against her brother's support of her husband, is hard to determine. In the light of later developments, Stewart appears to have been generally weak and amiable, rather than arrogant. Hence, it is probable that he simply acted as a sympathetic sounding-board for Margaret's complaints. His support of her righteous indignation doubtless bolstered her in her determination to take a stronger stand.

In any event, she stood immovable against all suggestions that she might relent against Angus. His letters to her begging forgiveness for 'anything wherein he might have offended her' were returned without answer. He was forbidden to ride with more than forty men in his entourage, or to 'approach within certain limits of the court'. Since reconciliation between Angus and the Queen appeared impossible to arrange, Magnus and Radcliff at least tried to help the Douglas Earl to end his old feud with the Earl of Arran. Their efforts to do so were also frustrated by what they felt certain were the machinations of the Queen.

The Duke of Norfolk urged Archdeacon Magnus to act in his capacity as priest by 'giving her Grace some wholesome counsel, for her honour in this world, and for the wealth of her soul'. He should remonstrate with her for spurning her wedded spouse and openly consorting with another man. Magnus's efforts to cleanse her immortal soul of these sins brought little appreciation from this 'lost sheep'. She began hinting strongly that, since he and his companion had delivered her brother's messages to her court, they might as well now go home. As Magnus sadly reported to Wolsey, she made it quite clear that 'she would full fain we were both again in England'. While refusing to leave till their mission was more nearly accomplished, however, they tactfully stayed out of court for the time being.

Meanwhile Parliament opened in the Tolbooth on November 14th 1524. Everything went smoothly for the Queen. The Duke of Albany's governship was declared at an end and Queen Margaret's regency was confirmed. In accordance with her wishes, ambassadors were chosen to go to London at once and to arrange for the long-term peace agreement and possible alliance with England. She thus carried out her brother's requests. On the other hand, the Douglases were accused of having broken Scottish law by leaving France and going to England without their ruler's permission. As a result, their actions were to be further restricted.

Angered by these proclamations, Angus, helped by the Earl of Lennox and the Laird of Buccleuch, determined on revenge. Slipping over the city walls before dawn on November 23rd, they opened the gates to their men, four hundred of whom entered the town and marched boldly to St. Giles' Church. Here the leaders proclaimed their right to take part in Parliament and denounced the legislation just passed against them.

Aroused from her sleep by tidings of this invasion, the Queen dispatched a messenger to the castle, commanding the gunners to fire the five brass cannon there upon the invaders. Simultaneously, she herself prepared to defend Holyrood. Magnus and Radcliff, likewise awakened by the clamour, went out into the street. Here they were met by the Bishop of Aberdeen and the Abbot of Cambuskenneth, who begged them to go with them to dissuade the Queen from having her cannon fired upon the town. Arriving at the gates of Holyrood, they found four or five hundred men, preparing to defend the palace by placing 'afore the outer gates such small guns as they had'. Margaret herself was bustling about giving directions. She paid scant regard to the pleas of the clergymen and ordered the two Englishmen 'right roundly to depart home to their lodging and not meddle with Scottish matters'.

While she was talking, a loud boom was heard from the direction of the castle, followed by the sound of shrieks and yells. Word came that the castle gunners had followed their orders, but had hit, not the Earl of Angus or his men, but 'two merchant men, a priest, and a woman'. (Apparently the aim of the Scottish artillery had not improved since Flodden.) This tragedy convinced the Queen that a general bombardment of the town would do more harm than good. She sent a message to the castle to cease firing, and the day passed without further casualties.

Finally, at four in the afternoon the Earl and his men, finding insufficient support for their plans, obeyed the King's command to leave. They marched out of the city and withdrew to Tantallon. Margaret and James then rode up from Holyrood to the castle on the hilltop. By the light of flaring torches, they entered through the great stone gates and had the portcullis lowered. Here they would be more secure than in the less fortified palace below.

The Queen now wrote to inform her brother that, as she had foreseen, the Earl of Angus was creating great problems. She hoped Henry would 'not assist any Scottish subject, except at the King of Scots' desire'. She emphasized her own success in managing affairs by reporting that ambassadors were being sent at once to treat with the English King for peace and she hoped its permanence could be assured by a marriage between his daughter and her son.

Angus sent his own version of affairs to Wolsey and to Henry, complaining that his 'humble' efforts at reconciliation were met with scorn by his shrewish wife. 'I have made my offers to ye Queen, as your Grace commanded me, in my most lowly manner ... but she will on no wise hear of no concord, but seeks all ways she can for my utter destruction'. He trusted Henry would keep his promise 'to take his part against her if she would not listen to his counsels . . .'.

At the same time the Queen let Cardinal Wolsey know, in words she had not dared use to her brother, what she would do if he did continue to support Angus: 'Many wonder that' the King, for whom she had been doing everything, 'now abandoned her by sending in Angus'. She 'must keep herself from her unfriends; and if they get assistance against her, she must make friends of her foes'; by this, she meant, of course, the French. Caught in the crossfire between husband and wife, Wolsey may have begun to feel like an unsuccessful marriage counsellor.

Another who was beginning to fear that this marriage was one that could not be saved was Archdeacon Magnus. The Queen was so annoyed by his persistence on behalf of Angus, that she urged him and his colleague to go back to London at once. They therefore decided that one of them should acquiesce and go south, but that the other would stay in Edinburgh to persevere in their difficult assignment. Radcliff was the lucky one who returned home, where he was to report in person on affairs in the North. They had begun to suspect that their 'posts had been taken by the way', so that their messages, which were largely uncomplimentary towards Margaret, were not reaching London. They hoped that 'when Wolsey understood their minds more fully, he would not think they had had here a commodious and pleasant pastime'. Quite the reverse! Not only had they been verbally assaulted by the Queen, but also by other women of Edinburgh. A dozen wives of the town, outraged by reports of English ships having seized some Scottish vessels, accosted the two ambassadors and demanded the return of their husbands and sons who had been lawlessly captured by English seamen.

Understandably, it was the Queen who received most of the blame by the unhappy ambassadors for the hopeless breach between her and her spouse. Her husband's actions which had originally broken the marriage, his involvement with Lady Jane Stewart and his seizure of his wife's properties were conveniently forgotten by the would-be conciliators. However, Magnus soon found himself obliged to reprimand Angus for his similarly lawless occupation of the monastery of Paisley. He also urged the Earl to avoid further acts of violence, such as his recent invasion of the capital city on November 23rd. Magnus had to admit, too, that, except when he persisted in lecturing her as a fallen woman, Margaret was pleasant and reasonable. Although she kept reminding him that there was no longer any need for him to stay on in

Edinburgh, she acted the part of a gracious hostess whenever he visited her and her son.

Her son, he reported to the English King, was a most promising youth. The Queen had taken Magnus and Radcliff to Leith one day to watch him 'stir his horses, and run with a spear among his lords at a glove', activities in which he exhibited great skill and daring. Also, 'he sings, dances, and shows familiarity among the lords; than which nothing can be better in a young Prince not thirteen till next Easter'. The Archdeacon diplomatically added that 'in person, face and manner', James resembled Henry VIII, and he 'liked the manners of England better than those of France'. Young James himself, according to this account, was learning how to be diplomatic.

Although Margaret may thus have been teaching her son how to deal tactfully with foreign ambassadors and to maintain control over his Parliament, she seems to have neglected other features of his training. In fact, the boy's formal education apparently ended with his 'erection' as King at the age of twelve. Heretofore, he had been tutored by a series of very capable men, particularly the poet, Gavin Dunbar, later Archbishop of Glasgow. Under such scholars he learned Latin and French, although not English; his mother, as Magnus remarked, had to translate messages received from his uncle's court.

He also became a good musician, playing the lute and singing. These skills were acquired from Sir David Lindsay of the Mount, the Prince's closest companion from the days of his infancy. First as Master Usher, then Master of the Household, Sir David became in effect a substitute father for the boy, as he reminisced later:

> When thou wast young I bore thee in mine arme,
> Full tenderly, till thou *begouth to gang* [began to walk]
> And in thy bed oft *happit* [wrapped] thee full warm,
> With lute in hand, syne, sweetly to thee sang.

Later, the kindly poet also entertained the Prince with stories, telling him over and again his favourite tales of heroes, such as King Arthur, Alexander, Caesar and Hercules.

Thus he probably influenced James greatly in his desire to become skilled in martial affairs. Throughout the many shifts of guardians during James's unsettled childhood, Lindsay remained the one constant. He was still Master of the King's Household at this period, although the boy had little time now for leisure pursuits. He was, after all, the King, a position for which he felt quite ready. At the age of eleven, he had reminded his Parliament 'that former Kings of Scotland had governed well when they were as young as he'. Nevertheless, the Queen was, of course, the real authority, who not only controlled the decisions of government, but also influenced her son to favour the nobles that she preferred and to scorn those she hated.

These observations of Margaret's supervision of all Scottish affairs continued to pervade the letters written to England by Archdeacon Magnus. The latter was still in the Scottish capital at Christmas, when French ships arrived, bringing some of Albany's officers with supplies for the French stronghold of Dunbar. The Queen also let it be known that 'the French King had sent her 30,000 crowns', and added, 'it would be long before she had as much from England'. Moreover, according to rumours, she had received an offer of additional pecuniary support, and even a proposal of marriage from the now-widowed Duke of Albany, who would, of course, first arrange with the Pope for her divorce from Angus. Margaret would have been delighted to accept this latter proposal, but not marriage to the Duke. She also balked at another condition, that she return to the 'Auld Alliance' instead of continuing to press for one with England. She was loyal to her brother, as long as he continued to support her regency and desisted from giving aid to Angus.

On the other hand, Magnus, learning that the French were making tempting offers to various noblemen, wrote to warn the 'Earl of Anguisshe' not to let himself be 'circumvented by the French'. Angus's reply to this warning was acid. He briefly stated that he would 'keep his promises to England', but he hoped Magnus remembered 'the King of England's promise to him, that if the Queen would not follow her brother's counsel, he would take Angus's part against her'. This letter, as well as other correspondence between Angus and Wolsey, makes it quite evident that Margaret's suspicion was correct: her brother had agreed to support her husband against her. It also indicated that the Douglas Earl was by now gaining so much strength that he felt able to retort somewhat sharply to the Archdeacon's messages.

Angus was, despite his assurances to Magnus, now veering to the pro-French party as the best means of working towards the power which he was determined to attain. He corresponded with the Archbishop of St. Andrews, who had remained opposed to the Queen and was gathering a large following among the nobles who were angry at the present government.

The opportunity for this group arose when the embassy returned with the terms of the new peace agreement with England. In order to get real confirmation of this pact, so vital to the plans of both

King Henry and his sister, it was necessary to call a meeting of the full Council, including the dissident faction led by the Archbishop. The latter faction, of whom Angus was now a prominent member, refused to attend the meeting called by the Queen in Edinburgh on January 23rd 1525. Instead, they convened a counter-Parliament which met at Stirling two weeks later. Ominously, the notables assembled there were fully armed. Both sides sent appeals to Archdeacon Magnus, insisting on the rectitude of their intentions and their sincere desire for peace with England. Magnus reported to Wolsey that, since the Archbishop now had more influential partisans and, in particular, the Earl of Douglas, the Queen would have to accept some accommodation with Angus in order to achieve unity.

Margaret, however, was not one to give up without a struggle. She wished to ride with James to Stirling. There, confronting the enemies in their own camp, the young King would command them to join in the Parliament which he had called at Edinburgh Castle, or be declared rebels. James was quite ready to carry out this daring measure. He was willing to follow his mother's lead in all things, particularly when she planned such an exciting adventure. He would wear the new sword his uncle, Henry, had sent him. No, it was too small for a King! He wanted a man-sized weapon! Where was his father's sword?

The reference to his father brought back to Margaret the hideous recollection of Flodden. She began to quail. She was a Queen, but she was also a mother. The opposing forces now outnumbered hers. Angus and his party dared not harm her boy, but they might take this opportunity to seize him and declare that they were quite loyal to King James, and were only 'saving his majesty from his evil counsellors', the time-worn formula adopted by almost all rebels in those days when the 'King could do no wrong'. Realizing that in an armed confrontation, she might easily lose her son and even find herself imprisoned, Margaret regretfully relinquished this spirited project.

Instead, the next move was made by the opposing party, who came from Stirling to Dalkeith, a small town near to the capital. Interpreting this move as an aggressive action, the Queen, in a fury, ordered her nobles, Arran and his colleagues, to march out and drive off the foe. They respectfuly declined to attempt this enterprise, unless young James would accompany them so that if fighting erupted they could claim that they fought in defence of their sovereign lord. These remnants of the old feudal code still had great value. One could always use some age-old rule of conduct to cover up the real reasons for refusing to fight — such as the likelihood of being beaten. As they expected, Margaret did not want to run the risk that James might be captured.

Like a Queen in a game of chess who is driven by a more powerful opposing player into a fatal corner of the board, Margaret yielded one step at a time. She sent a deputation, headed by the Bishop of Ross, to inform the opposing group that they might now all (including the previously excluded Angus) safely enter Edinburgh to join the Council deliberations, provided that they would agree not to lessen her authority as granted by the last Parliament. They accepted the proposal. After all, they were merely making a promise that could always be broken later, on one pretext or another.

When news came of the peaceable ending of the impasse, the officials of Edinburgh joyfully opened the gates to the dissidents. At midnight on February 14th 1525 the Earls of Angus and Lennox, heading an array of 600–700 horsemen, entered and took up lodgings in the city. The next day the other nobles followed, with a well-armed force of 2,000 men. They all took up quarters in the city, but, as Magnus remarked in his report to Wolsey, they selected places that were 'without the danger of gunshot from out of the castle'. This time the marksmanship of the cannoneers might have improved. To make doubly sure of their security from cannon-balls, they threatened terrible reprisals against the relatives of the castle marksmen if they should fire their guns. Having control of the citadel, Margaret found, did not really gain her much advantage.

Forced back another step, she called on Magnus and at last granted him the long-sought permission to convey to the 'Earl of Anguisshe' an invitation to be received by his estranged wife. The Earl, sensing victory, sent back a gracious reply, since during his sojourn in France, he had learned all the polite manners and phrases with which a courtier could mask his real intentions. The delighted Archdeacon was, therefore, next requested to take the Earl a ring as a token of Margaret's reconciliation. Magnus afterwards reported this to Wolsey with becoming modesty: 'Thus I, without help but myself, continued in suit between these great parties', until, on February 21st, the pacification was finally concluded.

According to the agreements made with the rival faction, Margaret was to continue as her son's chief guardian, but with other nobles placed about him, chosen by the lords with her agreement. She should continue to have control over the granting of benefices and should receive the various feudal 'aids'; moreover, she should retain the principal authority in matters such as treaty-making and appointments to state offices. In all these areas, however, the Council was to share her authority.

The opening of Parliament on February 23rd 1525 dramatized

the reconciliation of the hostile forces that had so long disputed supremacy over the kingdom. Each of the leading contenders in this recent struggle was given a prominent role in the procession that entered the Tolbooth. The Queen walked beside her royal son, preceded by the Earls of Angus, Arran and Argyll, who carried respectively the crown, the sceptre and the sword of his Majesty. Beaton, Archbishop of St. Andrews, was restored to the post of Chancellor and given a position on the Council of regency appointed to supervise the business of the kingdom. Margaret headed this Council and was to oversee the young King's movements. She was still to remain with him at all times, but his residence was to be Holyrood rather than the Castle. Moreover, henceforth, the cannon of the latter fortress were to be fired only with the consent of the Council. The fatal shots of November 23rd were not forgotten.

The chief business for this session was to be the conclusion of peace with England. Argument, however, arose over the timing of the marriage alliance between James V and his cousin, Mary Tudor. Magnus, speaking for King Henry, urged that peace be established immediately — the marriage would follow later. After all, the bridegroom was not yet thirteen, and his proposed fiancée was nearly four years younger. Nevertheless, the Scots insisted that no peace treaty could be considered secure, until all parts of the agreement were completed. Also they wanted time to obtain the permission of their 'auld ally' to make such a long-term agreement with England. Finally, it was decided that the Scottish embassy should return to London to arrange for an eight-month extension of the truce.

This decision was a disappointing conclusion to the treaty proposal, particularly for Margaret. In hopes of a permanent Anglo-Scottish peace, she had agreed to the public reunion with her estranged husband. Now, it seemed her self-sacrifice had been in vain. Moreover, as events progressed, she began to realize that, despite all the conditions she had insisted on to safeguard her own supremacy in the new regime, she had lost real control over the kingdom. In actual fact, the brief reign of Margaret, Queen Regent, was now over.

CHAPTER 17

THE RED DOUGLAS STAR IN ASCENDANCY (1526–1527)

Who was more high in honour elevate
Than was Margaret, our high and mighty princess?
Such power was to her appropriate —
Yet came a change within one short process —
That pearl preclair, that lusty pleasant queen,
Long time durst not into the court be seen.

The above excerpt from a contemporary poem refers to the collapse of Queen Margaret's regency in 1526. Her downfall was certainly precipitated by the political opposition headed by her husband. Yet actions of her own definitely hastened her loss of power.

Some of her critics maintain that she might have made a success of her reign and established real union with England, if she could only have overcome her repugnance for her husband and renewed a real marriage relationship with him. In view of Angus's own actions later, after he had gained the upper hand, this happy solution seems most unlikely. In fact, his treatment of his stepson substantiates the opposite theory held by some historians that, once James became old enough to assume kingship, Angus would have arranged some accident to remove the young monarch permanently from the scene. Then Angus might have made use of his powerful position to seize the throne personally, for the Douglases boasted of royal descent, albeit through the female line. The fact that several others had still better claims to the royal title (the Duke of Albany, the Earls of Hamilton and of Lennox) would scarcely have deterred him from such an attempt. In view of this grim possibility, Margaret's wariness of her erring husband appears more rational, based on legitimate fears for her son's safety.

Moreover, even by attributing the purest of motives to Angus, and supposing a perfect reconciliation between him and Margaret, what guarantee was there that together they could have succeeded in allying Scotland permanently with its ancient foe? After all, the Queen had been in perfect accord with her husband and with her brother in 1515, when she and Angus had been overthrown and driven out by the hostile nobles and their French allies.

The above survey of possible theses makes it apparent that Margaret alone was not to blame for the breakdown of Anglo-Scottish accord. Nevertheless, her own fall from power in 1525 can certainly be traced, not only to Angus's machinations, but also to her foolhardy stubbornness. 'The Queen . . . is so blinded with folly . . . that to have her ungodly appetite followed, she doth not care what she doth'. This acid comment by the Duke of Norfolk typifies the criticism of Margaret made by the English court throughout this time. This harsh judgement undoubtedly rested on the highly biased charges made against her by the Douglas faction. Yet even her most sympathetic partisans have been forced to admit that this period of her life shows her at her worst.

To begin with, she encouraged Harry Stewart to accompany the royal household when it was moved in February 1525 from Edinburgh Castle to Holyrood. It became obvious, even to her, that she could scarcely continue a liaison with him in the same court circle which now included her publicly reconciled husband. Hence she soon sent the young courtier to Stirling — far enough away to 'maintain the appearance of circumspection, but near enough for an occasional brief rendezvous.

It disturbed the Queen to note the progress Angus was making. He quickly built up a coterie of his own followers in the centre of influence. Early in March the rumour of a plot to steal the young King from Edinburgh afforded a pretext for changing James's guardians. Several of Margaret's staunch supporters were removed from this group and replaced with nobles more subservient to the Douglas Earl. Angus was soon also made Warden of the East and Middle Marches.

As she observed his gradual but steady acquisition of power, and the consequent diminution of her own authority, the Queen became increasingly nervous. How long would she be able to maintain her own independent status? At the time of their first steps towards reconciliation in February, she had insisted that Angus's return to public life in Scotland must not entail resumption of his personal relationship with her. She had finally agreed to limit this proviso to a given time span — until Whitsuntide [June] 1525. Till then Angus had promised to make no effort to resume his full rights as her husband. Nothing was promised, or even mentioned, beyond Whitsuntide.

Why had the Queen agreed to accept this early date for ending the six-year separation from her husband? The answer of course was that, at the time of signing these terms, she was confident that before June 1525 she would have her long-sought divorce in hand. To this end she had early in the year resumed a friendly correspondence with the Duke of Albany. She declared that she would do anything necessary to help France, and would even give up the proposed Anglo-Scottish alliance, in case Henry should help Angus return to power. But Albany must, on his part, secure her divorce. The Duke's response, as well as replies she got from similar appeals to the French King and to the Pope, assured her that she would at last attain this official freedom from the hated bonds of matrimony. However, she then planned at once to re-enter this 'blessed state', as wife of her new love, Harry Stewart. (He, incidentally, was meanwhile divorcing his own wife in preparation.) All these plans and correspondence were conducted in what Margaret thought to be the strictest secrecy.

But weeks continued to pass without the hoped-for result. Whitsundide was fast approaching. How should she fend off the undesired advances of her spouse? Actually, she need have had little fear of any physical resumption of her marital status. Angus had small desire to share the bed of his long-absent wife; he much preferred that of Lady Jane Stewart of Traquair. Now he took more pains to keep that affair hidden than he had back in 1516–18. He knew better than to ruin his chances of keeping the support of King Henry in his efforts to regain the legal status of his sister's husband. The conjugal right for which Angus was aiming, was the title to his wife's properties. Even before Whitsuntide he began entreating Wolsey to permit him at once to receive the rents from her estates.

The English court became more favourable to the Douglas Earl. He was, so far as they could determine, behaving with utmost propriety, whereas his wife appeared on the contrary to be quite shameless. Magnus's letters from Edinburgh tended to support the unfavourable accounts of Margaret being circulated in England by Lord Dacre. The Warden was in London at this time, and still diligently supporting his kinsman Angus. But the final blow to Margaret's reputation came as the result of her own actions. Some of the letters which she had written to France requesting help in her divorce suit had been intercepted by the English. It is easy to imagine the effect they had on her brother. In a positive fury he wrote her a scorching epistle, which he sent her by way of Magnus. The Archdeacon delivered it to the Queen, who was at the time with her son in 'St. Johnstoun' [Perth].

Magnus first informed her and her court of the disastrous defeat recently suffered by the French at Pavia. Francis I had not only been beaten but taken prisoner by the imperial forces. This news, Magnus reported to Wolsey, confirmed the rumour which had already reached Scotland and severely shook those around the Queen who had been leaning toward France. Margaret herself

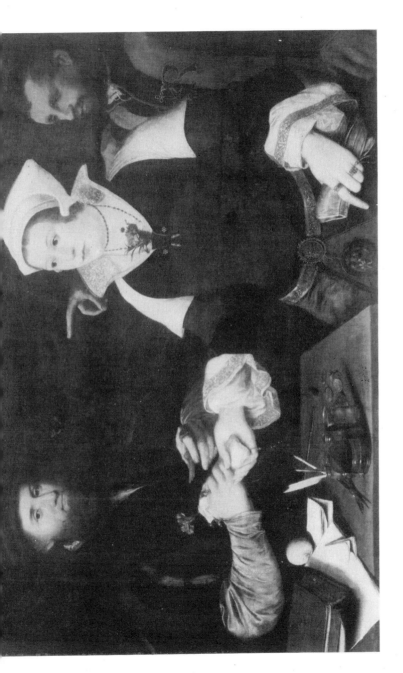

Margaret Tudor, with the Earl of Angus on her left. The man he is pointing to has been identified by some as the Duke of Albany, but is more probably Harry Stewart.

(From a private collection)

heard it with pretended indifference. Then, in a private interview with her, Magnus handed her the angry letter from King Henry.

This missive 'her grace received in full honourable manner', but upon opening it could not conceal her reaction: '. . . after Her grace had over seen and read five or six lines of the same, she altered her countenance in such manner that it was an hour after, 'ere her grace could sober herself from weeping; and long it was, and with much pain, or that her grace could bring the said letter to an end'. When finally she was able to stop sobbing enough to speak coherently, she gasped that 'such a letter was never written to any noble woman'!

Far from granting her any sympathy, the Archdeacon sternly admonished her to 'note every part of the said letter, and to be as well content with the same, as the King's Highness, my Master, was with her letter' to the French in which she declared that she would never send ambassadors to England if the 'Erle of Anguisshe' were allowed to enter Scotland.

Margaret's only rebuttal to this evidence that her secret letters to France had been intercepted was to appeal to her son. He, she said, would assure Magnus that she had always supported England. In similar vein she finally wrote also to her brother, reproaching him for his 'right sore and sharp' words. In reply to his accusations, she merely emphasized her devotion to him and gave as proof a lengthy recapitulation of all the exertions she had made to establish her son as ruler instead of Albany, and her efforts to forward the alliance with England.

This episode marked one of her periods of deepest humiliation. Though the French continued to make her attractive overtures, she realized that in their own distress after Pavia they could not possibly fulfil these offers. It seemed to her now that her appeals to Albany and King Francis had brought her disgrace without any compensation, for there was still no divorce, and Whitsuntide was hard upon her.

In desperation she seized upon a pretext to absent herself from the court. Angus gave her this opening by illegally granting a bishopric to one of his brothers without first obtaining the Queen's consent. Declaring herself deeply offended by his breach of the recent articles of agreement, she withdrew from Edinburgh to Stirling. Here in her own dower castle, she felt secure from any unwelcome advances by her husband and close to the comforting support of her lover. However, her absence from the capital also removed her from the society of her son — and from the centre of power. True enough, she had obviously been losing influence in the government as Angus built up his strength. By now he had gained the adherence even of her old ally, the Earl of Arran. Nevertheless, her complete absence from the Council table could only hasten her eclipse. Eventually, as she steadily refused to come to its meetings, or to those of the national assembly, the lords decided to carry out all measures without the formality of her signature on decrees.

In May, Magnus wrote to persuade her to return to take part in the discussion of the peace with England. Since Henry had refused to agree to the eight-month truce proposal, there was urgent need for a peace agreement. She sent a vigorously worded admonition to the Council to make every effort for peace. They simply postponed a final decision till Parliament should meet in July.

The Queen's absence probably had little effect on the outcome of these deliberations. However, it certainly weakened what little support she still had among the nobles and made it easier for the Douglas party to continue its steady growth. She wrote in vain beseeching the Council to prevent Angus from seizing her rents. To her frequent reminder that he was under a papal summons of divorce, he paid no heed, and when she wrote that she was afraid to come to meetings in Edinburgh for fear of him, he retorted in a speech to the Council that he should 'treat her Grace at my power so long as we are undivorced as law, conscience, and honesty of her Grace requires'. Moreover, he reminded them that the Queen was 'bounden and obliged by the law of God and the holy Kirk' to return peaceably to her lawful husband.

Unfortunately for Margaret, the Council was made up entirely of men. Whatever their political views might be, they fully supported the law which gave the husband control over his wife — body, soul and property. With this comfortable masculine view of affairs, they felt under no compulsion to defend her or her income from the control of her legal spouse. Instead, at the close of Parliament Margaret was declared to have forfeited all her authority through her persistent absence. The young King desperately protested that he 'trusted the Queen his mother had not so highly offended'. This appeal only caused the decree to be delayed for twenty days, before it was passed. Since Margaret still refused to return to the capital during this period of grace, she lost whatever chance she had at this point to regain some control over affairs.

As Margaret reached the nadir of her career, her husband simultaneously continued his rapid ascent to power. His opportunity to achieve complete dominance came through a new decree. The decree stated that a group of nobles should be chosen to attend and supervise the young King, and that its members should change at each quarter of the year. One of those in charge during the first term was Angus, who swiftly moved to assume for himself the chief functions of this supposedly shared office. Then, when the time came for him to relinquish his post to the next contingent, he simply refused to do so.

This *coup* succeeded because the Douglas faction was by that time supreme. However, it brought the inevitable reaction: resentment by those nobles who now found themselves over-reached. Arran, disgruntled by losing his own turn in authority, retired to Linlithgow, along with others who were also jealous of the new regime. Here they received word in January 1526 from the Queen. She had, during her recent eclipse, moved far to the north of Scotland, where she had been building a party of her own, including the Earl of Moray and the Bishops of Ross and of Moray. They and their adherents, who numbered around 600, planned to join Arran and his party at Linlithgow, but Angus prevented any successful union of these two dissident groups. With the help of Lennox and Argyll, he gathered 7,000 men. Moreover, he held the key piece to this chess game — the King himself. The boy was forced to ride at the head of the forces moving against his mother, while all her adherents were declared to be rebels. In face of these overwhelming odds, her allies dispersed. Margaret fled north again, while Arran and Moray surrendered to the successful Douglas.

During this period of renewed husband-wife controversy, ne-gotiations were continuing between Edinburgh and London for the long-sought peace. As a condition of peace, both Margaret and her son begged the English King to demand the Queen's right to her dower, as stipulated in her original marriage contract with James IV. Henry yielded to these pleas. Apparently, he felt that she had now suffered sufficiently to expiate her recent transgressions in seeking French help for her divorce. According to Magnus, 'the King's sharp and quick words had brought [her] to some better order then [than] her Grace was in afore'. Magnanimously Henry now came to her support by insisting that his sister's rights must be respected — or there would be no peace. The important provision that her husband must not share in her property was long opposed by the Scottish nobles, who were now obedient to Angus. However, they — and he — eventually yielded. This provision was, after all, merely a written agreement. Its enforcement was another matter — as had been proved by Margaret's previous difficulties in trying to obtain payment of her rents. So Angus himself now acted the part of a magnanimous gentleman. He even promised to accept a divorce — 'if sufficient grounds for it were found to exist'. Since apparently none had been found after years of effort by his wife, they might never appear. Anyway, if the Pope did finally grant the decree, there would be no escaping its verdict. Meanwhile, it would do no harm to make a virtue of necessity and thus regain favour with the English court, for Angus had lately been losing ground with the Council there. His ability to rule was beginning to appear scarcely better than that of his wife. Lawlessness was again becoming rampant, especially on the Borders where he had been given specific authority. Lord Dacre had died in October 1525, and therefore his support was now lost to the Douglas Earl. Angus's smooth manner and humble appearance still kept Archdeacon Magnus sympathetic to the 'noble Earl of Anguisshe', but he obviously needed to repair his reputation with Westminster.

To accomplish this effect, he continued his show of respect for King Henry's sister, assuring her that she need not fear undesired advances or injury from him if she chose to return to the capital. Therefore, after the articles of peace were finally signed at Berwick in the winter of 1526, the Queen at last returned to Edinburgh. She longed to see her son, who was overjoyed by the reunion with his mother. Magnus took this opportunity to exhort Margaret in the future to use her obvious influence over young James to uplift his character and judgement. She should, he told her, 'every day first . . . give unto him her most loving blessing, counselling his said Grace to love, dread and serve God and to love and favour his good lords and subjects'. Thus she would train the young monarch to do justice 'to the comfort of all good men, and to the dread and terror of all evil-disposed persons and malefactors within his said realm'. She should, on the other hand, refrain from urging James to take the side of any person she liked, or to act against those she opposed. Very noble advice, no doubt, but not likely to have much effect on Margaret Tudor! Her ability to sway James to her views was her chief asset in this struggle. Though Angus now had the King's person in his control, she had his affection, an advantage she was not likely to abjure.

The Archdeacon had to admit that in her outward deportment the Queen was the model of propriety. To observe her when she appeared in public beside her husband, one would suppose her the most devoted wife in the world. Alas! Magnus was once again disillusioned. He discovered that the entire reason for her apparent sweet deference to her husband was but a show put on to win his assistance in gaining a divorce. Ah, the dissimulation of woman! The good clergyman shook his head over it, and regretfully confessed to Wolsey that her grace still seemed quite unreformed.

He did not apparently notice a similar discrepancy between the humble letters and the high-handed actions of her husband. Margaret, however, quickly discovered that all Angus's promises to accept the solemn language of the recent treaty of peace had no effect on his subsequent actions. True, he made no unwanted invasion of her bedroom, but he proceeded quite freely to seize her rents. Although she procured a papal 'cursing' against any who might interfere with her property while the divorce suit was pending, her husband paid no more attention to this than he did to orders of the Council to the same effect. He now took measures to elevate his own power above any possible interference by the Council or other government authority. On June 14th 1526 he successfully persuaded Parliament to declare that James V was of full age to rule. This act meant that the fourteen-year-old King now could appoint new officials to all departments of government, since all previous holders of such positions were forced to give up their titles. Angus, however, simply delayed the business of choosing new officers. Instead, he assumed all their powers for himself.

In desperation, Margaret left the capital city, to make a fresh attempt at overthrowing her husband. A number of discontented nobles joined her, the most influential and capable being James Beaton, Archbishop of St. Andrews. This prelate had previously been opposed to the Queen, because she had early in her own regency imprisoned him for refusing to desert Albany. Now that he was ousted from his post as Chancellor by Angus, he forsook the Douglases and became henceforth Margaret's foremost champion. The Earl of Lennox also joined her. At long last the tide was beginning to turn.

Nevertheless, her return to power was destined to be a long and arduous struggle. Angus was a more formidable and ruthless adversary than the Duke of Albany had been. In July 1526 Lennox and Buccleuch made an attempt to rescue the young King from his stepfather. Their opportunity finally came when Angus left the security of Edinburgh for the Borders in order to punish the rampant crime there of which the English were constantly complaining. Afraid to leave his royal pawn out of his own sight even briefly, he took James with him on this expedition. On their homeward journey they were met by Lennox and Buccleuch, who rode up with a considerable following and declared that they wished to 'do honour to their sovereign'. When Angus forbade them to approach, they attacked his party with the obvious aim of seizing the King, but were driven off in spite of outnumbering the Douglas forces.

The failure of this attempt disappointed no one more than James himself. He hated his stepfather, who kept him a virtual prisoner. He could neither see anyone without Angus's express permission, nor leave the palace grounds without a formidable guard of Douglas supporters surrounding him. His riding and hunting were limited to a narrow area, and he felt hemmed in and restricted at every turn.

Angus tried to capture the boy's friendship by 'indulging him in every propensity, and allowing him every gratification that did not interfere with his own ambitious views'. This latitude encouraged the teenager to experiment with vices which were to mar his character in later years. However, it had no effect on James's feeling for his stepfather whom he continued to regard as his gaoler and as the usurper of his own rightful position.

His mother was naturally concerned about his unwholesome situation. She and Lennox complained to the members of the Council that Angus was holding the King captive, and sent deputies to demand that he be freed of these intolerable restraints. Angus boldly referred to them and their letters in a Council meeting and declared 'if so were that his highness was in captivity, there should be no baron of the realm of better will to put his grace to liberty . . .'. If any peer present wished to accuse him of harming his Majesty, he proclaimed he would submit the matter to immediate trial. Since this Council was dominated by his own supporters, none dared speak out against him. He then took Margaret's emissaries to meet James and ask him openly whether he were being mistreated. The boy replied that 'his mother needed not to be anxious respecting him, for he could not lead a more pleasant and cheerful life than he did, with his good cousin, the Earl of Angus'.

Nevertheless, James soon after this was able to get letters smuggled out to Margaret, Lennox and Archbishop Beaton. In these he confirmed their suspicion that he had been forced by his stepfather's threats to give the answer that he had. Contrary to this coerced statement, he was miserably unhappy and begged them to secure his release.

Galvanized into immediate action by this plea, the Queen and Lennox plotted to kidnap the King with the help of the Master of Kilmaurs. He was the Treasurer, who had been serving in Angus's government, but now wished to defect from his imperious regime. He agreed to help James to escape from Holyrood to the Burgh Muir. Here they would be met by Lennox and a band of two hundred horsemen who would convey them to Stirling. Alas! the Earl got wind of the plot in time to circumvent it. He sent at once for the Treasurer, but by his quick thinking James was able to save his friend. He 'conveyed the said Master [of Kilmaurs] through the coining house, and so he made escape at the Holyrood House'. The young King was less fortunate. Although technically he could not be punished, his stepfather took measures to prevent a renewed attempt at escape by removing him from the palace to a mansion in the city. Here he was guarded closely by a picked band of forty soldiers, supervised by George Douglas. This stern brother of

Angus was now made Master of the King's Household in place of David Lindsay. Bereft of the poet who had been his one constant guardian since his infancy, the boy felt friendless indeed.

Spurred on by news of her son's misery, Margaret persevered in her efforts to rescue him. Her adherents were increasing in number almost daily, as Angus's rule became more intolerable to the other nobles. Finally, on September 3rd 1526, an army led by the Earls of Lennox, Crawford and Casillis, and a number of other noblemen, marched towards 'Edinburgh to take the King'. As they neared Linlithgow, they were intercepted by Angus and Arran, and a sharp encounter ensued, during which the Queen's forces were defeated. They were badly hampered in attacking their opponents by the fact that the young King was himself in the van of Angus's army, for they feared that in their assault they might injure him. James himself was looking for an opportunity to make a dash for freedom by galloping over to his mother's army, but George Douglas prevented this. Catching the reins of the boy's horse, he angrily 'bade him beware, for they would rather tear him in two in their struggle to keep him, than relinquish him into the hands of their foes'. This grim warning reinforced James's fear and hatred of his gaolers. The Douglas family were long to regret this terrible example of *lèse-majesté* by one of their members.

So the young King had to witness the failure of his mother's army to free him. Another sorrow for him was to learn of the death of the Earl of Lennox, slain in the fracas — or murdered after the battle, as it was later rumoured. Many other prominent leaders of the Queen's army also lost their lives. Exhilarated by their victory, the Douglases, still maintaining the fiction that they were fighting to dispel his Majesty's enemies, and still bearing the unhappy monarch in their midst, laid siege to Stirling Castle. When the Queen's stronghold surrendered, she was nowhere to be found. She and the Archbishop of St. Andrews had left the region after the disastrous Battle of Linlithgow. At this juncture it was obvious to them that there was no hope of success in a further resort to arms.

Instead, Margaret again tried the tactics of graceful submission. When she received an invitation from Angus, eagerly seconded by the young King, to return to the capital, she graciously accepted. She was very anxious to be once again with her son. Also she was excited by an offer from her husband. He would withdraw all opposition to a divorce if she would promise not to oppose his complete control over state affairs, nor to try to reinstate Beaton as Chancellor, or others of her party in positions of influence. In addition, she would yield the lucrative wardship of the Earl of Huntly to Angus. She was slightly reluctant to have to promise to give up the company of Harry Stewart, but did so because it was a proviso which was easily circumvented in practice. Although her favourite did not accompany her to Edinburgh, he remained in Stirling, and was near enough for her to visit frequently.

Her entrance into the capital on November 20th was cheered by the commoners, who still felt affection for the widow of their best-loved monarch. Her son met her joyously and escorted her to Holyrood, where she was given the attractive apartment which the Duke of Albany had formerly occupied. Here she was able to see James daily, a privilege he enjoyed as much as she. When they went hawking and hunting together, she was delighted with his horsemanship. Like his father, he was able to vault into the saddle without putting his feet to the stirrups, and easily managed even the most spirited steed. For his sport, he wanted some specially trained hounds, which, he had heard, were available in the north of England. With his mother's help, he now sent a request for these dogs to his young cousin, Henry Fitzroy, Duke of Richmond. The latter was son of Henry VIII and Bess Blount, the lady-in-waiting whom Margaret recalled seeing in Catherine's apartments during her visit to England back in 1516–17. Her child had been elevated to the nobility with great ceremony in 1525. Many people had then surmised that the King, despairing of a legitimate male heir, since Catherine was by then past child-bearing age, had decided to legitimatize his natural son and rear him as the future ruler, instead of his daughter Mary. This six-year-old boy now lived with a great retinue in Pontefract Castle. The Queen wrote to ask her young nephew for some greyhounds and bloodhounds for the King of Scots. The request was graciously granted. James wrote his cousin a letter of thanks, besides sending to him in return 'two brace of hounds for deer and smaller beasts'.

This pleasant state of affairs continued throughout the winter of 1526–27. With James's assistance, Margaret was able to recover some of her former influence. She could be very persuasive when she exerted her charm and thus was able to get Angus to permit her ally, Beaton, Archbishop of St. Andrews, to return to court. However, she overreached herself when she also tried to have Harry Stewart admitted to Holyrood. It was not only Angus who objected to this. Patrick Sinclair, who at one time had been Margaret's most trusted emissary, had been alienated by her siding against him on behalf of young Stewart. Shifting his support to King Henry, Sinclair had become a trusted messenger between him and Angus, and in addition had gained the confidence of young King James. He frequently brought messages and gifts to James from his uncle Henry. Trying to influence James along the lines indicated to him by Wolsey, Sinclair drew the boy's attention to his mother's apparent interest in Harry Stewart and told him that, for her own good name, she should cease seeing this courtier. Hence, when Margaret, early in the spring of 1527, asked her son's permission to invite Harry to Holyrood, the young King refused. She tried to persuade him; he remained firm. In a burst of temper, she collected her belongings and moved to Stirling, followed soon afterward by the Archbishop.

Fortunately this foolish quarrel with her son — the first time he had refused to yield to her — was only temporary. After a few weeks' absence, during which their tempers cooled, she returned, although just for a visit. Thenceforth, she travelled back and forth between Edinburgh and Stirling, but she kept her chief domicile in the latter castle. It was well that she did so, as later events were to prove.

News of his sister's refusal to get rid of her lover, in spite of his injunctions, infuriated Henry VIII. He had also learned that she was still industriously corresponding with the Duke of Albany in pursuit of her divorce, and the subsequent discovery that she apparently intended to remarry outraged him. At this time he had an interview with Turenne, the French ambassador in London, who told him that the Duke of Albany, worried by the news of Angus's misgovernment in Scotland, was considering urging his own followers in Scotland to restore Margaret to the regency. To the ambassador's surprise, the English King, far from appreciating this proffered help to his sister, retorted that if Margaret gained control of the government in Scotland, he would do his best to overthrow her. He also urged the French not to assist her in any way, for, he declared, 'that her folly and ill-government were a disgrace to himself and all his race and that her conduct could not be more shameful'. He added that he had heard that she would marry Albany once she gained her divorce. The startled ambassador replied that he felt sure the Duke would not wish to marry any woman with such a character as the King described.

Turenne would have been still more amazed if he had known of another meeting which King Henry had just had with his Lord Chancellor. For the very pious monarch, who had just shown such outrage over his sister's immoral behaviour, had in that same month of May 1527, informed his trusted work-horse, Wolsey, that he wished him at once to get to work to procure him a divorce from his Queen, Catherine. The reason? Henry now wished to marry a lady of the court — a vivacious young girl named Anne Boleyn.

CHAPTER 18

THE FALL OF THE RED DOUGLAS (1528)

Then durst no man come nearhand the king
But the surname of the doughty Douglas
Who so royally in this region did reign
Spending the king's rightful income

.   .   .   .   .

For nothing that time that fell among us
But was taken by Archybaldy earl of Angus.

In the above verse, Lindsay summarizes the rule of Angus, who, by the beginning of 1528, had reached the zenith of his power in Scotland. Named Chancellor by his puppet-King, he had in turn installed his own henchmen in all other important positions, a large number being his own relatives. An uncle, Archibald, was royal Treasurer as well as Provost of Edinburgh. One of his brothers, William, was Abbot of Holyrood and Prior of Coldingham; another brother was Master of the Royal Household. James Douglas of Parkhead was Master of the Royal Larder, while James Douglas of Drumlanrig presided over the royal wine-cellar. To George Douglas was assigned the all-important responsibility of supervising the care of the young King himself.

Consequently James V, now in his sixteenth year, found himself completely surrounded by the Douglases who controlled his every movement, and prevented any activity which they opposed. Because he was cut off from the companionship of those whom he felt he could trust, and closely guarded wherever he went, it was not surprising that he now turned to the unwholesome indulgences with which Angus tried to distract him. But neither gambling with the Douglas retainers, nor learning about sex from the ladies to whom they introduced him, could long divert the royal boy from his chief aim: assumption of the kingship on his own. Hence he listened when Patrick Sinclair urged him to abondon the evil habits he had begun to acquire. Sinclair, one of the few in whom the young ruler felt some confidence during this period, told the boy that his uncle, King Henry, was much displeased by reports of his delinquency. The same messenger also reproved Angus himself, telling him that the English monarch did not wish his Scottish nephew debauched by association with the rough soldiers with whom George Douglas had surrounded him. The Earl retorted that his stepson was better supervised under his care than he had been previously.

A few months later, Sinclair reported to Wolsey that his reprimands had been successful, at least so far as the young King himself was concerned. The next time he saw James, he declared him 'far altered, and given to virtuous and good manners'. The boy had now returned to his favourite martial pastimes, improving his horsemanship and his facility with weapons. He had by this time acquired the man-sized sword he had demanded, and was now able to draw it easily from the scabbard. As he wielded this great blade, over a yard in length, he amused himself by imagining that he was whacking off the heads of all his Douglas gaolers. Somehow, sometime he would be free of them. Then let them beware!

At the moment, however, these dreams of vengeance appeared hopeless. Angus had, after the Battle of Linlithgow, divided the spoils with Arran. In order to keep him and the rest of his family loyal to him, Angus had persuaded Parliament to give the Hamiltons the lands of the western nobles who had just been vanquished, while the Douglases themselves took those of the east and the north. As long as these two families worked together, they appeared invincible. The other nobles realized that their helplessness would continue while the King remained in the control of his stepfather.

Meanwhile, what of his mother? Although she returned on brief occasions to Edinburgh, she now stayed most of the time at Stirling. Here, in December 1527 she at last received the divorce which she had so long been seeking. In her joy, she forgot to be annoyed when she learned that Pope Clement VII, prodded by the Duke of Albany, had actually granted the decree almost nine months earlier. Its delivery to Scotland had been delayed by the tumultuous events then occurring on the continent. As soon as she received the papal decree, the Queen took it to Edinburgh and had it validated by the Scottish Church court. Angus no longer opposed it, since he had already acquired on his own all the power he wished. As for the King of Scots, he was delighted that his mother was freed from any ties with the Douglases.

James was much less pleased when Margaret used her new freedom to marry Harry Stewart. This wedding took place secretly early in 1528. When Margaret announced it in March of that year, her son was so exasperated that he sent troops to besiege her castle of Stirling, demanding the person of Harry Stewart. The accounts of this action vary. One version (found in Lesley's history) includes a moving scene in which the Queen ran out of the gates to throw herself on her knees before her son, pleading for her husband. A more prosaic account is given in the letter from Lord William Dacre to Wolsey, dated April 2nd 1528. Dacre, now Warden ·of the Northern Marches, wrote simply: 'Harry Stewart hath maried the Queen of Scots, as she hath confessed herself; and for that cause the King her son caused the Lord Erskine and a certain company to lie about the castle of Stirling to attack him; and thereupon the said Queen delivered him out, and so he is put in ward by the King's commandment'. In the absence of other contemporary evidence, Dacre's letter must be accepted as the more credible version, although certainly Margaret would have enjoyed enacting the melodramatic scene described by Lesley. However, young James was apparently not with the troops at Stirling to provide the necessary supporting cast for this scenario. Moreover, as in most cases during this period, the entire attack was probably initiated by Angus, although he issued the orders in the name of his puppet-King.

Another person outraged by Margaret's remarriage was her brother, who at once asked Wolsey to write remonstrating with her against her behaviour. Henry himself was at this point too busy penning love-letters to Anne Boleyn to have time to write to his erring sister. The Cardinal's epistle threatened the Scottish Queen with the 'danger of damnation to . . . [her] soul', and begged her 'to relinquish the adulterer's company with him that [was] not, nor might not be of right [her] husband'. Did Wolsey, as he wrote this letter, reflect upon its irony? The same King who reminded Margaret of 'the divine Ordinance of inseparable matrimony first instituted in Paradise', was, in that same April 1528, making every effort to break the inseparable chains which linked him to his wife of nineteen years' standing. No one was more keenly aware of this fact than the Cardinal. He was now striving with all his might to enable his master to marry the sister of his recently discarded mistress, using the argument that Henry's first marriage was invalid because it had been to the widow of his deceased brother Arthur.

This reason had been indignantly refuted by Catherine herself, when her husband had first voiced it in the preceding year as he broached his new plans for their future. She had also refused Henry's kind offer of a comfortable convent where she could spend the rest of her life with great dignity and honour, provided that she would simply agree to an annulment and adopt the role of nun. The heart-broken wife rejected this sixteenth-century equivalent of a retirement home. Instead she would fight to the last breath for her own reputation and for the legitimacy of their daughter, Mary. Catherine wrote to ask her nephew Charles, the Holy Roman

Emperor, to prevent the Pope from granting this divorce. Since Charles's troops controlled Italy at this time, the Pope was afraid to offend him by yielding to the demands of King Henry. Therefore, in the winter of 1528, Wolsey's emissaries to Clement VII had only succeeded in bringing back a promise that a Legatine Court would soon be held in England to resolve the question of this divorce. The Cardinal hoped against hope that this measure would be soon enough and successful enough to save his own neck. The wrath of King Henry if he continued to be frustrated in pursuit of his new passion was fearful to contemplate. Ruminating on all these developments, Wolsey must have been filled with bitterness as he wrote to the Scottish Queen about the wicked divorce which Pope Clement had just granted her.

The Cardinal's admonitions had, predictably, no effect whatever on Margaret. Unlike her brother, she felt little concern either for her soul's salvation, or for her worldly reputation. Henry always felt compelled to ennoble his actions, covering his true motives with sanctimonious declarations of piety. Hence he told Catherine and later announced to the public that he was personally devoted to his faithful wife. But how could he continue to live with her now that he realized that their marriage was a sin? Holy Scripture specifically forbade carnal relations with his brother's wife, and the fact that he had thus been sinning for over nineteen years had been punished by their marriage being childless. (Mary did not really count, being only a daughter.) Henry did not try to explain why his fear for England's security under a female successor had not galvanized him into action some seven years earlier, when it was already obvious that Catherine could no longer bear children. Nor would he admit that his childless state and the scriptural reason for it had struck his conscience only after Anne Boleyn had refused to accept the role of a mere mistress, and insisted on being wife and Queen.

Margaret did not bother to justify her behaviour as her brother did. In seeking her divorce, which, to her credit, she had commenced years before she fell in love with Harry Stewart, she had only sought a legal basis on which she could attain it. As her real reasons for wanting a divorce had failed to convince the Pope that he must break their marriage bonds, she sought some other ground. One particularly bizarre suggestion which she tried was that her first husband had still been living when she married for the second time. This, she said, she had reason to believe because of the widespread rumours among the people that James IV had not died at Flodden. When this far-fetched reasoning failed to get results, she fell back on more ordinary legalisms. The final decree was based, as it frequently was in those days, on an already existing contract; in this case, Angus's betrothal to Lady Jane Stewart of Traquair. The Queen had at first resisted the use of this cause of annulment for fear it would result in making her daughter illegitimate. Finally, however, Pope Clement declared this stigma should not affect Lady Margaret Douglas because her mother was, at the time of her marriage, ignorant of Angus's pre-contract.

Lady Margaret herself had meanwhile been seized by Angus. He stole his daughter away from her mother while he was in power, perhaps because the Queen was planning to betroth her to a nobleman of her own party. Angus had already made his other daughter, Lady Janet Douglas, child of his mistress, Lady Jane Stewart, his heiress. Nevertheless, he also wanted the control of his daughter by Margaret. Being King Henry's niece, she could be very useful to her father — possibly as a marriage prize for one of his confederates, or else as a means of keeping King Henry's support.

Though Margaret was unable to recover custody of her daughter, she redoubled her efforts to free her son from her ex-husband's contrcl. With the help of the Archbishop of St. Andrews, she laid new plans. In these James himself played a dominant role. The young King summoned a meeting of the Council in which he reproved Angus for his failure to execute justice. Angered by these reprimands, the Earl set out with an armed force, ostensibly to repress the lawlessness still rampant in the Borders. James, however, felt sure Angus's real purpose was to attack those nobles who had supported the King at the recent meeting. Whatever the reason for the Earl's departure to Lothian in June 1528, the young King now made haste to seize the opportunity offered by his absence. Archbishop Beaton, who had recently feigned sympathy with the Douglas party, summoned George Douglas to St. Andrews. With the leading Douglases thus occupied away from Edinburgh, James now made his break for feeedom.

He first declared his intention of going on a great stag hunt at Falkland, to which he invited several noblemen. The night before this announced event, he retired early, in preparation for an early start the next morning, and urged his gaoler-companions to do likewise. Their leader, James Douglas of Parkhead, came to bid the King goodnight and finding him already in bed, retired also. However, as soon as everything was quiet, the young monarch rose and put on a suit of clothes which he had earlier acquired from a stable boy. In this disguise he was able to elude his guardians. He reached the stable, where a trusted groom had a horse ready for him. Accompanied by only a few loyal attendants, the King made good his escape and at once galloped off to Stirling. Here his mother, who had provisioned the castle and garrisoned it with her own followers, was anxiously awaiting him. At his signal, she commanded the drawbridge to be lowered; he and his companions clattered across into the courtyard. He was free at last!

Meanwhile at the palace his absence was discovered. When he failed to appear for the announced hunting expedition and his room was found empty, various explanations were suggested as to his whereabouts. Some of the men-at-arms felt sure he had gone 'to Banbreich to ane gentill woman', a lady in whom he had expressed much interest. Others, however, quickly guessed the King was seeking, not an amorous adventure, but his liberty, a conclusion which was confirmed by reports that he had 'passed the bridge of Stirling'. George and Angus, returning from their separate errands, discovered that they had at last been outmanoeuvred by a sixteen-year-old.

They at once gathered their forces for an attack on Stirling, only to learn that again their monarch, counselled by his mother, had forestalled them. As soon as he had gained the security of Margaret's hilltop fortress, he had issued a decree forbidding any of the Douglases to return to court on pain of treason. Therefore those nobles who had previously feared to resist Angus at last rushed to the standard of their liberated King. Followed by a splendid retinue, James returned to the capital city. Riding beside him and once again sharing the plaudits of the crowd, was Queen Margaret. She had helped to restore him to his kingship; she was once again his chief counsellor.

To show his complete forgiveness for her marriage to Harry Stewart, James soon raised her new husband to the peerage as the Earl of Methven. The newly created Earl was also given a number of royal offices and received several landed estates, some of which had previously been part of Margaret's dower properties.

In spite of the restoration of his royal powers and the evidence of his own popularity with both lords and commoners, King James remained apprehensive that his recent gaolers might return. During the few weeks that he remained in Edinburgh after his triumphant re-entry into the town, he kept a guard before his chamber door each night, commanded by several of his loyal nobles. Soon, for greater security, he and his mother returned to Stirling, whose more isolated location and powerful fortifications reassured them both. His counsellors also urged him to stay in the castle, or close to its protective shelter, until the forces of the Douglases were vanquished, for the latter had broken into open rebellion. They had been ordered to yield to their sovereign the castles then in their possession, three-quarters of which were legally the Queen's property which her ex-husband had seized while in power. Instead of obeying this command, the Douglases fortified all their strong-holds, gathered their tenants into an army, and started raiding lands belonging to those who were loyal to the King.

Therefore, when Parliament met in September 1528, Angus and his family were accused of treason and summoned to come to Edinburgh under a safe conduct to defend themselves against the charge. When they refused to appear, they were declared traitors for having kept 'the King against his will these two years', and were dispossessed of all their estates. These lands, when captured, were divided among the nobility of the royalist side. Neither the Queen nor Methven, however, received any of the confiscated lands, though Margaret did secure the return of her own estates which Angus had held illegally.

To prevent King Henry from again supporting the cause of the Douglases, James at once wrote to his 'dearest, maist tender and best beloved brother and uncle, King of England'. After briefly recapitulating his reasons for having banished the Earl, the young King urged 'that if Angus or his adherents seek help in England it may be refused'. In order to explain matters in greater detail, Patrick Sinclair was sent to carry this letter to London. Just as James and his mother had expected, Angus had lost no time in applying again to England for help in recovering his lost powers. In response to his request both Henry and Wolsey wrote to the young King to reaffirm their complete reliance on the Earl and to try to persuade James to restore him. Naturally such a request fell on deaf ears. Angus, fearful of being driven from Tantallon by royal forces, next demanded sanctuary across the border. He asked the Earl of Northumberland to prepare chambers for himself, for George and Archibald Douglas and their families, and for his daughter, Lady Margaret.

The little girl followed her father from one dreary refuge to another. A few months after this, Angus sent her on to Norham Castle. By July of 1529 she had become the guest of one Thomas Strangways, Captain of Berwick, a pensioner of Cardinal Wolsey. This residence was well chosen because Lady Margaret was Wolsey's goddaughter. She and her servants were therefore given board and lodging in Strangways' house without charge to her father. Her host told Wolsey that he was allowing the girl as much freedom as possible, but was maintaining close watch over her to prevent any Scottish attempt to take her back across the border to her mother. What Lady Margaret's own preference may have been is of course not mentioned.

Meanwhile, the Earl continued to harry his Scottish foes, sending, as he boasted, 'four-score men to burn the country about

James V, King of Scots
Artist unknown

(*Scottish National Portrait Gallery*)

Edinburgh, that the King might have light to rise with on Friday morning'. This raid brought retaliation, and for some time the Borders were kept aflame as Angus attempted to hold out at Coldingham Priory and royal forces were sent to wrest this area from him and his brother William. Though William was killed in the siege of Coldingham, Angus was able to escape with two hundred men. His castle of Tantallon was also besieged, but its mighty walls and its position on the cliffs above the sea made it nearly impregnable. As its owner proudly commented later: 'Never was so much done in vain to win one house'. When James's artillery had proved unsuccessful against the great red-stone walls of this castle, the young King retired to Edinburgh. His enemy then surprised the royal forces which had been left at Tantallon, killed the King's popular captain, and captured his cannons.

While these hostilities were in progress, plans for peace negotiations between Scotland and England were continuing. In October 1528 commissioners were sent to a 'diet on the Scotch Borders'. These men were instructed to do all they could to restore the Earl of Angus to his lands and position; they were not, however, to press their demands to the extent of endangering the peace. Instead they should 'send privately some discreet person to Angus and persuade him to come into England, and tell him that by so doing he can recover his authority'.

Even Archdeacon Magnus, who had been sent to try to encompass the Earl's restoration, wrote to Wolsey after a meeting with Angus, that he felt 'it would be a pity to alienate the King of Scots for the sake of Angus'. He added that the English borderers had no very high opinion of the Earl, who had made an unsatisfactory job of maintaining order in that area throughout his administration. Nevertheless, in the same period the Archdeacon wrote to Margaret begging her to intercede with her son for the sake of her former husband. He felt sure, he wrote, that 'she would be sorry to see [the Earl of Angus] pursued to utter destruction'.

Margaret replied that she was surprised Magnus should expect her to exert herself on behalf of the husband who had wronged her in the past in so many instances. Despite these injuries, she continued, she had 'forborne to make evil report of him', and would take no vengeance against him if he and his friends would be 'good subjects to her son'. The young King himself, however, had no intention of permitting the return of the man who had caused him so much misery throughout the period when he had been in power. James was 'so perplexed and pained' to hear reports spread by George Douglas that Henry would not make peace unless the Douglases were included, that 'he braste oute of weping that the teers came rennyng downe by his chekes'. He commissioned Magnus to go to his uncle Henry and to repeat the account of all the indignities that he had been forced to endure under the Douglases.

The Archdeacon had himself begun to lose his old admiration for the 'noble Erle of Angwisshe', perhaps as result of hearing the Scots' own account of the arbitrary way in which he had managed affairs wholly to the advancement of himself and his kinsmen during his two-year regime. Magnus now urged King Henry and his advisers to give up their demands that the Douglases be reinstated and instead to work simply to establish the long-awaited peace treaty with Scotland. These recommendations were eventually followed and a peace agreement was signed in December 1528. This pact contained complete recognition of the rights and properties of Queen Margaret, but no provision for her former husband.

As for Angus, James told Henry VIII in a letter the following February, he had been offered a pardon, but had refused it, 'meaning to cause a breach between the realms'. More details of his evil conduct were also given to Magnus when he met the King of Scots later that month. James said that instead of giving up Tantallon to his ruler, as he had previously offered to do in return for a pardon, the Earl continued to use this fortress as a base for raids upon the King's subjects in that area. Finding that the boy was still resolutely opposed to any reinstatement of his former stepfather and gaoler, the English emissary turned to other subjects. Rumours of marriage plans for the youthful monarch had been circulating for some time, Magnus told him. Was it true that he was considering espousing a French Princess or one of the imperial family? Why was he no longer interested in his uncle's offer of his cousin Mary as his bride? The boy replied that he had also heard rumours, from England, that the Princess was being offered to the Duke of Orleans, but if instead she were still available for him, 'there was no marriage that he more desired'.

While in Edinburgh, the Archdeacon discussed these marriage plans with Margaret. She was, as usual, delighted by the idea that her son might gain the hand of her royal niece. In fact, Magnus was well impressed with the Queen's entire attitude on this occasion. Now that the vexed question of her divorce had been settled in her favour, she no longer had any quarrel with the old Englishman. Hence he found her the most charming and delightful hostess imaginable. 'I have not at any time found the Queen of Scots more inclined to the devotion of England or to the pleasure of her dearest brother, the King's highness, than her grace is at this season . . . and, being in right good favour . . . with the King's grace her son, she is clearly given to the advancement, furtherance and setting forward of the same'.

Leaving this pleasant scene of contentment and concord — so unusual in the Edinburgh court — the Archdeacon made the journey back to Berwick. On his trip he found himself much endangered by the hostilities which were still keeping the Borders in ferment. The cause of this turbulence, he explained to his masters, was, even as James had told him, none other than Angus. He was 'at this moment burning and doing displeasures in Scotland; and Earl Bothwell, appointed Lieutenant of Lothian, [was] doing all the displeasures he [could] to remove him'. Magnus concluded that he could not 'see how the Earl can continue, as he depends only on the King [of England]'.

True to this prediction, the 'Erle of Anguisshe' found it impossible to return to power in Scotland. King James was now in full control of affairs and never could he forget or forgive those who had made his life miserable for two years. The most he would do for his hated former stepfather was to spare his life by conniving at his escape into England, whither the ruined Earl at last retreated. There he was of course received by the King who had first set him up in authority in Scotland. Henry eventually also provided a home for his young niece. In 1531 Thomas Strangways brought her to London. Since his patron, Wolsey, had died in 1530, there was no one to pay for the upkeep of this girl, the Cardinal's god-daughter. Doubtless her mother would have been overjoyed to have Margaret returned to her, but Angus was determined not to permit his ex-wife to have their daughter again. King Henry, who now was pensioning his protégé Angus, therefore sent young Lady Margaret Douglas to live in the household of her cousin, Princess Mary Tudor.

The two girls had much in common. Being nearly the same age, both were suffering the fate of children in a divorce: separation from one or both of their parents. Margaret, who had spent all of her early years with her mother, seldom seeing her father, had now been deprived of her mother's company. Mary, also now separated forever from the mother who had been so devoted to her, was in this period just beginning the life of unhappiness and controversy she was to endure. Although she did not actually witness the events which were then occurring, she must have learned of them from those about her.

In the summer of 1529 the long-expected Legatine Court had begun the sessions which the King and his anxious minister, Wolsey, hoped would produce the divorce. Queen Catherine, however, refused to attend it, after one brief appearance at its opening. The sessions continued, with the chief issue of debate being the question of her first marriage to the King's older brother. Had this union actually been consummated? Although the Queen persistently denied it, witnesses came forward to prove the contrary. Various courtiers declared they had heard Prince Arthur boasting the day after his wedding of having 'been in the midst of Spain' the night before. One of those who demeaned themselves by repeating this coarse rumour was Charles Brandon, Duke of Suffolk. He, like most of these witnesses, wanted to remain a favourite of his sovereign. Not so Brandon's wife, Henry's beautiful younger sister. She was disgusted by her brother's infatuation with the 'Boleyn hussy'. Loyal to Catherine, Mary withdrew from court and lived in seclusion on one of the Suffolk estates.

The Legatine Court finally adjourned without arriving at any verdict. (Catherine's nephew, Emperor Charles V, still controlled Italy and the Pope.) Wolsey was therefore deposed, and, not long after, having already been accused of treason, died while on the way to his trial. Sir Thomas More received the powerful but dangerous post of Chancellor, while Thomas Cromwell became chief adviser to the King on his new plan to gain the divorce through Parliament.

The 1530s thus opened with scenes of conflict and confusion in England. The happy, carefree court in London which Margaret had so enjoyed on her visit in 1516–17 was now darkened by tension and suspicion. The Tudor women whose happiness she had so envied were now scattered and suffering as the result of their King's 'Great Matter'. Henry's elder sister knew little of what was occurring in her homeland to the south. In far-off Edinburgh, on the contrary, the Scottish Queen now basked in the glow of long-awaited success. Her son, finally King in his own right, continued to look to her for counsel and smiled favourably upon her new husband. Angus and all his hated followers had at last been overthrown and driven from the kingdom. After the storms of the past years, sunshine had broken through the clouds, and Margaret rejoiced in its unaccustomed warmth.

Part Three

WHEN THE HURLY-BURLY'S DONE (1528–1547)

CHAPTER 19

THE QUEEN DOWAGER
(1528–1537)

For several years after she had shared her son's triumphant entry into Edinburgh in 1528, Margaret was supremely happy. Her heart swelled with maternal pride as she observed the young monarch's vigorous efforts to suppress crime and restore law and order to his realm. Sometimes when he visited the Borders at the head of an armed retinue, she would accompany him at least part of the way. Thus in 1532, when he set out southwards on a hunting party, she rode with him as far as her estate in Ettrick Forest, where she stayed to hold a 'forest court'. During this process she ousted the Laird of Buccleuch from the governorship of her castle in Newark because of his incivility to her, and replaced him with her husband. This transfer of the control of her property was one she was later to regret.

While his mother was thus bickering with her tenants, James proceeded to hunt down his real quarry: those malefactors who continued to keep the Borders in turmoil. Some of the worst of the offenders had already been eliminated, including Johnny Armstrong. This notorious outlaw had committed many depredations on both sides of the border, and boasted that he recognized neither the King of England nor the King of Scots as his ruler. Such a challenge was certain to bring retribution from whichever of the monarchs thus insulted could first reach the braggart. The English Warden of the North had tried time and again to capture him, but in 1530 the Scottish King himself had at last been successful. Having seized the culprit, James wasted scant time on his trial. His guilt for numerous crimes was so widely acknowledged that it would have been impossible for him to prove innocence. His only recourse was to throw himself on royal mercy, but this was in vain. Johnny was hanged on the nearest tree, and so became the hero of many folk tales. Whether or not there is any truth in the ballad which claims that King James captured the outlaw by treacherous means, it is certain that his uncle, Henry VIII, would have endorsed the method. This is indicated by the number of victims of English justice in those harsh times who perished as a result of trusting the good faith of a monarch's safe conduct. Never was the advice, 'put not your faith in Princes', more applicable than in sixteenth-century Europe.

Hence the emissaries sent from London to Edinburgh throughout the 1530s complimented the Scottish King's thoroughgoing measures to eliminate disturbers of the peace, and pleaded for one group of Scottish outlaws only: the Earl of Angus and his followers. The Douglases, now refugees in England, continued to be the centre of controversy between the two nations. King Henry's persistence in urging James to restore them to favour was a major cause of the resentment which the Scottish King developed against the English ruler. He was particularly exasperated because the Douglases remained close to the Borders, just across the frontier, from whence they could lead raids into Scotland, then retire into their sanctuary across the Tweed.

In addition, they kept encouraging other Scots to rebel and join them in attacks on their own country, and they urged King Henry to 'allure' a number of Scottish noblemen to his service in order to prevent their accepting the pardon James offered to all those (except Angus and his family) who would repent and return to the obedience of their rightful King. In the early 1530s the Earl of Northumberland, Warden of the East and Middle Marches, reported to his monarch that the frontier war with Scotland was caused to a large extent by the Douglases. This was not surprising, since King Henry himself promised Angus on August 25th 1532, that in return for the Earl's serving England in any war against Scotland and swearing 'allegiance to him [Henry] as supreme lord of Scotland', the English monarch would 'pay him yearly £1000 until he had been restored to his lands in Scotland'. The royal expense accounts of England prove that this sum was regularly paid to Angus, while similar pensions were given to his relatives who also sought refuge in England. Finally in 1537 even the Duke of Norfolk, by then Warden of the North, urged his ruler to move Angus and his brother away from the Borders, as a necessary preliminary to the restoration of peace in that region. Henry reluctantly agreed they should be sent south, but not far enough to prevent their returning whenever this seemed advisable.

During the same period, Queen Margaret did her best to restore good relations between her son and her brother. Early in 1532 she wrote to Henry to offer her services as a mediator. He thanked her for her 'gentle letters', though he felt it beneath his dignity to correspond with 'the mother of our enemy'. In 1534, peace was restored through the assistance of the French ambassador to Scotland, France being then temporarily allied with England. A few months later, Lord William Howard came as English emissary to

Edinburgh. He was instructed by his monarch to visit the Queen, greet her 'after the goodliest wise' he could, and assure her that Henry appreciated her 'cordial good will' and work towards peace.

Margaret was pleased by this evidence that her brother considered her important. She also enjoyed participating in the entertainment of ambassadors. James, like his father, loved tournaments and arranged for military sports contests between members of the English entourage and some of his own court. The Scots won most of these mock battles. Margaret then proposed an archery contest, in which she felt sure her compatriots would come off victorious. 'The King hearing this of his mother was contented of her game and got her to pledge ane hundred crowns and ane tun of wine upon the Englishman's hands and he incontinent laid down as much for the Scottishmen. The field and the ground was in St. Andrews'. Once again the Scots were victorious, despite the traditional superiority of the English with bow and arrow. Perhaps this apparent triumph of Scottish arms was an actual triumph of English diplomacy. In any event King James was so pleased that he was quite ready to discuss the more serious proposals made by his uncle's envoys, and the Anglo-Scottish peace was accordingly strengthened.

To cement these good relations, the English King next desired a personal meeting with his nephew. He sent commissioners to Scotland to propose this and to enquire if the Queen would help to arrange such a meeting. Margaret was delighted and replied: 'There could be no more pleasant sight in this earth . . . as [than] we to see our most dearest brother and our most dearest son, in proper personages together, and of one loving mind . . .'.

She sent at once for James, who was absent from home at the time. He returned to discuss the matter but turned down the invitation. Apparently he was dissuaded from meeting the English King by leaders of the Scottish Church. They feared their monarch might be tempted to follow his uncle's example of defying the Pope. This was the year 1534, and the famous 'Reformation Parliament', as it was to become known to history, had by now dissolved England's ties with the papacy and was even then declaring the King to be supreme leader of the English Church. As a result the heads of the English clergy were toppling, quite literally in some cases, although the executions of Fisher, More and others who denied the royal supremacy did not take place until the following year. The Scottish clergy feared that their turn might be next. James himself was profiting from the royal patronage of the rich church benefices which the Pope had granted him; he therefore yielded to the persuasion of his clergy.

Henry was disgruntled; his sister was heart-broken. She had made such plans for this meeting, in which she had visualized an important role for herself. She would accompany her son to her homeland, where she would participate in the fabulous splendour of a second 'Field of Cloth of Gold'. She begged Henry to persevere in his efforts to arrange it, and sent loving messages to him and to his new Queen, Anne Boleyn.

'Your grace is our only brother, and we are your only sister', she wrote, reminding him of the recent loss of their younger sister, Mary, Duchess of Suffolk, who had died at the age of thirty-seven, 'and since so it is, let no . . . report of ill-advised [persons] alter our conceits, but brotherly and sisterly love to endure, to the pleasure of God and weal of us both'.

Henry swallowed his pride sufficiently to reissue his invitation. When his envoys arrived with this message, Margaret reported to her brother that James was away and was just recovering from a case of smallpox. Nevertheless, on receiving his uncle's letter, which she had forwarded to him, James rose from his sick-bed and travelled 140 miles in only eight days to a place twenty miles from Edinburgh. James then asked his mother to send Henry's messengers to meet him. She not only did this, but she and her 'sad [said] spouse' set out together with the envoys, although it was a very difficult journey, 'in the most troublous weather' she had ever endured. However, as she later boasted to Henry, it was 'by our sole advice', that her son finally agreed to the meeting.

After this hopeful appearance of agreement, James nevertheless was not yet completely convinced that he should carry out the proposal. First, he wanted to know precisely what subjects would be on the agenda when he met Henry personally, for he did not want to hear anything more with regard to restoring the Douglases, nor would he listen to any arguments trying to change his religious establishment. Secondly, he wanted the meeting-place changed to Newcastle. York, which had been proposed, was so far removed from his own boundaries that he felt he was compromising his independence of action by venturing so far into what was traditionally regarded as enemy territory. Some Scottish clerics warned him that he would be kidnapped by the English. Henry haughtily refused to change any of his plans, or commit himself in advance to items for discussion. So the meeting plans broke down.

The Queen persevered, doing her best to persuade her son to trust her brother. Her persistent and repetitious arguments finally irritated James to the point of fury. In a burst of temper he accused her of having been bribed by Henry to lure him on to enemy soil. This accusation of treachery deeply hurt his mother, who decided she was no longer wanted by her son. She wrote to her brother and to Thomas Cromwell, now Henry's principal Secretary and adviser, begging permission to come into England alone and make a visit without her son. Cromwell sent back her messenger, Otterburn, with the answer that the English King could not welcome his sister into his territories without her son, unless the latter gave his express permission for her to travel south.

Margaret was deeply hurt by this curt rebuff and wrote to her brother to complain of his Secretary's rudeness. When Cromwell then assumed the role of injured party and complained that he had only delivered the message dictated by his sovereign, she was forced to apologize. She had not intended to criticize Cromwell, she assured both him and Henry, but only wanted to request that hereafter any such message be sent to her privately so that 'no Scottishman' should learn, as Otterburn had, that the English Princess was unwelcome in her own brother's kingdom.

One more plan for the much-debated meeting was proposed: that the three Kings of France, England and Scotland should confer personally on the establishment of permanent good will amongst themselves. Henry was at this time gratified on at least one point. Both Francis I and James V had acknowledged the validity of his divorce from Catherine and his marriage to Anne. Their acceptance of this *fait accompli* was based, not on moral or ecclesiastical grounds, but on their firm conviction that any monarch had the right to free himself from an undesired wife and choose another. Their agreement on this royal and masculine view of affairs did not, however, afford a sufficient basis for lasting friendship. Before the three rulers could actually confer, other matters arose on which they differed, and this proposed summit meeting never took place.

Once again the Scottish Queen had lost the long-desired opportunity to revisit her native soil, but it was not only this disappointment that grieved her. She was now suffering again from a more chronic problem: lack of funds. As usual in such a situation, she appealed to her brother. Her letter requesting financial help was phrased with even more ingenuity than before. She needed money — quite a lot of it, in fact — for several reasons. For one thing, she had spent large sums on a whole new wardrobe in anticipation of the meeting she had striven so hard to arrange. She had done this for Henry's sake, and was it not just that he should now pay for these clothes? Moreover, her tenants had for several years been unable even to live on her lands because their farms had been so badly ravaged and their crops destroyed during the recent fighting on the Borders. This damage had been committed by 'broken men of

England'. Hence she required compensation from the English King for her inability to collect rent from this property.

To this elaborate argument she received no answer. She wrote again and again, both to her brother and to his Secretary, Cromwell, her pleas becoming increasingly urgent. Finally, she admitted to having fallen severely into debt in order to buy the now useless wardrobe for the expected meeting. As a matter of fact, she was in such straits that she owed over £20,000. 'Derrest bruder', she wrote, 'we bezeik your grace help us now ... and let us not be dishonoured ... since we must either be helped by you or else without remedy'. This letter, incidentally, was paid for on delivery and the English royal expense account for 1536 includes a payment of £10 'to a Scot for bringing the King a letter from the Queen of Scots'.

At last, in July of 1536, the English monarch wrote to tell his 'dearest sister' that he marvelled 'that ye should be so far behind the hand, as that ye should make such allegations ... as though the cause thereof had sprung of us and our realm'. He assured her 'that albeit we do in heart esteem you as our natural and loving sister, and will in all things ... so use you ... yet we desire you neither to think that we should disburse, upon so light a ground, any such notable sum of money; nor that we should willingly hear, that ye our sister should either have so far impledged your honour, without consideration for the redemption of the same, or allege unto us for a cause thereof, that thing which can toward us be imputed no cause of such inconvenience'. He added that if her losses were caused by the war, which he had been forced to wage for the defence of his subjects, this was the fault of her son, the King of Scots. Henry concluded therefore that Margaret should apply to her son, not to her brother.

All this was reasonable enough, no doubt, but of very small comfort to the worried Queen. She dreaded having to confess her extravagance and its consequences to James. For, although he resembled his father in some respects, the young King of Scots was far more like his English grandfather, Henry VII, when it came to financial matters. Such indebtedness as Margaret had incurred would be sure to aggravate the strained relationship between mother and son which had resulted from her unsuccessful efforts to arrange his meeting with Henry.

Another difference between them arose over James's marriage plans. Margaret's hopes for her son's bethrothal to her niece, Mary Tudor, had been utterly dashed, although this was as much the fault of the English King and his diplomats as it was of the Scottish monarch. When the Princess had first been offered to James, she

was already pledged by a very solemn betrothal to Emperor Charles
V. Then after Charles had eventually broken off this engagement so
that he could marry the heiress of Portugal, Mary was again urged
on King James by the English ambassadors. By this time, however,
the Princess was further humiliated by the divorce of her mother,
Queen Catherine. Parliament declared that her daughter was
therefore illegitimate, and Henry even forced the unhappy girl to
take an oath acknowledging the fact that she was a bastard.
Catherine's nephew, Charles V, refused to accept this view, and
instead he and his English ambassador, Chapuys, always referred
in their correspondence to the new Queen, Anne Boleyn, as 'the
concubine' and to her daughter, Elizabeth, as 'the little bastard'.
Charles continued trying to arrange royal matches for the cousin he
had himself jilted years before. Nevertheless, even he and Chapuys
had to admit that Mary's standing in the European marital market
had plummeted. Instead of an Emperor or a King, at best she would
probably now have to settle for a Duke for a husband.

Even without the stigma of illegitimacy, Mary would not have
been James V's choice for a bride. His growing antagonism towards
his uncle strengthened his decision to look elsewhere for his Queen.
Many different propositions were offered: several from the Holy
Roman Empire, a sister or a niece of Charles V, as well as at least one
from Italy, the Pope's niece, Catherine de Medici. However, the
young King of Scots himself seemed from the beginning to be most
interested in Madeleine, daughter of Francis I. This match had
been first arranged when the Treaty of Rouen, made by the Duke of
Albany, was ratified in 1521. After James had finally secured his
own control over Scotland, he began reminding King Francis of the
promise of his daughter's hand. Francis hestitated, for he was then
allied with England, against his traditional foe, Emperor Charles,
and the English definitely opposed a marriage alliance between
France and Scotland. Moreover, Francis was genuinely devoted to
his daughter, who was so frail and sickly that sending her to chilly
Scotland might prove fatal. He told James she was too young. She
was then only fourteen, but James's mother and his grandmother
had both been married when even younger.

The Scottish monarch became impatient. It was necessary that
he marry, he wrote the Duke of Albany, not only to provide legal
heirs to the throne, but also *pro éviter la procréation des bâtards*. This
was indeed a valid point. James was even more promiscuous than
his father had been; while still in his teens he had sired at least three
bâtard sons that are recorded. His precocity in sexual affairs was one
of the unfortunate results of his two years' domination by the
Douglases. Of course, as it turned out, marriage was to prove no

lasting cure for this problem. Meanwhile, since his application to King Francis seemed to have been indefinitely delayed, the King decided his best solution would be to marry his favourite mistress, Lady Margaret Erskine. She was so beautiful and charming that she had held James's affection longer than any other. Being a Scottish noblewoman, she would certainly be no more ineligible as Queen than several earlier Stewart Queens, or than Anne Boleyn of England. There was one problem; she was already married. This seemed to pose no real difficulty, however, as the Scottish Kirk readily granted James's chosen lady a divorce from her husband, so that she could then wed the King. Unfortunately, the Pope refused to accept this presumptuous action by his ecclesiastical subordinate, the Archbishop of St. Andrews, and declared the divorce invalid.

James reluctantly accepted this decision. He had observed the difficulties his uncle had recently encountered in trying to gain papal consent to his divorce and remarriage, and James had no wish to go to such lengths as King Henry in order to marry the lady of his choice. For one thing, James lacked the principal spur which had driven the English ruler to continue his course. Unlike Anne Boleyn, Lady Margaret had not insisted on being given the rank of wife and Queen, rather than accept the role of mere mistress. Hence the Scottish King had already shared her bed, and was confident he could continue to do so even after his marriage to someone else — some Princess who would bring him a good dowry. So why not have his cake and eat it too?

In retrospect, it might have been better for him and for his kingdom if he had been permitted to marry Lady Margaret. His son by her, whom he named James Stewart, would probably have proved an excellent ruler. Years later, as the Earl of Moray, he helped his half-sister, Mary Stuart, to govern Scotland, and after her abdication acted as Regent for her infant son. But history cannot be re-written. In 1534 King James again scanned the continental marriage market.

His mother was greatly relieved. She had strongly disapproved of her son's project for marrying his mistress. Moreover, she still had hope of strengthening the ties with England by a match there — if not with her unfortunate niece, Mary Tudor, then with someone else from that country. She wrote to her brother reassuring him that she was using all her influence with James to get him to seek his uncle's advice in choosing a wife. She still remained confident that he would do so even after the Scottish King set sail for France in 1535.

James went to France with the ostensible intention of proposing in person to the lady who had recently been offered to him by King Francis as an alternative to his consumptive daughter Madeleine. This alternative was Marie, the daughter of the Duc de Vendôme. Although James had sent emissaries to arrange for his marriage to this lady, he had not been fully satisfied with their reports. The promised dowry of 100,000 crowns was sufficient — always an important consideration — but the replies to his questions about Marie's personal qualifications were somewhat evasive and contradictory. There was only one way he could be quite sure that her figure was not ungainly, her complexion was not pockmarked, or her breath unpleasant: he must go himself. According to Pitscottie, James made quite sure of getting the truth by entering the ducal palace disguised as a servant. Pitscottie recounts that the lady, who had a portrait of the King of Scots, recognized him despite this subterfuge, went directly up to him and demanded that he take his proper place at the head of the Scottish company. Chagrined by this embarrassing revelation, James then embraced his hostess and made a great show of enjoying the entertainment prepared for him.

Nevertheless, he had determined privately not to wed Mademoiselle de Vendôme, whose appearance fell far below his standards. He soon left her father's court and went to pay a visit to the King of France, whose eldest son had recently died. Despite his grief over this loss, King Francis received James with the greatest show of honour and soon permitted him to meet the one lady he had really come to France to see: Princess Madeleine. Although this *demoiselle* had been ailing — as indeed she was for most of her brief life — she rose at once from her sick-bed and came to meet her persistent suitor. According to Pitscottie, the meeting was a case of love at first sight. After meeting James the Princess declared that she was determined to marry him, and no advice from either her father or her physicians could dissuade her. If she died, as they warned her she probably would, as a result of leaving sunny France for colder climes, she would at least die as a Queen, and the fulfilment of this ambition was, she said, the one thing that made her life worth living.

Madeleine was not the only one who was impressed by the good looks and athletic physique of the Scottish King. The French poet, Ronsard, depicts him as having 'royal bearing', and a face expressing both 'sweetness and strength, as if Venus and Mars had shared in his creation'. This was a court poet's hyperbole, but James, who had inherited his mother's fair skin and his father's auburn hair, keen grey eyes and clear aquiline profile, was handsome. This is evident from the portraits which were made at this time of his life, before sorrow had given his eyes the enigmatic, haunted expression of his better-known later pictures. Ronsard was also impressed by the Scottish King's proficiency in knightly feats of arms, as he demonstrated in the many tournaments now held in his honour. Soon King Francis yielded to the entreaties of his daughter and gave her as bride to the persistent Scot. The marriage was performed on January 1st 1537, amid a magnificent display of pomp and lavish entertainment. Afterwards the young couple stayed on in France to await more clement weather before sailing. The Scottish King was absent from his home for nearly a year in all. He apparently enjoyed hs visit thoroughly, and seems to have left his father-in-law's elegant court with almost as much reluctance as his daughter Mary Stuart was to evince many years later, when she too left her *douce France*.

During the King's absence from Scotland, Queen Margaret helped to look after affairs for her son. She was much displeased by the French marriage, into which he had entered so precipitately without consulting either with her or with his uncle Henry. She wrote to her brother to confess her chagrin over this match. But James was not the only man who had disappointed Margaret during this period. Another who had used her far worse was — predictably — her husband. Harry Stewart, now Earl of Methven, had, like both her previous spouses, proved unfaithful in marriage, and was now keeping a mistress, the Earl of Atholl's daughter, Janet, on one of the properties which he had gained from his wife's generosity. Moreover, he was, like Angus before him, appropriating the income from her estates for himself, money which the Queen desperately needed to pay off her own debts. Once again, Margaret, poverty stricken, begged her brother for money. James would soon return home from the magnificent French court bringing a most elegant French bride, and as the King's mother she needed new clothes in which to meet her daughter-in-law. Surely Henry would want his sister to be properly dressed for this occasion — the honour of the Tudors was at stake!

One may imagine King Henry's thoughts on receiving this doleful epistle. What was he to do about this sister who was always in trouble, always at odds with her current husband, no matter who it might be, always expecting him (Henry) to pick up the tab for her debts, her needs and her clothes? What had happened to the lavish wardrobe that had set her back £20,000 just a short while ago? Did Margaret never consider that her brother might also have financial difficulties, or marital problems?

For instance, he may have ruminated, he had been badly deceived by Anne Boleyn. To win her love, he had discarded his faithful wife, illegitimated his daughter, demolished his Church, broken with his allies, and executed heaven knew how many wretches — all for the sake of that black-eyed hussy!

Yet how had she requited all this? She had deceived him, convincing him that she would bear him the longed-for heir to the throne, and then producing instead another mere girl, followed by one false hope after another — all born dead! Surely this was a sign of God's judgement against her and proved that she must verily have been a witch, who had kept the King under her spell all those years. So Anne had finally paid for her sins, after the King's court had been convinced by evidence produced by Thomas Cromwell that she was guilty of having betrayed her royal husband with no less than five men.

Thus Henry was once again free — completely free, since Catherine also had died, stubbornly insisting to the very last breath that she was the King's true wife. Why would she never yield and admit that their marriage had been illicit and that they had been committing incest by living together for over twenty years? How unreasonable she had become! Was there no woman in the world who was reasonable? Ah yes, just one, a lady-in-waiting whom Henry had discovered in the entourage of his second wife. Jane Seymour was sweet, gentle and submissive, the complete antithesis of that termagant, Anne.

The thought of his present wife, Jane, whom he had married as soon as the Boleyn hussy was out of the way, perhaps brightened the King's outlook, and brought him a feeling of tenderness that could encompass even his tedious, querulous sister. He would help her once again, bail her out of debt if necessary, even buy her some new clothes.

Before actually dispatching the requested sums, however, the King wished to make sure that his sister needed them. He had received such conflicting reports from Scotland that it would be best to receive a new, completely unbiased account. He therefore dispatched one of his gentlemen of the Council, Ralph Sadler, to Edinburgh, to seek out the Scottish Queen and inform Henry what her circumstances actually were. Was his sister really being neglected by her son and mistreated by Methven, or was she only using this complaint to prey on his sympathy?

When Margaret received a visit from Ralph Sadler, she was delighted to see someone from her brother's court, who came for the express purpose of inquiring after her welfare. She revelled in the opportunity of recounting all her tribulations to a sympathetic audience. Sadler thus reported to his master that it was very true: the Scottish Queen was suffering privation as the result of

Methven's assumption of her rents, which he used for his own purposes, and mainly to support his concubine and their children.

When Henry received this testimony, he sent his messenger on to the French court. The purpose of this mission was ostensibly to deliver the King's felicitations on his nephew's recent marriage, but mainly to take advantage of the bridegroom's happy mood and to make two requests of him: one, that he forgive and reinstate the Earl of Angus and his relatives; the other, that he ensure that his mother would receive proper treatment from her husband. Despite all Ralph Sadler's tact in bringing these matters to James's attention, the latter could scarcely veil his annoyance at having the sore subject of Angus raised once again. He refused to consider making any change in the status of that nobleman. On the other topic, however, he demonstrated the utmost civility. He was shocked to learn that during his absence his mother had been suffering deprivation because of her husband's misconduct, and agreed that he would immediately set the matter straight in person.

As a result, Margaret soon afterwards received a solicitous message from her son. He also sent orders to his Council and to Lord Methven to see that her income was immediately restored so that she should lack for nothing. The Queen happily reported to her brother that she and her son were now in complete accord, a situation which would continue unless some evil counsellors should prevail upon James. As for Harry Stewart, she was through with him. She had determined to divorce him; then he would no longer be afforded the slightest pretext to appropriate the income from her estates. She would tell James these plans as soon as he came back from France.

Because she thus kept up a correspondence with King Henry's court, and assured emissaries from England that she would let them know whether the Scots were contemplating war with their neighbours, some of her biographers accuse Margaret of spying on her son and betraying his confidence. Her frequent admonitions to her brother and his officials not to let any Scots know about her letters do appear to substantiate this charge. So does her occasional insistence upon elaborate precautions which King Henry's emissaries must use to keep their visits to her secret when they were on official business in Edinburgh. For example, when Henry Ray went to Edinburgh in 1537 during James's absence in France, he wished to visit Margaret and learn how she was being treated by her son and by Methven. She sent him word that in order to come to her he must 'change [his] apparel, and put upon [him] a cloak and a hat after the Scottish fashion and should come to her ... secretly ... at nine o'clock at night'.

The secret messages which she then imparted to him were simply that none of her son's councillors gave him 'any good counsel towards England', and that these same evil advisers suspected Henry of planning to intercept James's ships on their way home from France. She also told Ray of her determination to divorce Lord Methven, and therefore asked him to implore the Duke of Norfolk that, if he did intend to start any war against Scotland, he should postpone it until her divorce had gone through — 'which shall be within a month. For if the war should be before the said divorce were made, the lords of Scotland will suffer him to occupy my living'.

This interview indicates that Margaret's conspiratorial measures were taken to keep James's counsellors from learning of her meeting with Ray and probably to prevent her husband's finding out about it. Also her interest was apparently confined to recovering her property from Methven, rather than any concern over international affairs.

There is no actual evidence, here or elsewhere, of her giving to the English any information that could cause harm to her son or his kingdom. The probable explanation of her extreme concern over secrecy is that James's counsellors distrusted her as an English-woman; hence every time she was reported to have conferred with an ambassador they would suspect her of treachery. Her letters complaining to her brother of her own ill-treatment by any Scots might also cause resentment if known in Scotland, and therefore should be kept secret. It cannot have been easy, after all, for Margaret to spend a lifetime in a nation that was so frequently at odds with her native land.

Margaret's real loyalty to James is illustrated by her concern for his safety. While he was in France planning soon to return home with his bride, a letter was brought to Queen Margaret containing gossip from the north of England. Included in this was a rumour of a threat to 'do him [James] a displeasure before he came to Scotland again', as a retaliation for his refusal to meet King Henry in York. Margaret at once called together the Council to inform them of this danger, and they promptly forwarded the information to their King in France.

On his return to Edinburgh from Paris, the Scots King had hoped to be able to traverse the north of England. This trip would be an easier route than going all the way by sea from France to Scotland. Hence he wrote to his uncle, requesting a safe conduct through his realm. King Henry, however, brusquely denied the request, basing his refusal on the following grounds. He reminded James that when the latter had refused to meet him in York, one reason given had been the Scottish clerics' suggestion that the English might kidnap him. Therefore, if harm should come to James in England, the Scots would claim it was his uncle's fault. Another reason was that no Scottish King had ever come to England on a peaceful errand without first admitting he was a vassal to the English crown, a humiliation that James was not likely to endure, whatever the excuse.

A third reason, which Henry did not give, was probably the fear that if James travelled through the north of England he might be met there by English malcontents requesting him to lead them in rebellion against their own tyrannical ruler. For in 1536 the beginning of the dissolution of the monasteries sparked a rebellion in the northern parts of England. Known as the 'Pilgrimage of Grace', it was a gathering of people, mostly peasants, to beg their ruler to cast off his 'evil advisers' and to spare those religious houses which he had not already abolished.

The Duke of Norfolk, commander of the royal forces in the area, felt incapable of suppressing the movement at once. He therefore issued what amounted to a free pardon to all the pilgrims, along with an implied promise that their wishes would be granted if they at once returned peacefully home. Simultaneously he wrote to his monarch, apologizing for this apparent weakness, saying, 'take in good part whatsoever promise I shall make to the rebels . . . for surely I shall observe no part thereof'.

Accordingly, as soon as the movement subsided, Norfolk carried out the King's orders to 'cause such dreadful execution upon a good number of the inhabitants, hanging them on trees, quartering them, and setting the quarters in every town, as shall be a fearful warning'. Over two hundred people in all were executed, including the leaders, who had gone to London under a safe conduct expecting to confer with King Henry about the implementation of the reforms which his agent, the Duke, had promised.

This retribution certainly crushed the 'Pilgrimage', but left much bitterness. News of this discontent spread to Scotland, and explains the warning which Queen Margaret told the Duke's envoy to relay to his master. If Norfolk were contemplating any incursion against Scotland, he had better first 'be sure of the commons'. She of course knew none of the details of the 'Pilgrimage of Grace' or of its suppression, only that it had been a rising against her brother. Obviously, with every ounce of her Tudor blood she resented any assault on royalty by 'the commons'.

Certainly these considerations must have helped to determine Henry's refusal of his nephew's request to travel over English territory. King Francis then put in his own plea for the young couple, asking his brother monarch of England to let them traverse his terrain for the sake of his fragile daughter. Henry replied that Princess Madeleine would of course be welcome, but not her husband, and it would scarcely be seemly for a bride to travel by a different route from her husband. As a result, James finally brought his wife home by sea. As they passed northwards along the Northumbrian coast, a boatload of English from the disbanded 'Pilgrimage of Grace' came aboard the Scottish flagship to beg James to lead them against their ruthless monarch. Disgruntled though he was by his uncle's rude treatment, the Scots King would not join in any such scheme.

James arrived in Scotland loaded with rich gifts from his father-in-law, including several suits of gilded armour, two completely outfitted ships and a dowry of 100,000 *livres*. King Francis seemed much pleased with James, whom he said he loved as his own son. It was with sorrow that he had watched the young couple leave, for he knew that it was the last time he would see his daughter. If Madeleine herself felt any qualms, she hid them heroically. When, on May 19th 1537, she was able to step ashore at Leith, she knelt down upon the sand, lifted a handful of it, and kissed it — the soil of Scotland, the country whose Queen she had at last become.

Upon reaching Edinburgh, they were met by those of the leading nobles and prelates who had not already accompanied their sovereign on his journey, and also by Margaret, henceforth known as the Queen Dowager. She was resplendent in a new gown of cloth of gold, heavy with gem-sprinkled embroidery and bordered with fur. Her brother had responded to her plea and had sent her £200 with which to buy clothes for the occasion; she was thus able to meet her daughter-in-law in a style which befitted a Tudor.

Madeleine did not long enjoy her coveted role of Queen. She became ill soon after arriving in her husband's country, and died on July 7th aged sixteen. The entire country mourned her passing, which the poet David Lindsay eloquently described in his *Deploratioun of the Deith of Quene Magdalene*. The bereaved husband paid his deceased wife the highest compliment possible. He proved how deeply he missed her by determining at once to fill the empty place by his side. He wanted another French lady, if possible, who would help to maintain the close ties he had established with the French King. Consequently, Francis had scarcely received the sad letter telling of his daughter's passing, before another Scottish messenger arrived with instructions to request the mourning father to help find his son-in-law a new bride.

At the same time, James's mother was again making every effort to escape once and for all from matrimony. She felt confident that her son would approve of this step, since he had originally opposed her marriage to Harry Stewart. When, shortly after James's return from France, she first mentioned her intentions for divorce, he did indeed seem agreeable to this idea, for he had been quite angered by the news which Henry had sent him of Methven's mistreatment of the Queen. Later, however, James reversed his stand completely, as Margaret wrote to her brother in August 1537. She had found twenty 'famous provers' to support her allegations against Lord Methven, and as result had promptly been granted a divorce by the Pope. Yet her son refused to permit this decree to be published by the Scottish Kirk, because he was afraid that, once she was free, she would marry Angus again. This fear, she told Henry, was absurd, the utmost falsehood which had been invented by Methven. In fact, it was a very clever move on the latter's part. He knew that even if he had treated Margaret badly, King James would never let her divorce him if she might then use her freedom to remarry his hated stepfather. Like her second husband, Harry Stewart too had discovered the way to wealth and power through marriage to the Queen, and had no intention of losing the fringe benefits of his position as her husband.

His strategy was successful. So angry and disappointed was Margaret that she was ready to leave the country. She begged Henry to let her come into England. Her situation in Scotland had become intolerable because her income and many of her estates had been taken over by Methven and she had sold some others to her son. At the age of forty-nine, she lamented, she had no residence to call her own, but must travel about the country like a poor gentlewoman, not like a Princess. She might have to become a nun and live in a convent. She would rather be dead than be forced to exist as she was having to!

Once again King Henry sent a messenger to verify his sister's complaints. The report showed that some of the lands which Margaret alleged had been taken from her were ones she had herself given to her husband in moments of foolish fondness. James, apprised of her unhappiness, now made sure that those properties which were rightfully hers should remain hers. He also arranged a reconciliation between her and Lord Methven. Gradually domestic tranquillity returned.

James's instant reaction to the supposed threat of his mother's re-marriage to Angus was understandable. It was only one of many examples of his phobia concerning the Douglases. In the summer of 1537, he received several alarms involving this proscribed family. Eight or ten men were executed for having attempted, during the King's absence in France, to rebel and bring George Douglas into the realm. More lurid was the charge against Lady Glamis, Angus's sister, and her third husband, the Master of Forbes, who were accused of having plotted to kill the King by poison. Since Lady Glamis was already suspected of having poisoned her previous husband because he refused to assist her brother, she was the more vulnerable to this new accusation. The court found both her and her husband guilty. He fell to his death while trying to escape; she was burned at the stake — the usual sentence for those convicted of this crime. Since she died quite bravely, professing her innocence to the last, many sympathized with her. It was whispered that, but for the King's hatred of her brother, her life might have been spared.

Another Douglas was in difficulty during these years. Young Lady Margaret had, as previously mentioned, been placed in the household of her cousin, Princess Mary Tudor, with whom she developed lasting ties of friendship. Faithfulness to the Catholic Church was one of the bonds that held them together throughout their lifetime. Their aunt, Mary, Duchess of Suffolk, acted as kindly protectress to these two nieces, and both girls were deeply grieved when the Duchess died in the summer of 1533.

In September of that year, Princess Elizabeth had been born to Anne Boleyn, and Lady Margaret was made an attendant of the royal infant. She was at this time in high favour with King Henry, who even suggested her to the French ambassador as a possible bride for the Duc d'Angoulême. The ambassador had asked, in the Duke's name, for the hand of Princess Mary, but her father harshly denounced his daughter for refusing to acknowledge Anne Boleyn as Queen — a stubbornness for which 'he would take care to punish her'. Instead of Mary, King Henry said, 'he had a niece, daughter of the Queen of Scotland, whom he keeps with the Queen his wife and treats like a Queen's daughter . . .'. 'He would make her marriage worth as much as his daughter Mary's'. The ambassador added, 'I assure you the lady is beautiful and highly esteemed here'.

Nevertheless, the French ambassador did not make an offer for Margaret. She might not have been too enthusiastic about leaving England then, even for such a distinguished marriage. She was at this time falling deeply in love with a member of the Queen's household. This gentleman was Lord Thomas Howard, a brother of the Duke of Norfolk and young uncle to Anne Boleyn. As long as Anne remained in the King's favour, fortune smiled upon her relatives. Therefore when Henry first learned of the attachment between his niece and Lord Thomas he seems to have looked benevolently upon it, but as Anne's decline in the royal favour became marked, in 1536, the young couple realized that they must act quickly to snatch at happiness. They secretly became betrothed, or possibly even married, an action which was to cost them dearly.

In July 1536, the imperial ambassador, writing to Charles V about the news of the English court, stated that the Duke of Norfolk's younger brother had been condemned to death 'for having treated a *mariage par paroles de présent* with the daughter of the Queen of Scots and the Earl of Angus. A statute had also been passed making it treason to treat for marriage with anyone of royal blood without the King's consent. The said personage of royal blood [Lady Margaret] was also to die, but for the present had been pardoned her life considering that copulation had not taken place . . . .'.

Both Lord Thomas and his fiancée (or wife) were at once imprisoned in the Tower of London. The reason for this severity was that Margaret's descent from King Henry VII made her dangerously close to the English throne. When Queen Anne was sentenced to death, her daughter, Princess Elizabeth, had been bastardized by Parliament, thus removing her as well as her half-sister, Princess Mary, from the line of succession to the throne. This move to prevent either Princess from becoming Queen after King Henry's death should clear the way for the new heir to inherit the crown, the male child expected to result from Henry's next marriage, to Jane Seymour.

However, if this marriage produced no children, then the next in line of royal succession could well be Lady Margaret, since she was the only other living Tudor who had been born on English soil. When the King and his counsellors realized this possibility, they at once took steps to prevent such an occurrence. Parliament declared Lord Thomas guilty of treason for having committed the crime of 'treating for marriage with one of royal blood without the King's consent'. The fact that Thomas had done this before the statute had been passed made no difference. (It was not until 1689 that the Bill of Rights would prohibit such *ex post facto* laws or condemnation to death without trial, by mere legislative action.)

To make quite sure that Lady Margaret herself would have no chance to inherit the throne, the same statute referred to her as 'illegitimate', since her mother's marriage to Angus had been annulled. The ingenious lawmakers added that Queen Margaret herself was at this time trying 'to come into this realm, to be restored to the Earl of Douglas, her late husband', in order to legitimate their daughter. There is no proof of any such intention, although this parliamentary statement may be the basis for the rumours that Margaret wished to divorce Methven so as to remarry Angus.

Certainly Queen Margaret herself said nothing to indicate such a desire. On the contrary, she wrote to Henry begging him to send her daughter back to Scotland. This request was part of the letter she sent to her brother in August 1536, as soon as she learned of her daughter's dire predicament: 'Dearest brother, we beseech your grace ... to have compassion and pity of us, your sister, and of our natural daughter and sister to the King your dearest nephew; and to grant our said daughter Margaret your grace's pardon and favour, and remit of sic [such] as your grace has put to her charge'. She concluded with the plea to send the young girl back to Edinburgh, 'so that in time coming she shall never come into your grace's presence'.

This latter petition Henry ignored. He was too close a friend of Angus to let his daughter return to his former wife's care. Nevertheless the King did relent somewhat in his severity toward his niece and her lover. Neither of them was executed, although both became severely ill in their unhealthy and dismal prison. From the window of her room Lady Margaret could see the very spot where Queen Anne had rcently been decapitated, a view that certainly did not make for ease of mind. Eventually her mental and physical health became so endangered that she was moved to somewhat pleasanter quarters, Syon Abbey, a place on the Thames often used by King Henry to house his female prisoners of high degree. Her fiancé was less fortunate. On October 31st 1537 he died 'of intermittent fever, contracted during close confinement in the Tower of London, and aggravated by want of air and exercise'.

Even before his death, Lady Margaret had written to Secretary Cromwell begging him 'not to think that any fancy doth remain in me touching him [Lord Thomas], but that all my study and care is how to please the King's grace and to continue in his favour'. According to some rumours of the time, Cromwell himself had hoped to marry the daughter of Angus and Margaret, but there is no evidence to prove this. Eventually, after the birth of little Prince Edward, Margaret was released from Syon, and she and Princess Mary were reunited at Beaulieu. They later both became ladies-in-waiting to Anne of Cleves and Katherine Howard in turn. Princess Mary had, some time earlier, yielded to her father's commands and threats and accepted her illegitimacy, a status she now shared with four-year-old Elizabeth. Lady Margaret's bastardy was also now officially established. King Henry sent Lord William Howard (brother of ill-fated Lord Thomas) to Scotland to collect all the data necessary to prove that this girl had no claim whatever on the English throne, regardless of her Tudor descent.

Queen Margaret meanwhile was immeasureably relieved to learn of her daughter's release from prison, and wrote to her brother thanking him 'for the nobleness he had shown her daughter, who would never have her blessing if she did not all he commanded'. Henry replied somewhat stiffly that so long as Lady Margaret conformed to his 'convenience', he would treat her well. There is no doubt that the young lady sincerely wished to stay in his good graces. The trouble was, it was difficult to keep abreast of his current wishes — so frequently and so drastically did he shift his favour from one noble family to another, depending on which lady had most recently achieved his regard. And Lady Margaret was still young enough to attract and be attracted to male admirers. How could she be sure that one of these who today was acceptable to her royal guardian would remain so tomorrow? Margaret's daughter must have often wished herself back in the colder, but safer, country of her mother.

CHAPTER 20
CLOUDY SUNSET (1537–1541)

'Though I be forgot in England, yet never will I forget England!' These plaintive words typify Margaret's feelings during the last years of her life. To the English emissaries who occasionally came to Scotland from King Henry's court she complained sadly of her brother's neglect: 'It had been but a small matter,' she sighed to Sir Ralph Sadler, 'to have spent a little paper and ink upon me and much it had been to my comfort; and were it perceived that the King's grace my brother did regard me, I should be the better regarded of all parties here'.

Henry's failure to write to her she felt undermined any pretence she might make of being really important to either England or to Scotland. Unfortunately by this time it was pretty obvious that she was no longer of real value in diplomatic affairs, for she had lost her influence over her son. This fact, which had been illustrated by James's choice of Madeleine as a wife, was re-emphasized by his determination to maintain the French connection by his second marriage. Although Margaret kept assuring her brother that this time her son would follow her advice and King Henry's, James showed not the slightest inclination to do so. On the contrary, he was most anxious to keep the patronage of King Francis I.

Undoubtedly the French monarch was a most generous father-in-law. He promised not only to pay to the royal widower all of Queen Madeleine's remaining dowry, but also to arrange a second marriage for James with a wealthy French lady. This was Marie de Guise, just widowed by the death of her husband, the Duc de Longueville. James learned that the lady was very attractive. At the age of twenty, she was 'lusty and fair and has had one child by her husband'. Child-bearing ability was most important in a Queen. Evidently Marie was far stronger physically than the fragile child-bride he had just lost, for his emissary to France assured him that the Duchess was 'stark and well-complexioned' and might 'endure travel'. The King was so well pleased with all these details he did not this time take the trouble to go to France personally to inspect the bride in advance. He promptly asked King Francis to close the deal, provided of course that a good dowry was included. His father-in law handsomely took care of this, giving 150,000 *livres* as *dot* for Marie, whom he designated as an honorary 'daughter of France'.

These financial arrangements were eminently satisfactory to the prospective groom, and the French monarch therefore sealed the bargain with Marie's father. There then occurred a surprising complication: another suitor made an offer for the pretty widow — none other than King Henry VIII. He had also had just become a widower, following the death of Jane Seymour. That paragon of marital fidelity had kept her promise to him and on October 13th 1537 had presented him with a son, Edward. Unfortunately the baptismal ceremonies and celebrations had proved too much for the new mother, who had died on October 24th.

The loss of his Queen presented the King with what Cromwell felt to be an excellent opportunity to strengthen England's position in foreign affairs. He must find a bride who would establish a firm alliance against the crusade in which the Pope was calling all Catholic rulers to join for an attack on the heretics (the Lutherans and England). With France and the Empire now at peace such a combined attack might come any day. King Francis's support might be won if Henry were to marry a French noblewoman. Henry's marriage-agents reported on the virtues of the Duchesse de Longueville. The King was especially intrigued by her proven child-bearing capacity. Little Prince Edward seemed healthy, but might take after his poor mother in physical stamina, and with infant mortality so high, one could never be too well prepared. Then came word that this 'lusty' noblewoman had already been promised to the King of Scots. Far from discouraging Henry, this news seemed to fire him with greater determination to win her for himself. There was nothing like competition to stimulate the bidding, in the marriage market just as in the commercial one! A 'pretty comedy' was now enacted (as Castillon, the French envoy to England, described it to his master, King Francis). King Henry was 'so amourous of Mademoiselle de Longueville that he could not refrain from coming back upon it', despite Castillon's declaration that the lady had definitely been promised by her father to James V. Henry boasted that 'he would do twice as much for you [Francis] as the King of Scots would'.

Maybe the Duc de Guise had promised his daughter to the Scot, but what about the lady herself? Here the English suitor received encouragement. Marie's mother seemed to be excited by his offer, which she persuaded her daughter was far more advantageous than the Scottish one. True, James was younger and far better looking than his uncle, but England was a much greater and wealthier nation of which to be Queen. Marie's ambition for prestige and luxury apparently outweighed any romantic consideration — the dowager Duchesse de Longueville was a very practical woman.

Even the realization that she would be marrying a heretic did not deter her. Perhaps she thought she could reconvert him to the true faith. If she reflected on Henry's rather discouraging record as a husband — 'divorced, beheaded, died' — her mother perhaps reassured her that Marie would be the lucky one. She would achieve his gratitude by promptly giving the King a healthy second heir, and probably would have the luck to outlive the old 'Bluebeard'. Good health like Marie's was a prime blessing in the sixteenth century!

When Henry heard the rumours that the fair widow was interested in his offer, he was delighted. 'Now the King [Francis] . . . will have no excuse to refuse me her in order to give her to this beggarly King of Scots!' he told Castillon. Francis, however, was a man of honour who had already awarded this marriage prize to his son-in-law. He knew that a man like James would 'hazard his kingdom rather than suffer such a wrong' (as have his fiancée given to his rival). Francis did indeed have great fondness for James — plus a resolve not to break the 'Auld Alliance' for the sake of such a dubious ally as the English might prove. He ordered his vassal, the Duc de Guise, to keep his pledge to King James and told Castillon to inform Henry that his master 'would not lose such a friend as the King of Scots, whom he looks upon as his own son'.

Therefore Cromwell's emissaries continued to look further afield in Europe for a bride for their master, one from a princely house which would assist England if the country were attacked by the Catholic powers. The Duchy of Cleves seemed to hold a pivotal position in this religious controversy and was sympathetic to the Protestant cause. Anne of Cleves was accordingly singled out to be Henry's fourth Queen. Henry objected to buying a pig in a poke so commissioned his court artist, Holbein, to paint a portrait of the lady. This picture so pleased the much-married ruler that he agreed to send at once for the original. Perhaps Holbein had flattered her. In any case, when the King met his bride-to-be, he declared to his intimates that she 'did not please him' at all. This disappointment no doubt gave him additional reason to feel aggrieved against James. His bride, who arrived late in 1538, was acclaimed by everyone as a beauty, tall, graceful, with bright red hair and sparkling blue eyes.

The Queen Dowager of Scotland was again much chagrined that her son had selected another wife from France. Nevertheless, she wrote to her brother that she must have money for more new clothes in which to meet her new daughter-in-law in such style that she would 'do honour to our noble progenitors'. No answer came to this plea. Henry had decided enough was enough.

Whether or not Margaret managed to solve the problem of her inadequate wardrobe, she was pleased with this attractive French-woman who treated her with great deference. Marie soon inquired of her mother-in-law whether she had heard lately from her brother. (Perhaps Marie still was contemplating the passed opportunity to have become his wife.) Margaret answered with some embarrassment because, to be quite truthful, she had heard nothing from her brother for some time. Of course, she answered — not quite truthfully — she had 'but recently heard from him'; then she wrote to him to complain of his neglect. She also continued to bemoan her lack of income and the difficulty of collecting her rents. When Henry sent diplomats to James's court to confer with his nephew on various matters, they were instructed also to check on the 'old Queen'.

By 1540 their reports maintained that she was getting along pretty comfortably. James had finally managed to arrange a reconciliation between her and Lord Methven. They were now living together once more, although Margaret spent much of her time also at court, for she and her daughter-in-law had become fast friends. She was in Edinburgh when Ralph Sadler came there in 1540, and he told his superiors that he owed his comfortable quarters in the city to Margaret. He and his retinue had at first been given a shabby apartment, but when the 'old Queen' learned of this she at once brought it to her son's attention. As a result, the English emissary and his party were properly lodged.

One of Sadler's errands in Scotland in 1540 was to convince the Scottish King that he should follow his uncle's example by leaving the Church of Rome and establishing a national Church. Then he could give up raising sheep, as Henry understood James had been doing on a large scale on his lands, and become rich by confiscating and selling church property. This method had overnight trans-formed his uncle from a debtor into a wealthy creditor.

The proud Scot retorted that he did not keep sheep, although some of his tenants might do so. Moreover, he had no need to confiscate church property because he had plenty of income, from his own estates and from the generosity of his 'father, the King of France'. He would not stoop to so shabby a step as turning out the good monks and nuns from their abbeys and ending the charitable works they were performing for the poor and needy. Nor was he really impressed by the accusation Sadler made against some Scottish bishops who, he reported, were plotting to bring temporal as well as religious matters under the control of the papacy.

Although James thus refused in any respect to follow his uncle's example in breaking away from Catholicism, he was not blind to the faults of the established Church, which Sadler dwelt upon in detail. In fact, James several times urged reforms, and encouraged a spirit of criticism of the widespread abuses in the Scottish Church. He applauded his poet, David Lindsay, for his vigorous depiction of these abuses in his poetry, especially his *Satyre of the Thrie Estaits*. This play made fun of the laxity and immorality of many monks and other clerics. It was enacted at the palace of Linlithgow in 1540, and is similar to other Renaissance satires on the established Church of that day, such as Chaucer's famous *Canterbury Tales*.

Although the King recognized the need for reforms, and frequently commanded his clergy to carry them out, he himself was too much a participant in the very abuses he decried to enforce any real improvements. The Pope let him bestow many rich benefices on his various bastards, and permitted him to tax his clergy, ostensibly to establish his well-known College of Justice, but in practice much of the money collected actually remained in the royal purse.

In return for the favours which he received from the Pope, James continued to protect Catholicism and agreed to legislation to defend it against heresy. James's personal inclination was fairly tolerant. In some cases he tried to mitigate the sentence imposed on heretics condemned to be burned at the stake, but was informed by his bishops that the royal power of pardon could not extend to such cases. During his reign there were therefore some Protestant martyrs, although very few in comparison with France or the Empire. Certainly Scotland was then a far more tolerant country than England. At least, in Scotland the ground rules were clear: so long as a person remained orthodox and neither read, published, nor distributed proscribed literature, he was safe. In England, on the contrary, one could be hanged, drawn and quartered for being too Catholic (for such crimes as denying the royal supremacy), or burnt at the stake for being too Protestant (for denying the validity of transubstantiation). Thus in July 1540 an equal number were executed for occupying each of the two sides of the religious *media via*. Moreover, unfortunately, the rules did not remain constant, so that what was acceptable belief one day might be forbidden the next. The Scots were probably fortunate that their King did not follow his uncle's example in religious matters.

Marie de Guise was a devout Catholic as the Duke of Norfolk reported to Cromwell in 1539: 'the young Queen is all papist, and the old Queen nearly as much so'. There are several indications that Margaret was at this late stage of her life taking a deeper interest in religion. One example of her good works is her letter written to King Henry on March 1st 1541, on behalf of a monk who had previously been Sacrist of the Church of the Holy Sepulchre in Jerusalem. He wished to collect alms for the redemption of this Church, and hoped to travel through England to do so. The Queen Dowager requested a safe conduct for him to traverse England, for she had heard that Roman Catholic clergymen were not always safe in her brother's newly Protestant territory. A number of English clergymen had fled into Scotland to escape punishment for preaching the old faith. Henry had demanded that James extradite such fugitives, but the younger monarch had refused to send them back for punishment, an action which pleased both of the Scottish Queens.

The 'old Queen's' apparent devotion to her faith may indicate that in her later life Margaret had repented of the very casual attitude toward religion that had typified her youth. Was she perhaps making a belated effort to prepare for an easier ascent from purgatory? This does not seem likely as probably no Tudor ever doubted that Saint Peter was waiting to give him (or her) a royal welcome. It is more likely that Margaret was simply trying to please her daughter-in-law, whose reputation for piety seems to have been well founded. Certainly the Queen Dowager enjoyed the friendship of her son's second wife. She forgot her earlier disappointment that he had selected a Frenchwoman rather than an Englishwoman, eloquent testimony to the tact and graciousness of the 'young Queen'. Marie made the 'old Queen' feel not only respected, but wanted and needed — a remarkable accomplishment for any daughter-in-law.

Consequently Margaret spent much time at court, wherever it was. Like her French daughter-in-law, she admired the way in which James was embellishing and adding to each of his residences. At Linlithgow he changed the main entrance from the east to the south side, where a magnificent new gateway was erected. He also had the intricate fountain built in the courtyard. The influence of the French Renaissance on his taste is likewise apparent in the renovations to the palaces of Falkland and Holyrood. The great hall and other apartments at Stirling owe much of their beauty to his direction. The effect of his year in France can also be seen in other features of his reign. He had the crown of his ancestors remodelled, and the sceptre embellished. Margaret, with her Tudor love of display, applauded her son's work in making his residences more princely, his court more lavish. Like his maternal grandfather, Henry VII, James, for all his frugality and acquisitiveness, was willing to spend freely for the elegance and splendour which could help to impress visitors from abroad.

His chief hope was realized in May 1540, with the birth of his first legitimate heir, a son. When this news reached England, it must have turned King Henry quite green with envy. His new bride, Anne of Cleves, was so unattractive, he told Secretary Cromwell, that he could not even bring himself to have marital relations with her — much less beget another heir to the throne. The Secretary recalled the fate which had threatened his predecessor, and started feverishly planning ways to remove Anne without ruining relations with her homeland, Cleves.

Marie de Guise's child-bearing potency was again proved in the following year, when a second Prince was born. However, this joyous news was soon blotted out by a tragic reversal of fate. The new baby and his older brother both died very suddenly, within a few days of each other, though they were living in completely separate establishments at this time. So heart-broken were the parents that Margaret found her time completely occupied trying to comfort them. She wrote to Henry apologizing there was not time to send more than a brief note. (This last was a circumstance which her brother found possible to bear with reasonable equanimity.)

James was even more despondent than his wife over the deaths of the two infants. It was at this stage that his face began to wear the haunted expression so noticeable in his later portraits. His health had also begun to decline, ever since a nearly fatal hunting accident in 1537. Was he too perhaps fey, like his father?

Certainly a summary of the diplomatic developments throughout his personal reign shows striking resemblances to the chronology of the events that led up to Flodden. In both cases there was the international background of rivalry within the eternal triangle, England, the Empire and France, with England tending to side with the Hapsburgs against the traditional foe, France. The latter, in turn, looked to its 'Auld Ally' for support. As in the reign of James IV, efforts were made to preserve the peace, which had been re-established by the treaty of 1534. James pleased his uncle by his energetic suppression of border raiders and his expeditions to the Western Isles and later to the Northern Isles to reaffirm his control there. Henry had been concerned by rumours that residents of these outer fringes of Scotland might assist the Irish. The chronic rebellion in Ireland challenged his power from time to time, especially when urged on by the papacy as a result of England's break with Rome.

For a while after the Pope had excommunicated him, the English monarch feared an attack by the combined Roman Catholic powers, especially at times when the usual rivals, Francis I and Charles V, were at peace. During such intervals, Henry courted Scotland, which could constitute a real danger as a spring-board for such a combined invasion. His emissaries delivered gifts that Henry knew would please his sports-loving nephew: falcons, hounds and horses. In 1535, he even awarded James the coveted Order of the Garter. The young King accepted this honour, but without taking the oath customarily administered in such ceremonies. He would take this vow of fealty later, he said, after he had established his own knightly order, with which he would honour his uncle. At that time he and King Henry could make reciprocal pledges. Not even in a symbolic ceremony would the proud Scot declare himself to be the inferior of the English ruler. Henry's reference to him as a vassal (as on the occasion where he was refused the safe conduct through England) must have been especially galling to the younger man. A statement of this sort could undo the effects of years of careful diplomacy, nor could all the gifts in the world remove its sting. Margaret found that her efforts to establish any lasting accord between her brother and her son were as hopeless as similar attempts with Henry and her first husband had been.

Though the Queen Dowager certainly lamented her son's growing reliance on Francis I and his simultaneous divergence from King Henry, she was quite unconcerned by his relations with his own subjects. From them James V acquired two contrasting nicknames: the 'King of the Commons' and the 'ill-beloved'. Each of these apparently contradictory titles was appropriate to that part of the population by which it had been invented. The ordinary people adored him, because with his personal assumption of power they were delivered from the chaos of his minority into a reign of law and order. Moreover, he won their hearts by travelling abroad amongst them to an even greater extent than his father had done. Sometimes he would appear at a Highland castle disguised as a solitary huntsman, as in Scott's *Lady of the Lake*. More often he used the role of a simple farmer. As 'the Gudeman of Ballingeich' he would visit the homes of his humble subjects, acquainting himself at first hand with their problems, so that he could then resolve them. (Also, quite frequently he made particular acquaintance with their daughters, if they chanced to be attractive.)

This picture of the kindly monarch devoted to the well-being of his people contrasts sharply with the record of his severity towards the nobility. He showed them no mercy whenever they appeared to be in the wrong (as frequently occurred). When they disrupted the peace with their feuds, he attacked their castles, imprisoned the offenders and seized their estates. When they retaliated by joining with other malcontents in rebellion, he used all the force at his disposal to overpower them. Once defeated, they were dispossessed of their lands, stripped of their authority, and sometimes executed.

This severity towards aristocratic offenders helped to make James beloved by the poor tenants who suffered most at the hands of these unruly landlords. Such Robin Hood policies would perhaps have made him successful as a modern politician. They were, however, fatal to a ruler of sixteenth-century Scotland. In a nation which was still largely feudal, the King was forced to rely upon his nobles to supply his army with men and to lead them into battle. Unlike his father, who won the love of all classes, and led his nobles to sacrifice themselves for his sake, James V tried to force them into obedience. This was the cause of his eventual failure and explains the tragedy that concluded his brief reign.

His hostility to the lords of the realm is easy to understand. As a class they appear throughout the early history of Scotland to have been motivated primarily by self-aggrandizement rather than patriotism. During his own childhood, these leaders had baffled and infuriated his mother. Her complaints of their fickle and sometimes treacherous behaviour must have been a familiar refrain in her advice to her intelligent son. Then, when he was forced under the control of Angus, these early impressions were multiplied a hundredfold. The hatred for the Douglases which resulted from the two years spent under their domination became an obsession. Unfortunately, this hostility towards one family marked his attitude towards the entire class they represented.

Only one nobleman seems to have become a confidant of the King, George Gordon, fourth Earl of Huntly. The origin of their friendship can be traced to their youth. George as a boy had been Angus's ward, and had like James been held in subjection by that harsh guardian. Their shared hatred for the Earl brought the two boys together, and explains why the Gordons of Huntly joined the King's forces so readily to help him to suppress the unruliness rampant during his reign.

Otherwise, James turned for advice and support to the non-noble ranks. These men were referred to contemptuously as the 'King's *mignons*' — a word then used to denote sycophants, the ruler's favourites on whom he lavished favours actually due to those of higher rank. It did not then imply homosexuality, which was not among James V's vices. His amorous affairs were conducted with the opposite sex. But naturally James's preference for men whom they considered as their social inferiors added to the nobility's hatred of their monarch.

Evidently James failed to realize how his alienation of the hereditary leaders of his country was undermining his strength for any international conflict. With the proud defiance that character-ized him, he maintained his allegiance to his French father-in-law without making sufficient effort to propitiate his powerful English uncle.

Henry, in the summer of 1541, was making a final effort to establish a reconciliation with Scotland. Knowing that soon he would probably be once again at war with France, he tried to gain King James's support, or at least a guarantee of his neutrality. By now he had forgiven his nephew for having snatched the attractive Marie de Guise from his grasp. Henry's own affairs had at last straightened out most satisfactorily. He had rid himself of Anne of Cleves. Cromwell had once again succeeded in removing an unwanted wife, this time by less drastic means than with the Boleyn witch. After all, this fourth wife was a foreign Princess, and severe diplomatic repercussions might follow if she were handled too roughly. Besides, there was no way 'the Flemish mare' could have been accused of infidelity to her husband. No one who saw her would have believed it. Even the most docile members of Henry's Council could not have found her guilty. Cromwell's solution was an annulment, granted by the King's own Church, and agreed to by prior arrangement with the lady in question. She was so relieved to keep her head, that she was simply delighted with the liberal provisions made for her: a luxurious household of her own, with all expenses paid for the rest of her life, and the honorary title of the 'King's beloved sister'. This title suited Henry much better than that of his wife. (How incredulous the monarch would have been had he realized that it suited Anne a lot better too.)

Of course, Secretary Cromwell had had to go. Any minister who put his ruler through what Henry had had to endure in that marriage must be guilty of something treasonable! So Parliament had 'discovered' that Cromwell had tried to convert the King to Lutheranism. Too much Protestantism was just as bad as too much Popery. To celebrate the elimination of his Secretary, the King had immediately entered into a marriage of pure pleasure. A beautiful eighteen-year-old had been brought to his attention by the Duke of Norfolk and some other ambitious members of her family. (The Howards had been trying to engineer a return to power ever since they had lost all their influence with the downfall of Anne Boleyn.) It was true that Katherine Howard was Anne Boleyn's cousin, but she was completely different from that sharp-tongued virago: she was all meekness and gentleness, as well as being curvacious and red-haired. She was, her elderly bridegroom proclaimed, a 'rose without thorns'.

In order to show off this lovely new Queen, he would entertain her in York with a replica of his famous 'Field of Cloth of Gold'. The purpose of this spectacular show was to meet at long last with the King of Scots. Thus, in one move the English monarch, on his first personal visit to the principal city of the north, would dazzle the eyes of the repentant 'Pilgrims of Grace' with Tudor splendour, and also convince his nephew that he must henceforth follow the lead of his omnipotent uncle.

Emissaries were once more dispatched to Edinburgh to invite James to this rendezvous. Once again, the Queen Dowager eagerly seconded her brother's persuasions and urged her son to accept this exciting invitation. She again began to plan her wardrobe for the magnificent occasion. Henry was as optimistic as she that this time the summit meeting would take place. He himself therefore undertook the arduous journey to York, the furthest north he had ever travelled in his kingdom. Here elaborate preparations were already under way for a repetition of the 1520 'Field of Cloth of Gold'. Tents made of this gorgeous material were erected, pavilions built, and fields marked out for tournaments. The country round about was scoured for victuals of all kinds to provide for the expected feasting. All to no purpose; the chief guest, for whom these lavish arrangements were made, failed to appear. His expectant host, after waiting in vain for nearly two weeks, rode back to London in utmost fury.

Thus Margaret's hope for a visit to England was ruined — forever, as it turned out. In the autumn of that year she became ill. Pursuivant Ray reported to King Henry that she was taken sick 'upon the Fryday before night at a place that is called Meffin [i.e. Methven], and dyed upon the Tuesday before night after' (October 18th 1541). Her final illness was described as 'a palsye' (probably a stroke), and was not at first considered to be very serious. Margaret therefore did not send for her husband or her son, nor did she make a will. When at length she realized that this was indeed the end, she sent 'for the Kyng her son, being then at Falkland, to come to her', but she expired before he could reach her.

Meanwhile, feeling death approach, she called for 'the *Frères*, that was her confessors, that they should set on their knees before the King, and to beseech him that he would be good and gracious unto the Earl of Anguyshe, and did extremely lament, and aske God mercy, that she had offended unto the said Earl as she hade'.

This surprising statement has convinced some of her biographers that Margaret had genuinely changed her attitude towards Angus in later life. They assert that she did indeed want to divorce Methven in order to remarry her second husband. This interpretation is of course possible, but it seems strange, if such was her desire, that she had never admitted it to Henry. The latter, she knew, favoured Angus and would have done everything possible to arrange for her reunion with him, possibly to the extent of inviting her to make the much-desired visit to London for such a purpose. Yet neither to Henry nor to anyone else did she ever suggest such an idea. It appears more likely that her last request was, like many other deathbed confessions, a complete renunciation of what she then apprehended might be considered as her previous sins. In her last moments, she thus responded to the solemn appeal by the Friars that she freely confess every sin and any person she might have wronged. In any event, her appeal to James to restore the Douglases certainly fell upon deaf ears.

Another person of whom Margaret thought in her final moments was her daughter, from whom she had long been separated. She desired 'her said confessors to solicit the King her son, from her, to be good unto the Lady Margrat Douglas, her daughter, and that she might have of her goods, thinking it most convenient for her, forasmuch she never had no thing of her before'. In this instance also the Queen's last wish was disregarded. Her son apparently considered that her jewels were heirlooms belonging to the Stewart family, and they went to his Queen. So far as money was concerned, Margaret died as truly poverty-stricken as she had for years been complaining. Pursuivant Ray declared that 'the said Queen had no mor redy money at the time of her departen, but 2500 markes Scottes'.

Nevertheless the 'old Queen' would have been gratified to know of the splendid funeral her son provided for her. She was interred in Perth, in the Carthusian monastery where many members of the royal family of Scotland were buried. All the leading nobles and prelates of the country were commanded to attend, clad in black, a funeral custom just recently established in Scotland. The clothes of their servants and the trappings of their horses and chariots were likewise of sable. What Margaret herself wore for this her last appearance upon earth is not recorded. For once in her long career she did not care.

CHAPTER 21

AFTERGLOW

Margaret Tudor died in October 1541. However, two of the monarchs with whom she was so closely associated survived her. Each of them was enmeshed that autumn in personal sorrow of such proportion that her decease had little impact on them. Her son was still sunk in the melancholy which had engulfed him after the recent loss of his two little heirs.

Meanwhile her brother had returned from his disappointing visit to York to receive a real blow: Katherine Howard was unfaithful to him. She had, it was said, shared her favours both before and after her marriage with such abandon that there was no way it could be kept hidden from her husband. The courtiers, knowing that failure to inform the King of such treason as she had committed would in itself be labelled treasonable, dreaded having to break such bitter news to him. Archbishop Cranmer, the one person for whom the often-fickle monarch seemed to have a deep respect and affection, generously accepted the dangerous responsibility for telling him. On hearing Cranmer's revelation, Henry was incredulous — furious — heartbroken. He had truly loved his 'rose without a thorn', but such _lèse-majesté_ as hers could not go unpunished. Katherine's lovers and accomplices were executed, followed at last by the terrified and repentant girl herself.

As usual, the downfall of the Queen affected other innocent victims, including Lady Margaret Douglas. This luckless girl had again fallen in love with the wrong man: Queen Katherine's brother, Charles Howard, cousin of Margaret's unlucky first fiancé, Lord Thomas. This time she had not gone so far as to become betrothed. Therefore, instead of being imprisoned in the grim Tower, she was sent to the less dreadful reformatory of Syon Abbey. After a few months' confinement there, she was allowed to return to court, although she was first reprimanded. Cranmer was sent by her uncle to warn her that this was the second time she had been indiscreet, and to 'beware a third offence'! The unhappy girl may well have decided it was too risky a business, falling in love with a relative of any of her uncle's wives; their tenure was too uncertain. Therefore, although she became a lady-in-waiting to the King's sixth bride, Catherine Parr, in 1543, Lady Margaret carefully avoided flirting with any of this Queen's family. She would henceforth wait for her uncle to choose a husband for her, although she probably hoped he would do so before too long.

Meanwhile, the Howard family fortunes had plummeted once more. The Duke of Norfolk, who had saved his position — and maybe his neck — by presiding over the court that had condemned his niece, Anne Boleyn, to death, now performed a similar office for his other niece, Katherine, whom he loudly excoriated for having betrayed her magnanimous lord and King (and for having incidentally ruined all her family's hopes of advancement).

Even if Norfolk had not made these righteous pronouncements, he would hardly have been eliminated at this stage of affairs. He was, after all, the best general in the nation, and his monarch had an important assignment for him in 1542: to go north and teach the Scots a lesson. King Henry had firmly determined on war against France, but first had to secure his northern frontier against a diversionary action on the part of Francis I's Scottish son-in-law. Since foolish young King James had scorned his uncle's pacific overtures and had refused to meet him at York, it was clear that there was only one way to deal with him — by force!

Having reinforced their castles along the Borders in 1541, the English launched their attack in August 1542 by making a large-scale raid into Teviotdale. This attempt, under Sir Richard Bowes, was driven back with heavy losses by James's capable friend, the Earl of Huntly. The Duke of Norfolk himself led the next incursion, but was unable to reach Edinburgh or other important goals. He merely burned a number of villages and returned across the Tweed.

It was now the Scottish monarch's turn to attack. He was understandably furious about the unprovoked attempts at invasion, particularly since they were accompanied by the English declaration that James was merely a disobedient vassal of King Henry. James's first effort to retaliate failed because the nobles accompanying him balked (as they had under the Duke of Albany) when they were commanded to cross over into England. This humiliation merely fired the stubborn King with renewed determination. He gathered a new host and started south again in November 1542.

One detachment was sent eastwards, but accomplished little. The main force, in the west, was to have been commanded by the King himself, but at the last moment he was prostrated with a severe illness at Lochmaben. In this dilemma he made the mistake of transmitting his orders through an unpopular subordinate, Sir Oliver Sinclair. The nobles, believing the entire command had been given to this commoner, refused to follow his orders. The resulting battle of Solway Moss was Scotland's most disgraceful defeat. When their ailing monarch learned that 'two earls, five barons and five hundred lairds' had surrendered, in addition to many lesser followers, his shame became unbearable. In utter dejection of spirit, he returned from Lochmaben, and, after several weeks spent aimlessly visiting first one, then another of his residences, he finally halted in early December, at Falkland.

At this favourite palace he had spent many happier days hunting; this time he had come here to die. He bitterly rejected all efforts by his attendants to rouse him from his despair. Among the last messages brought to the King was one from Linlithgow, telling him that his wife had given birth to their third child. Even this news failed to cheer him, for the baby was a girl. 'It came with a lass — it will end with a lass', was his mournful comment as James V turned his face to the wall and expired on December 14th 1542.

It is to be hoped that the heart-broken ruler did not learn that in the vanguard of the victorious army from the south rode his old *bête noir*, the Earl of Angus. He and his brother, George Douglas, loyal to their pledges to King Henry, had fought for him against their own nation. Soon after James's death, they were successful in having their titles and estates restored. The Earl became a leading member of the Council, widely noted for his support of the English interest, and for urging that the young Queen, Mary Stuart, should marry Edward, heir to the English throne.

In 1543 Angus himself married Lady Margaret Maxwell. A year later his daughter, Lady Margaret Douglas, was wed to another pro-English Scot, Matthew Stewart, Earl of Lennox, who had been finally selected for her by her uncle, King Henry. This latter was eventually successful in his last war against France, in which his forces captured Boulogne. In Scotland, however, he overplayed his hand. His brash declaration of suzerainty eventually turned even such Anglophiles as the Douglases into Scottish patriots, and the Queen mother, Marie de Guise, was able to maintain the 'Auld Alliance'. Not until the reign of Henry's daughter Elizabeth, the unwanted female child of Anne Boleyn, did Scotland become firmly Protestant and pro-English.

When Henry VIII died in 1547, he left a will providing for the succession to the throne. According to this document, which Parliament ratified, Prince Edward was to inherit the crown, to be followed, if he died without heirs, by each of his half-sisters in order of their birth. In case all three of his children died leaving no issue, Henry decreed that the throne should pass to the male heir of his younger sister, Mary, Duchess of Suffolk. Noticeably omitted from this list of possible future monarchs of England were the descendants of his older sister. Yet 'the best-laid plans' of even such an autocrat as the second Tudor can go 'agley', especially when he is no longer around to enforce them in person. King Henry's last surviving child, Elizabeth, died in 1603. The Virgin Queen, like her half-brother and half-sister, left no issue. Hence, Parliament kept the promise which Elizabeth's ambassadors had secretly made before her death to James VI of Scotland, and invited him to become King James I of England.

James V's famous deathbed prophecy therefore proved false. The Stewart line had indeed 'begun with a lass' (when the first Stewart gained the throne through his marriage to Bruce's daughter), but far from ending with Mary Stuart, it continued under Mary's son and expanded its rule over a double kingdom. The last British ruler surnamed Stewart was Queen Anne, whose successor was George I of Hanover. Nevertheless, 'German Geordie' was eligible for the British crown because his maternal great-grandfather was James VI and I (Stewart). Similarly, the present royal family, now surnamed Windsor, trace their claim to sovereignty to their Stewart ancestors.

Thus Henry's elder sister was in the final analysis successful beyond her fondest dream, although neither she nor the son for whom she had wished it lived to see her accomplishment. Moreover, Margaret had the unusual distinction of being a double great-grandmother to the first ruler of the dual kingdom. For James V's daughter, Mary Queen of Scots, chose as her second husband her cousin, Henry Stewart, Lord Darnley, the son of Lady Lennox (*née* Lady Margaret Douglas). Mary and Darnley's son was James VI and I.

Margaret Tudor has been denigrated by historians as headstrong, vain, fickle and selfish. Doubtless she deserved all these epithets, but she should also be credited with other qualities: determination and courage. Notwithstanding trials and disappointments that would have driven a weaker and gentler character to surrender or suicide, she never gave up. Somehow, she managed to endure hardship and disaster, sustained by the fierce Tudor spirit that refused to admit defeat. As a result she was able at last to see her son emerge triumphant in 1528 as King of Scots. It was her resolute determination which finally made possible the fulfilment of her father's wishes when he had first arranged her marriage to James IV: the establishment of the United Kingdom of Great Britain.

NOTES ON THE SOURCES

Despite Margaret Tudor's pivotal importance in the establishment of the United Kingdom, she has received slight notice from historians. Generally she is mentioned briefly as the mother of James V, and her regency is dismissed as one of the particularly dismal attempts at government during the King's minority.

Moreover, her career has been overshadowed by the more spectacular reign of her brother Henry VIII and by the more melodramatic fate of her granddaughter, Mary Queen of Scots. Consequently, in comparison with these two much studied monarchs, Margaret has drawn the attention of very few biographers.

In 1850 Agnes Strickland completed the first volume of her *Lives of the Queens of Scotland and English Princesses*, which includes a life of Margaret Tudor. This author used many original sources, but her portrayal of Margaret is 'inaccurate and a little malicious', according to the *Dictionary of National Biography*, which itself is far from complimentary in its appraisal of this Queen. With stern Victorian righteousness, Strickland condemns Margaret as the female epitome of falsehood, treachery and immorality. In contrast, the next writer to publish a series on *Princesses of England*, Mary Anne Everett Green, is sympathetic to the Queen Regent of Scots, explaining in careful detail the many problems she faced in her long career. Green's work is approved by the *Dictionary of National Biography* as 'extraordinarily thorough and careful'.

The most recent biography of Margaret is an admirable, though rather brief, account by Hester W. Chapman. In *The Sisters of Henry VIII*, Chapman shows that Henry's 'stolid' elder sister had difficulties which forced her into some of the devious ways she took.

To carry out my aim of portraying this Queen as an imperfect, but very human individual, and to describe in detail the many phases of her stormy career, I have used chiefly Green's work, along with the copious store of correspondence available in the *Letters and Papers of Henry VIII*, Volumes I–XVII. The *State Papers of Henry VIII* contain fewer letters, but, since these are printed verbatim, they are useful for additional details omitted by the resumés in the *Letters and Papers*, as well as for imparting the realistic flavour given by the writer's own words and inimitable spelling. Other complete letters are given by M. A. E. Green Wood's *Letters of Royal and Illustrious Ladies* and Ellis's *Original Letters*.

All these sources are occasionally quoted throughout the book. In addition, an invaluable source for Part I was Leland's *Collectanea*, which gives the contemporary account of Margaret's betrothal and the full particulars of her journey to Scotland in 1503. For the many additional books which proved helpful in the preparation of *Margaret Tudor Queen of Scots*, see the selected bibliography.

SELECTED BIBLIOGRAPHY

The Acts of Parliaments of Scotland, Vols. II, III. Ed. T. Thompson and C. Innes. Edinburgh, 1814.

ANGLO, SIDNEY. *Spectacle, Pageantry, and Early Tudor Policy*. Oxford: Clarendon, 1969.

BACON, FRANCIS. *The History of the Reign of King Henry VII*. Ed. J. R. Lumby. London, 1881.

BAIN, J., ed. *The Hamilton Papers*. Edinburgh, 1890–92.

BINGHAM, CAROLINE. *James V, King of Scots*. London: Collins, 1971.

———. *The Stewart Kingdom of Scotland, 1371–1603*. New York: St. Martins, 1974.

BROWN, P. HUME. *History of Scotland*, Vol. 1. Cambridge: University Press, 1909–11.

BRUCE, MARIE LOUISE. *The Making of Henry VIII*. New York: Coward, McCann & Geoghegan, 1977.

BUCHANAN, GEORGE. *The History of Scotland*. Transl. & ed. by James Aikman. 4 Vols. Glasgow: Blackie, Fullarton, 1827.

BURTON, ELIZABETH. *The Pageant of Early Tudor England 1485–1588*. New York: Charles Scribner's Sons, 1976.

CAW, J. L. 'Portraits of the First Five Jameses.' *Scottish Historical Review*, VII (1909), 113–18.

CHAPMAN, H. W. *The Sisters of Henry VIII*. London: Jonathan Cape, 1969.

CHRIMES, S. B. *Henry VII*. Berkeley: U. of Calif. Press, 1972.

CLIFFORD, A., ed. *The State Papers and Letters of Sir Ralph Sadler*. 2 Vols. Edinburgh: Constable, 1809.

CRUDEN, STEWART. *The Scottish Castle*. Edinburgh: Nelson, 1960.

DICKINSON, W. CROFT. *Scotland From the Earliest Times to 1693*. Edinburgh: Nelson, 1961.

DICKINSON, W. C., DONALDSON, G., and MILNE, I. A. *A Source Book of Scottish History*, Vol. II. Second ed. London: Nelson & Sons, 1958.

DOLMETSCH, MABEL. *Dances of England and France from 1450 to 1600*. London: Routledge & Kegan Paul, 1949.

DONALDSON, G. *Scotland, James V to James VII*. New York: Praeger, 1965–66.

———. *Scotland, the Shaping of a Nation*. Newton Abbot: David & Charles, 1974.

———. *Scottish Kings*. London: Batsford, 1967.

ELLIS, H., ed. *Original Letters*, Vols. I, II. London: Harding, Triphook & Lepard, 1825.

ELTON, G. R. *England Under the Tudors*. London: Methuen, 1962.

GIUSTINIAN, SEBASTIAN. *Four Years at the Court of Henry VIII*. Transl. Rawdon Brown. London: Smith, Elder & Co., 1854.

GREAT BRITAIN H.M.C. *The Manuscripts of the Luke of Hamilton, K.T.* London: H.M.S.O., 1887.

GREAT BRITAIN P.R.O. *Calendar of the State Papers Relating to Scotland.* Ed. M. J. Thorpe. London: Longman, 1858.

——. *Calendar of the State Papers Relating to Scotland and Mary Queen of Scots, 1457–1603.* Ed. Joseph Bain *et al.* Edinburgh and Glasgow, 1898.

——. *Letters and Papers, Foreign and Domestic, of the Reign of Henry VIII,* Vols I–XVIII. Ed. J. S. Brewer *et al.* London: H.M.S.O., 1870–1920.

——. *State Papers of King Henry VIII,* Vols. IV, V. London: H.M.S.O., 1830–52.

GREEN, M. A. E. *Lives of the English Princesses,* Vols. IV, V. London: Colborn, 1849–55.

HACKETT, FRANCIS. *Henry the Eighth.* New York: Liveright, 1929.

HALL, EDWARD. *The Union of the Two Noble and Illustre Families of Lancastre and Yorke.* London: Richard Grafton, 1550.

HENDERSON, T. F. *The Royal Stewarts.* Edinburgh: Blackwood, 1914.

KENDALL, P. M. *Richard III, the Great Debate.* New York: Norton, 1965.

KNOX, JOHN. *The Historie of the Reformation of Religion Within the Realm of Scotland.* Ed. R. S. Walker. Edinburgh: Oliver & Boyd, 1940.

LANG, ANDREW. *History of Scotland,* Vol. I. New York: A.M.S. Press reprint, 1970.

LAVER, JAMES. *A Concise History of Costume.* London: Thames and Hudson, 1969.

LELAND, J. *De Rebus Britannicis Collectanea,* Vols. IV, V. Ed. Thomas Hearne. London: Benj. White, 1774.

LESLIE, JOHN. *The Historie of Scotland.* Trans. Father J. Dalrymple, Rev. E. G. Cody and W. Murison. Edinburgh & London: Blackwood, 1888–95.

The Letters of James V. Ed. R. K. Hannay and Denys Hay. Edinburgh, 1954.

The Letters of James the Fourth, 1505–13. Col. by R. K. Hannay, ed. R. L. Mackie and Anne Spilman. *Scottish Historical Society,* 3rd series, XLV (1953).

LINDSAY, ROBERT of Pitscottie. *Historie and Cronicles of Scotland, 1437–1575,* Vol. I. Ed. A. J. G. Mackay. Edinburgh: Blackwood, 1899.

LINKLATER, E. *The Royal House of Scotland.* London: Sphere, 1972.

LOCKYER, ROGER. *Tudor and Stuart Britain, 1471–1714.* London: Longman, 1964.

LYNDESAY, SIR DAVID. *Works.* Ed. J. Small and F. Hall. New York: Greenwood, 1969.

MACFARLANE, LELSIE. 'The Book of Hours of James IV and Margaret Tudor', *The Innes Review,* XI (1969), pp. 3–20. Glasgow: Burns & Sons, 1960.

MACKENZIE, W. MACKIE, ed. *The Poems of William Dunbar.* Edinburgh: The Porpoise Press, 1932.

MACKIE, J. D. *The Earlier Tudors, 1485–1558.* Oxford: Clarendon, 1952.

——. 'The English Army at Flodden: the Armies Compared — a Victory of Organization; the Secret of Flodden', *Misc. of the Scottish Historical Society,* VIII (1951).

MACKIE, J. D. *Henry VIII and Scotland*. London: *Transactions of the Royal Historical Society*, 4th Series XXV (1947), pp. 93–114.
——. *A History of Scotland*. Baltimore: Penguin, 1964.
MACKIE, R. L. *King James IV of Scotland*. Edinburgh: Oliver & Boyd, 1958.
MATTINGLY, G. *Catherine of Aragon*. New York: Vintage, 1960.
MAXWELL, H. *A History of the House of Douglas*, Vol. II. London: Freemantle & Co., 1902.
MORRIS, CHRISTOPHER. *The Tudors*. Glasgow: Fontana-Collins, 1955.
PAUL, J. B., ed. *Accounts of the Lord High Treasurer of Scotland*. Edinburgh: H.M. General Register House, 1900.
PINKERTON, JOHN. *The History of Scotland, from the Accession of the House of Stewart to that of Mary*, Vol. II. London: C. Dilly, 1797.
PLOWDEN, ALISON. *The House of Tudor*. New York: Stein and Day, 1976.
POLLARD, A. F. *Henry VIII*. London: Longmans, Green & Co., 1905.
RAE, T. I. *The Administration of the Scottish Frontier, 1513–1603*. Edinburgh: University Press, 1966.
RICHARDSON, J. S. and BEVERIDGE, J. *Linlithgow Palace*. Edinburgh: H.M.S.O., 1948.
RICHARDSON, J. S. and ROOT, M. E. *Stirling Castle*. Edinburgh: H.M.S.O., 1948.
RYMER, T. *Foedera*. 3rd Edition Reprint. Farnborough: Gregg P., 1967.
SCARISBRICK, J. J. *Henry VIII*. Berkeley: U. of Calif. Press, 1968.
SCOTT, SIR WALTER. *Poetical Works*. Ed. W. J. Rolfe. Boston: Houghton, Mifflin, 1899.
SINCLAIR, G. A. 'The Scots at Solway Moss', *Scottish Historical Review*, II (1904), 372–377.
STRICKLAND, A. *Lives of the Queens of Scotland and English Princesses*, Vols. I, II. New York: Harpers, 1873.
STEPHEN, LESLIE and LEE, SIDNEY, eds. *The Dictionary of National Biography*. London: Oxford U. Press, 1921–22.
STUART, M. W. *The Scot Who Was a Frenchman*. London: Hodge, 1940.
TYTLER, PATRICK FRASER. *History of Scotland, 1249–1603*, in 9 vols. Edinburgh: W. Tait, 1841–43.
VERGIL, POLYDORE. *Anglica Historia, A.D. 1484–1537*. Ed. and trans. Denys Hay. Camden Series LXXIV. Royal Historical Society. London, 1950.
WILLIAMS, NEVILLE. *Henry VIII and His Court*. London: Wiedenfeld & Nicolson, 1971.
——. *Henry VII*. London: Wiedenfeld & Nicolson, 1973.
WOOD, M. A. E. GREEN, ed. *Letters of Royal and Illustrious Ladies of Great Britain*. London: H. Colburn, 1846.

INDEX